GEORGE ORWELL

a personal memoir

GEORGE ORWELL

a personal memoir

=

T. R. FYVEL

MACMILLAN PUBLISHING CO., INC.
NEW YORK

to my daughter Susan

Contents

Illustrations

Acknowledgements

ANOTHER AND BELATED book about Orwell? My justification could be that the memory of my ten years of friendship and association with Orwell has remained in my mind, waiting to be put on paper, right through the years. I felt that this personal memory gave me at least some idea how behind his writings Orwell looked upon life. Orwell's unusual and sometimes dramatic experiences of life in colonial Burma, in Wigan or in the Spanish civil war played a more direct role in shaping his outlook than has sometimes been suggested.

Orwell was in the widest sense an autobiographical writer. In compiling this memoir, I have relied in the first place upon personal recollection, adding to this the picture of Orwell as it emerges from the four volumes of his collected essays, journalism and letters, edited by Sonia Orwell and Ian Angus; and, above all, on the many directly autobiographical passages found in Orwell's writings. In a sense these could be regarded as successive definitions of a partly fictional self, and they have indeed been taken as such; yet in my view these passages, as in *The Road to Wigan Pier*, are what Orwell would have called 'essentially true' as descriptions of his life and standpoint at various stages of his career. As such, at any rate, I have treated them. I felt that wherever possible, Orwell should be left to speak for himself and I am grateful to Secker & Warburg Ltd, and A.M. Heath & Co. Ltd, his literary executors, for permission to quote from his writings.

As for other sources, while Orwell's request for no biography delayed biographical writings for a number of years, I read with interest both *The Unknown Orwell* and *Orwell: the Transformation* by Peter Stansky and William Abrahams, and the full biography *George Orwell: A Life*, by Bernard Crick. While not necessarily agreeing with the picture of Orwell they presented,

I have from all three books learned some details new to me about his life. Equally I found that the essays by various hands collected by Miriam Gross in *The World of George Orwell* (a volume to which I was a contributor) contained some interesting ideas about him.

However, in addition to my own recollection, a major part in building up my picture of Orwell has been played by personal conversations. From a day spent in the early fifties with Orwell's redoubtable brother-in-law Humphry Dakin and his children, I learned much about Orwell's family background and his early life. In starting out on this book I also had the chance to talk to his widow, Sonia Orwell, before her, alas, premature death. I derived much help and benefit from conversations with the friends of Orwell's last decade – with Arthur Koestler, David Astor, Julian Symons and the late Fredric Warburg, with Susan Watson, Margaret Branch, Jon Kimche and John Beavan. Mrs Mabel Fierz, Michael Meyer and Stafford Cottman were able to throw light for me on various periods of Orwell's life and I have quoted valuable insights on him by Cyril Connolly, Malcolm Muggeridge and Richard Mayne. While I was greatly assisted by this testimony, the responsibility for the use I have made of it must, of course, remain mine. I am also grateful for the opportunity to use the Orwell Archive at University College, London, to refresh some memories.

In the shaping of this book I am much indebted, as on previous occasions, to the careful advice of Catharine Carver. On behalf of my publishers, Elizabeth Burke has been an admirably sensible and sympathetic editor. I am grateful to Ramona Darvas for the patience with which she took the dictation of this book. Finally, I am deeply indebted to my wife, both for sharing with me her memories of George Orwell and for facilitating the conditions of my work.

T.R. Fyvel
January 1982

Prologue

IN THE PRIVATE WING of University College Hospital, London, where between October 1949 and January 1950 I visited George Orwell a number of times, a square pane of glass was let into the door of each sickroom through which patient and caller could see each other. My first glimpse of Orwell was always through this glass and always with shock at the sight of his thin, drawn face looking ominously waxen and still against the white pillow. But then, as I knocked, a sudden slight smile and look of interest would bring his features back to life as he saw that another visitor was calling, and as one entered he would immediately launch into some practical suggestion: 'Hello, Tosco, help yourself to a drink. There should be whisky on the sideboard. I've just been reading the usual piece in the *New Statesman* attacking NATO ... By the way, I've just been listening on the wireless to a talk on Palestine – with all that's going on in the world, there's no point in your worrying about Palestine.' His need in this way to plunge straight into conversation, with which I was familiar, was more than ordinary shyness; it had something of the schoolboy about it and to the last, even on his sickbed, Orwell seemed to retain his boyhood traits.

He was certainly ill; just how ill it was hard to know because he stoically did not like to talk about his state except in mentioning the briefest facts. My wife, Mary, had reported how on an earlier visit, after a slight haemorrhage, Orwell had greeted her with the news, 'Last night I thought I was a goner', before calmly going on to talk of other things. To me he said that while his left lung was almost useless, his affected right lung – this was in the days before penicillin was widely used – had not responded well to the streptomycin treatment, at that time the drug used to combat TB.

In fact, as he lay stretched out in his bed, his body looked frighteningly thin and wasted. Looking at him, I felt once or twice that the grim scene in *Nineteen Eighty-Four* – the book he had completed with such difficulty on the Isle of Jura, when already critically ill – where the hero Winston Smith weeps in prison at the sight of his shrunken, tortured body, had been drawn from life; and that the relentless, intangible force which crushes Winston Smith symbolized not only the totalitarian threat Orwell feared and described, but also the intangible illness in his own wasted body. Yet he did not like talking about this. To the last he kept his form. He read the daily newspapers carefully, watching out as he always did for meaningless clichés and misuse of words and even noting down some instances. One sign that he was not fully himself, perhaps, as I discovered in talking to other visitors, was that he said some of the same things to them as he did to me. And once he said to me (as to one or two others) with a wry smile, 'Do you think one can die if one has an unwritten book in one's mind?'

He still took an interest in current affairs in sometimes unexpected directions. I remember that at the time of my visits, sections from *Nineteen Eighty-Four* were appearing in German in *Der Monat*, the American-founded monthly in Berlin (then edited by Melvin Lasky). Orwell had only the sketchiest knowledge of German, yet a surprising feeling for the language. I went over some pages with him. Having spent the war working in psychological warfare against Nazi Germany I could illustrate for him what he had not known in detail, namely that Goebbels had systematically developed a totalitarian Nazi version of German 'Newspeak', obligatory for the entire German press and radio he controlled. Orwell liked the confirmation of his idea about the possible domination of thought by artificial language.

Orwell's last weeks in University College Hospital are always associated in my memory with Sonia – Sonia Brownell, his second wife, whom he had so mysteriously married in his bedridden state in October. To the last three months of his life Sonia had brought a kind of strange, quite external glamour. Sonia was young and beautiful. She was highly intelligent; she had worked most capably as Cyril Connolly's editorial assistant on his famous war and post-war monthly, *Horizon*, where Orwell had met her, fallen in love, and first proposed to her four years earlier.

Although Sonia denied it, I felt sure that she had been a partial model at least for the composite figure of the girl Julia in *Nineteen Eighty-Four*, who brings unexpected love and warmth to the hapless, middle-aged Orwellian hero, Winston Smith. Whenever she arrived during my visits, bringing literary gossip, she seemed to light up the hospital room in which Orwell lay with her vivacity and laughter. I thought that Orwell desperately looked forward to her coming. As he said to me, he had decided on marriage because he thought it might give him an extra hold on life.

On the last occasion I saw Orwell he seemed particularly cheerful. It was, I think, a Friday. The following Tuesday he was due to leave for a sanatorium in Switzerland with Sonia and a young friend, the painter Lucian Freud. He was to go by special charter aircraft. The money from his books was by now pouring in and there was no problem about the cost of the flight. Everything was arranged; the Swiss authorities had agreed to facilitate all formalities. Up in the Alps he said he hoped to be allowed to work for an hour or two a day.

Perhaps there really was some hope. We stayed reminiscing about our early schooldays, his at his class-ridden Edwardian prep school, mine at a state school, democratic socially and authoritarian in methods, in German Switzerland. He talked a little about himself at Eton, relating some amusing incidents. Before I left he urged me to visit him in his Alpine sanatorium. I said I would come if I could manage it. I was the last, or last but one, of his friends to see him. (Paul Potts looked into his room later that evening but saw him asleep and did not go in.) The next morning I received the news that he had died suddenly in the night, within a minute or so after a haemorrhage.

In his will Orwell had asked that no biography should be written about him. During his last years he had made what seemed quite a number of good friends but had rather kept them in separate compartments and he had striven hard to continue to keep his personal life away from all publicity. In the course of his work he had written a good deal about his outward experiences, often in sharply social and political terms, yet about his intimate inner life as Eric Blair, which was his real name, he remained most secretive: he clearly did not want its details aired. Yet such mystery could not be maintained. Only a few months after his death I found myself writing a lengthy article about his life, including my thoughts about his earlier years before I met him, in *World Review*;[1] some time later, replying to critics of his work, I wrote another long essay about his life as a schoolboy and writer in *Encounter*.[2] Indeed, one by one his friends and acquaintances and subsequently younger writers who never knew him have had their say about him in articles, and some in books. Peter Stansky and William Abrahams wrote in biographical detail about his early life[3] and they were followed by the authoritative biography by Bernard Crick.[4]

A good deal is thus known about George Orwell, although I feel there is still much to be said.

I had spent the nineteen-thirties for the most part abroad, but already in that decade I had come to admire Orwell's first novels and his journalism, and I thought of him as the English writer whom upon my return to England I would above all love to meet. Our publisher, Fredric Warburg, brought us together in January 1940, during the dismal days of the phoney war, and our acquaintance extended over the last ten years of Orwell's life.

During these ten years, I saw a good deal of him. In 1940–1, together with Warburg, we edited the 'Searchlight' series of short books on war aims which Orwell led off with *The Lion and the Unicorn*. When, on my return from the war in 1945, I succeeded Orwell as literary editor of the then very independent socialist weekly, *Tribune*, he remained a regular contributor and often talked about his 'As I Please' column and the general policy of the paper. From early on in our acquaintance, my wife and I had become extremely fond of him. Yet the memory of him which has stayed with me most clearly is of those visits to him in hospital in the winter of 1949–50. Across thirty years I have carried in my mind the impression of a dedicated writer who remained to the end his unmistakable, incorruptible, quirky and eccentric self.

While I was somewhat accidentally brought into contact with him, my own ten years of acquaintance with Orwell have, even with the dimming of memory, left an impression unlike any other, a memory of an historic era which has already become remote and of a writer who saw into its essence and understood it.

In rendering this picture of Orwell, I faced two problems. First, when I met Orwell in January 1940, he was already a mature writer, but one influenced all the way by the remarkable direct experience of his life. Prep school, Eton, Burma, Wigan, Catalonia – these had all been essential in shaping his unique outlook, and they demanded mention. Secondly, since his death in January 1950, the impact of his work has increased many, many times over. He has become a popular classic in what could still have been his lifetime and his work has to be seen in those terms. My narrative is therefore cast into three parts. In the first part, I have dealt with his career up to 1940 and the main influences on him of his early life. In the second part, I survey the decade of our acquaintance, while in part three, I try to assess his work in the light of my knowledge of him.

PART ONE

The Wandering Years

ONE

Orwell's Background

ORWELL has himself described how, except for a brief period in his youth, which one could tentatively place as his last year at Eton and his first years as a police officer in Burma, he was always determined to become a writer.

In 'Such, Such Were the Joys', his memoir of his years as a small boarder at his prep school, St Cyprian's, he has related how in self-defence against his persistent unhappiness he developed an inner voice in which he described to himself precisely what he saw around him and what he did. I think that this inner voice remained with him throughout his adult life – hence his compelling feeling that a day without writing was a day wasted. As I recall him as a writer, one impression stands out: he always looked at the world from the perspective of his own personal and social situation and needed always to define and redefine where he stood and what he thought on any issue. I think that this preoccupation with his own personal position had several literary consequences. It followed that all his fiction had strong autobiographical elements. But it also followed, since he was always an imaginative writer seeking self-definition, that his straight autobiographical writings in turn had their touches of fiction, if only in their selectivity. Thirdly, he believed firmly in commitment – in committing himself unequivocally to whatever cause he took up and wrote about.

One can see this need for constant self-definition in the openings of his books and essays, where he seems to brace himself and to plunge in the very first sentence into a definition of the chief character and his predicament. This is so equally in his fiction and non-fiction. In fiction:

'It was a bright day in April, and the clocks were striking

thirteen. Winston Smith, his chin nuzzled into his breast in
an effort to escape the vile wind, slipped quickly through the
glass doors of Victory Mansions, though not quickly enough
to prevent a swirl of gritty dust from entering along with
him.'[1]

Or in non-fiction:

'Soon after I arrived at St Cyprian's (not immediately but
after a week or two, just when I seemed to be settling into the
routine of school life) I began wetting my bed. I was then
eight years old.'[2]

'In Moulmein, in Lower Burma, I was hated by large
numbers of people – the only time in my life that I have been
important enough for this to happen to me.'[3]

Winston Smith observed, Orwell himself observed.

Orwell's most striking instance of self-definition occurs in
The Road to Wigan Pier (1937) where he spends half the book in
explaining in often angry detail who he himself is – this writer
with his upper-middle-class background, education and accent
who in 1936, after viewing the Great Depression in the
industrial north of England, had now become a democratic
socialist. He relates much personal detail of class prejudice,
such as that in his childhood he heard it said that the working
classes smelt and that at his public school (carefully not
named) he was an odious little snob. It is only on a closer look
that we realize that in this long account of his childhood and
youth he does not provide a single definite fact about his
parents, his home and his family background.

About these he never wrote anything. That is, not anything
factual: to judge from his writings, it was as if the gaunt,
tormented figure of George Orwell had sprung abstractly from
a shabby-genteel 'lower upper-middle-class' background.
When I first met him, his mother was still alive and he was
seeing her and his two sisters, but while in our conversations he
would reminisce about Eton, Burma or Spain, he never
mentioned his parents or other members of his family. Well, if
he wanted to keep his origins out of sight of his literary friends,
he was certainly a man whose reticence one respected.

Still, without giving it much thought, I suppose I had a vague impression about these origins. I knew that his baptismal name was Eric Arthur Blair, that he was born in India where his father Richard Blair had been a minor Indian Civil Servant. For want of other evidence I took my ideas from what I considered Orwell's most directly autobiographical novel *Keep the Aspidistra Flying* (1936). In his novel, Orwell's anti-hero Gordon Comstock had like Orwell suffered by being sent to a school where the other boys were richer than he, and, like Orwell, had worked as a bookshop assistant. Orwell also endowed Gordon with a particularly ineffectual and dreary family which had risen from the working classes to insecure gentility, only to sink again. Vaguely I thought that the family sketched in this depressing picture was something like Orwell's own. I also recall his friend Cyril Connolly saying – it was just an unimportant remark, not meant to be slighting – that Orwell was reticent about his family because of their working-class connections. It was only some years after his death when I received a letter from Humphry Dakin, the widowed husband of Orwell's late elder sister Marjorie, complaining about an article which had mentioned Orwell's 'dreary' background, that I realized that the facts about Orwell's family and childhood were much more complicated than I had thought – as one should have suspected.

I drove to Nottingham, where I met Mr Dakin, a retired lesser Civil Servant in his sixties, together with his son and daughter, Orwell's nephew Henry Dakin, an engineer, and his niece Jane Dakin, a teacher. I was almost surprised to find them two normally optimistic, cheerful young people – I was interested in our conversation and took some notes. Dakin himself was short, stout, loquacious and extrovert. He thought that a portrait of himself appeared in the figure of George Bowling in Orwell's novel *Coming Up For Air* (1939) 'though I like to think it a misreading of my character'. As a youngster he had known the Blairs intimately when they lived at Henley-on-Thames (the landscape of his childhood which Orwell so lovingly described in *Coming Up For Air*) and later when they lived at Southwold where he married Orwell's sister Marjorie who was five years older than her brother. 'Like all the Blairs,' said Dakin, 'she was undemonstrative, but unlike Eric she was tolerant, warm, the sort of human being who instinctively invites confidences.' In her two children's recollection, too, Marjorie Dakin stood out as a warm-hearted mother.

Dakin clearly had some confused grievances against his young brother-in-law for having suggested (as in the famous passage in *The Road to Wigan Pier* about his 'lower upper-middle-class' origins) that he came from a shabby-genteel family wretchedly concerned with keeping up appearances without the money for it. Dakin was indignant that some critics had accepted at face value these aspersions on the respectability of that amiable, perfectly genteel middle-class couple, Richard and Ida Blair, whom he remembered fondly. Richard Blair after his retirement had volunteered for the First World War in which he had served as probably the oldest subaltern in the British army. He had been a popular old gentleman in Southwold, pottering round the town wrapped up eccentrically against the cold and playing much bridge. Dakin remembered Mrs Blair, who was partly French, as 'a woman of character and self-assurance who never let doubts about money or social standing worry her'. She had spoiled Eric as a child and in his struggles to become a writer had helped him financially in small ways when she could. So had his elder sister Marjorie – during his early literary struggles Orwell stayed with the Dakins for several periods and, although hard up at the time, they had been glad to give him hospitality as he sat typing away. In fact, said Dakin, Orwell could have no real grievance against his family.

Orwell's nephew and niece, who seemed amused at this whole discussion, supported the memory of Mrs Blair's gift for generous domesticity. Henry Dakin told me, 'From my sixth year till I was about twelve I used to dream about going to my grandparents at Southwold – it was always so jolly.' His sister Jane added: 'To me as a child, the Blairs were *home*. I thought grandmother a marvellous woman. When I recall her house, I always see the same picture of red and white curtains, a table looking just right and a cheerful Ideal boiler. I also remember a well-kept garden and dogs on the lawn. To this day, when I enter a house where a cosy atmosphere mingles with the smell of an Ideal boiler, I think of Grandmother Blair.'

As witness to the Blair family's social status, Dakin showed me his most valued possession, a late eighteenth-century family Bible whose inside covers contained the detailed family tree of 'The descendants of Charles Blair, Esq., and Lady Mary Blair (Fane)' to whose children their uncle, the Earl of Westmorland, stood godfather.

As I looked down the list of generations in this family Bible (which I think I was the first of Orwell's friends to see) it became apparent that Orwell's 'dreary' Comstock family with its working-class origin in *Keep the Aspidistra Flying* was no direct portrait of the Blairs. On the contrary, the Blairs resembled that other English social phenomenon which Bernard Shaw called an upper-middle-class 'downstart' family, with younger sons slipping successively a little down the social scale, but making it not so strange for Orwell to go to Eton on a scholarship.

Biographical literary criticism is always dangerous, but as I drove back to London from my visit to the Dakins, I felt I had some new ideas about the cumulative self-portrait which Orwell had built up in his writings.

His family background to be sure was deeply philistine: there was no evidence that, apart from one aunt, any member of his conventional Anglo-Indian family showed any understanding of the literary ambitions of this strange writer in their midst. Perhaps Orwell resented this; at the same time the Blairs were also much more of an ordinary middle-class family of that Edwardian and post-Edwardian time than a superficial reading of his writings might suggest. When he described himself in *Wigan Pier* as deriving from the 'lower upper-middle class', the reader's attention could have been focused, and deliberately so, too much on the adjective 'lower'. He might have come from its lower fringe, but in the educational spirit he imbibed early in life, Orwell belonged to that English upper-middle class which in that pre-1914 imperial heyday still faithfully preserved the values of the English landed gentry – the ideals of rural life, shooting and other field sports, patriotism, imperial assumptions and the rest.

I thought that this explained one passage in *Wigan Pier* which had stuck in my mind as slightly puzzling. It was where Orwell

said that belonging to the 'lower upper-middle class' at the
£400-a-year level was 'a queer business' which involved one in
what he later called doublethink:

> 'It meant that your gentility was almost purely theoretical.
> You lived, so to speak, at two levels simultaneously.
> Theoretically, you knew all about servants and how to tip
> them, although in practice you had one or, at most, two
> resident servants. Theoretically you knew how to wear your
> clothes or how to order a dinner, although in practice you
> could never afford to go to a decent tailor or a decent
> restaurant. Theoretically you knew how to shoot and ride,
> although you had no horses to ride and not an inch of ground
> to shoot over.'[4]

Decent tailors, restaurants, horses, shooting – I had wondered whether as the son of a minor Indian official on a pension
Orwell wasn't piling on the social demands a bit. Now it
occurred to me that what he really meant to convey was that it
was as a reporter educated to admire this upper-middle-class
life, with his mind filled with unreal demands on him, that he
had gone to look at working-class life in the depressed northern
England of the thirties. He thus felt he looked at it across an
unbridgeable gap.

Still, as far as Orwell's childhood and family were concerned
Wigan Pier lay far in the future. More immediately I found
myself thinking of his melancholy memoir of his years at his
prep school of St Cyprian's, 'Such, Such Were the Joys'. In this
memoir Orwell described how he believed at school that sin
was not something you had the power to commit or not to
commit but that sinfulness was simply a state of which you were
passively possessed. He also wrote about his grievance that his
fellow-pupils could boast of being so much richer than himself.

I felt that there was surely something to be added to the
story. By his own evidence he had already arrived at St
Cyprian's as a small eight-year-old boy preoccupied by feelings
of personal inadequacy and guilt. Why? Who can know? He
was also not unhappy *merely* because other boys were richer
than he. On the contrary, I thought, it was because he was
basically an unhappy child, for all the countless complex

reasons for which a child may be unhappy, that he seized upon
this disparity of wealth as a justification for his unhappy
condition. Hence, perhaps, his later need to caricature his
social background.

The evidence also suggested that he was more attached to his
family background than he made out. While he boarded at St
Cyprian's, home and family and holidays represented safety
and relative happiness. As an adult he went on visits to his
parents to stay with them until well into his thirties. He also
stayed several times with his elder sister Marjorie; and in his
last years, when he was ill on Jura, his younger sister Avril took
over his household. So he had his continuing links to the family
nexus. As to the question why he emerged from it – by his own
evidence – as such an unhappy guilt-haunted small boy: there
we are left without an answer. To be sure, the Blairs were a
conventional, unintellectual family. There was his father whom
he remembered as a gruff elderly figure always saying 'No'.
There was his mother whom he loved as small boys do love
their mothers, but in whom, he said, he just could not confide.
There were his sisters about whom he confessed to a feeling of
guilt because their education had been neglected for the sake of
his.

But all this is ordinary enough. What one is left with is
Orwell as a phenomenon – the fact that he emerged from his
ordinary middle-class family background of that Edwardian
day as a small boy imbued with a sense of guilt, of failure, of
being an outsider, perhaps doomed. Some of these feelings
stayed with him throughout life. In *Nineteen Eighty-Four*, written
at the end of his life, he has Winston Smith feeling guilty over
apparent childhood sins committed against his mother and
sister. Feeling himself from his own childhood on to be solitary,
an outsider, Orwell developed the talent of looking sharply at
the world from this situation; he developed his defensive inner
voice, his determination to become a writer and, fortunately for
his readers, he found in the end all the gifts necessary to achieve
his literary breakthrough.

TWO

Education of a Genius

HOW IT ALL BEGAN. Charles Blair, the man of property who married the daughter of the Earl of Westmorland, was Orwell's ancestor five generations back. To judge from the neatly-drawn family tree which Dakin showed me, the Blairs travelled far and married late. Orwell's grandfather Thomas Blair was born as far back as 1802, 101 years before him. As a younger son, he went in the custom of the day into the Church. This Thomas Blair was an energetic traveller. He was ordained in India and Tasmania and lived for a time at the Cape of Good Hope, where he married and had children before settling down as a vicar in a rural parish in Dorset, where his youngest son, Orwell's father Richard Blair, was born in 1857. Had Orwell heard in the family about his grandfather's rural life, and had it had a nostalgic appeal for him? In 1935, when still an impecunious and struggling young writer in London, he wrote a poem for the *Adelphi* which he remembered well enough to reprint in 1946 in his reflective essay on his own life, entitled 'Why I Write'. The poem began:

> 'A happy vicar I might have been
> Two hundred years ago,
> To preach upon eternal doom,
> And watch my walnuts grow.
>
> But born, alas, in an evil time,
> I missed that pleasant haven . . .'[1]

Richard Blair, Orwell's father, went off to India to serve as a junior officer in the Opium Department of the Indian Government, rising normally in the service before retiring in 1912. He married Ida Limouzin, the daughter of a prominent French businessman and an English mother, in Moulmein in Burma.

Richard Blair's two elder children, Marjorie in 1898 and Eric in 1903, were born in India, his younger daughter Avril in 1907 in England, where Mrs Blair and her small children had gone to live at the then little market-town of Henley-on-Thames. There is some doubt how old Orwell was when he and his mother and sister left for England and whether he had any memories of the bright colours and smells of India, but the fact that he was born in Motihari in Bengal in India on 25 July 1903 and came from an Anglo-Indian family was clearly of basic importance to him: Indian affairs and the question of Indian independence occupied him to the end of his days.

Richard Blair, retiring from the Service at the age of fifty-five, rejoined the family permanently at Henley in 1912 when Orwell was eight. The sudden arrival of an elderly stranger as rival for his mother's attention may or may not have had an emotional effect on him. At any rate, for several years Mrs Blair ran a conventional family life at Henley in which, according to her son-in-law Humphry Dakin, she spoiled her little son Eric, who reciprocated her love although, as he later wrote, he felt too shy to express his feelings for her too directly. He observed that some of his earliest memories were of loneliness. In a family like the Blairs (as Orwell later wrote somewhat scornfully), it was the son's education that counted, more than that of the daughters, or even at the expense of that of the daughters, a preference which was perfectly normal at the time.

Mrs Blair was energetically intent on giving her son the best educational start and the process which was to turn him into George Orwell may be said to have begun when, in 1911, Orwell then being nearly eight, she went to an interview with Mr and Mrs Vaughan Wilkes. They were the headmaster and headmistress and the proprietors of a small private preparatory boarding school, St Cyprian's, at Eastbourne on the south coast. There Orwell was to spend his next five years, from eight to thirteen, by and large unhappy years in his life.

For this unhappiness there were no immediately obvious outward reasons. If St Cyprian's embodied all the typical Edwardian class snobberies, it was also a fairly typical prep school of the time. It was a small private boarding school run

for profit and designed to prepare the sons of comfortably-off
and rich families for entrance at the age of thirteen into the
leading English public schools, while also imbuing them with
the right class-conscious, patriotic and sporting values. But St
Cyprian's also took in a small handful of boys at very much
reduced fees whose task it was to gain scholarships to the very
top public schools and so bring glory and the right reputation,
and ultimately profit, to St Cyprian's.

After Mrs Blair's favourable interview with Mr and Mrs
Vaughan Wilkes, Orwell was in 1911, as a bright boy from a
socially suitable Anglo-Indian family, accepted into St Cyprian's at such reduced fees and one can only say that he fulfilled
both his mother's and the school's expectations. Placed under
constant pressure by the school, which to be sure he certainly
resented, he worked hard in classics, taught by Mr Vaughan
Wilkes himself, and in 1916 at the age of thirteen he gained an
entrance scholarship to the respectable public school of
Wellington.. More than that, he also gained fourteenth place in
the Election (for a free place) to the College at Eton, then very
much England's top school. Mr Vaughan Wilkes, who had
accompanied Orwell to Eton to give him friendly moral
support before his entrance interview, was so delighted by his
pupil's achievement that he awarded the school a half holiday
for it.

Success therefore? Here we come to the paradox: in Orwell's
own view not at all. Thirty years later he described how,
although he had been outwardly successful, as he packed up his
things to leave St Cyprian's for good, his mood was one of dark
pessimism. He might now have a brief respite from his
torments, but it would not be for long:

> 'There was time for a bit of happiness before the future closed
> in upon me. But I did know that the future was dark. Failure,
> failure, failure – failure behind me, failure ahead of me – that
> was by far the deepest conviction that I carried away.'[2]

Orwell's American biographers, Stansky and Abrahams,
somewhat startled, see this passage as 'virtually an aria to
failure, the word itself turning up five times in a twenty-one

word sentence'.³ There is no reason to doubt the accuracy of Orwell's recollection in 1947 of a desperate childhood state of mind which had evidently seared itself into his consciousness so that he still remembered and wrote about it in his forties. The passage comes from his memoir 'Such, Such Were the Joys' which he sent to Warburg from Jura in the middle of 1947, at the time when he was deep in his work on *Nineteen Eighty-Four.*

With 'Such, Such Were the Joys' in fact one enters on a subject of some controversy. The memoir paints a picture of Orwell's childish sorrows at his prep school that seems almost too stark. It presents a bitter attack upon the whole institution of boarding prep schools as they existed in 1911–16, and in particular upon St Cyprian's as the place of Orwell's forlorn, guilt-haunted early loneliness. Above all, the memoir contains a portrait of the headmistress, Mrs Vaughan Wilkes, the real ruler of the school, who is depicted as a harsh and capricious despot. So sharply is the portrait of this lady drawn that one feels as if Orwell, writing thirty years later as a highly successful author amidst the wilds of Jura, still saw her as a baneful influence on his life.

Now, the miseries of his life at St Cyprian's which Orwell describes can seem so dramatized that some critics have taken the memoir as partly an arbitrary angry outburst, partly a desire to write satirical fiction. Here, from my own knowledge of Orwell, I would not agree – I think the sad story he told in 'Such, Such Were the Joys' is what he would have termed 'essentially true'. One has to consider the reason why, after brooding over his youthful grievances for all these years, he finally wrote and completed the memoir in 1947. As he pointed out, he had been irritated by the way in which his schoolfriend and contemporary, Cyril Connolly, had in *his* memoir let off St Cyprian's from the blame due to it. Having long escaped from them, Connolly had treated its miseries much too light-heartedly. He, Orwell, was now going to set the record straight (presumably even if this meant an interruption in his work on *Nineteen Eighty-Four*).

So, in a characteristic bout of self-definition, he sat down on Jura to define the figure of himself as a small boy at boarding school and how as this small boy he had looked upon what went on in the world and upon himself. In this task, I think, he succeeded only too well: defining not only all the guilt and unhappiness he had felt as a small boy but the roots of similar feelings he had harboured as an adult; and by doing so he defined how he first developed his defensive inner voice which he later turned into his writing. In fact, 'Such, Such Were the Joys' can be read as showing how the literary figure of George Orwell first took shape.

To explain this, one has first to view the broad background to his stay at St Cyprian's. To start with there was the money worship of the Edwardian age. As Orwell put it, the years leading up to 1914 were the last era in which the English rich, to whom he did not belong, could flaunt their wealth and power and equate them with virtue without any doubts or self-consciousness, as they could never again do following the disaster of 1914–18. As Orwell was determined to see it, those boys who were handsome and athletic and above all rich, with families that possessed Daimlers and enjoyed Scottish holidays, could pass without effort into the privileged world of their public schools, while he, Orwell, had to slave for an insecure place on their fringe.

Secondly, and Orwell felt this vividly, there was the often harsh psychological wrench experienced by eight-year-old boys as they were sent away from the warmth of loving families to face the cold discipline of boarding school with its lack of privacy. Orwell remembered how he suffered from this change in his life but of course not he alone. England being England – where everybody was at school together – among his fellow-pupils at St Cyprian's were another leading English writer, Cyril Connolly, the future editor of *Horizon*, and the future arbiter of elegant taste, Cecil Beaton. ('From Orwell I learnt about literature,' wrote Connolly, 'from Cecil Beaton about art.')[4] Connolly has described how at first at St Cyprian's he cried himself to sleep night after night. Cecil Beaton cried; there are reports of other future intellectuals crying. Of course, some tougher boys did not cry, and nor did Orwell. He evidently bottled up his feelings of loss and recorded that he only cried once.

A third circumstance was the remarkable personality of Mrs Vaughan Wilkes, called 'Mum', by all accounts a woman in her thirties at once very feminine and very dominant and as headmistress the unchallenged ruler of St Cyprian's. Her habit, as reported by Orwell and Connolly, was first to call nervous newly-arrived eight-year-olds harshly to order, often reducing them to tears, and after that to offer her embrace and love to them to establish her ascendancy. To be in her favour was to bask at ease, to be out of favour for a supposed offence or defect was to have a sense of being cast out. As Orwell and Connolly both reported, everybody at school 'sucked up' to her. Orwell, who inwardly resisted her blandishments, outwardly surrendered as well, while despising himself for it. It is interesting that both Connolly, whose deliberate charm usually kept him in favour, and Orwell describe Mrs Vaughan Wilkes as playing the role of Queen Elizabeth, casting her small charges in turn as Essex. More often than not, Orwell felt that for what he thought unalterable reasons he was out of favour with her and so an outcast.

This was the broad background. As Orwell recalled it in 1947, his sense of being an outcast began with his very arrival at St Cyprian's. After a week, he began nightly to wet his bed. As Orwell remarked, this was not at all an unusual reaction by a small child suddenly removed from home to a strange place, and by 1947 this fact was understood fairly sympathetically, but back in that Edwardian day it was considered, as he said, 'a disgusting crime' for which the proper cure was a beating.

'For my part, I did not need to be told that it was a crime. Night after night I prayed, with a fervour never previously attained in my prayers. "Please God, do not let me wet my bed. Oh please God, do not let me wet my bed", but it made remarkably little difference. Some nights the thing happened, others not. There was no volition about it, no consciousness. You did not properly speaking *do* the deed: you merely woke up in the morning and found that the sheets were wringing wet.'[5]

After the second or third offence, Orwell was warned that he would be beaten next time. He was summoned to Mrs Vaughan Wilkes's study where he found her chatting to a stranger, an intimidating lady with a riding whip. Looking at him with probing eyes – it was difficult to look her in the face without feeling guilty, Orwell later wrote – the headmistress told the lady that here was a little boy who wetted his bed every night and had to be beaten for it. By one of the misunderstandings of childhood, said Orwell, he thought it would be the lady with the whip who would beat him, and, thirty-five years after, he still remembered that terrible moment of standing as a small boy of eight in front of the two women, 'almost swooning with shame'.

Orwell then learned that it was not the lady who would cane him but Mr Vaughan Wilkes, the headmaster, and as such canings were frequent, this evidently brought back welcome normality. He came out of the headmaster's study, boasting that it had not hurt much, was overheard and caned a second time. He cried, for the only time during all his years at St Cyprian's. Not because this second, harder caning had hurt so much either. His grief was spiritual. Because it is so revealing, the passage from the memoir in which Orwell tries to remember his state of mind is, I think, worth quoting in full:

'Fright and shame seemed to have anaesthetized me. I was crying partly because I felt that this was expected of me, partly from genuine repentance, but partly also because of a deeper grief which is peculiar to childhood and not easy to convey: a sense of desolate loneliness and helplessness, of being locked up not only in a hostile world but in a world of good and evil where the rules were such that it was actually not possible for me to keep them.

'I knew that the bedwetting was (a) wicked and (b) outside my control. The second fact I was personally aware of, and the first I did not question. It was possible, therefore, to commit a sin without knowing that you committed it, without wanting to commit it, and without being able to avoid it. Sin was not necessarily something that you did: it might be something that happened to you. . . . I must have had glimpses of this idea even before I left home, for my early childhood had not been altogether happy. But at any rate this was the great, abiding lesson of my boyhood: that I was in a world where it was *not possible* for me to be good. And the double beating was a turning point, for it brought home to me for the first time the harshness of the environment into which I had been flung. Life was more terrible and I was more wicked than I had imagined.'[6]

The bed-wetting duly stopped. But what is one to make of this memory which so rankled in Orwell's mind all the way to his stay on Jura in 1947?

One cannot take 'Such, Such Were the Joys' absolutely literally; Orwell was, of course, looking at his childhood as an adult novelist and expressing his idea that the double beating was a turning-point for him more lucidly than an eight-year-old boy could have done. (It is almost as if he endowed himself as a small boy at boarding school with that sense of isolation felt by Winston Smith in the threatening society of *Nineteen Eighty-Four*; or alternatively as if he gave Winston Smith the memories of his own desolate feelings of guilt in childhood.) Even so, the clarity with which the memory of childish grief lived on in Orwell's adult mind is remarkable – it shows that in this respect the bed-wetting episode was indeed formative.

His friend Malcolm Muggeridge has suggested that Orwell was strongly influenced by self-pity. I don't think it is exactly that. 'Such, Such Were the Joys' represents simply another of his attempts at self-definition. What does emerge from this account is that Orwell already came out of his home with feelings of guilt and personal unworthiness which he carried with him to school, feelings whose origins must remain unknown. The evidence is that he loved his mother as a small child. There was in his infancy certainly no trace of any neglect or cruelty, as was the case with some other writers (Kipling, for example). If he said that his early childhood 'had not been altogether happy', how many childhoods are?

Many children who have such guilt feelings manage to shake them off. In Orwell's case, they seemed to become part of his fixed view of himself, of society, of life; one part of this view, at least. I think that the harm which St Cyprian's did him was both to provide a social rationale for these guilt feelings and to reinforce them. It provided this rationale by its faithful mirroring of the Edwardian class outlook. As seen by its upper classes, England in the years before 1914 was a great country with an Empire on which the sun never set. As seen at St Cyprian's, for a boy not to pass on into one of the leading public schools, the pride and buttress of this England, was like dropping into outer darkness. Such a boy could at best become a little clerk sitting on a stool in an office, a fate depicted as that of an outcast.

But this outer darkness was something which Orwell says he always vaguely felt he belonged to and perhaps was drawn to. His sense of guilt was next directly stimulated further. He had been at the school for two years, with three more to come, when he was told what he named 'the shameful secret': he had been accepted at St Cyprian's *at much reduced fees* as a favour bestowed by Mr and Mrs Vaughan Wilkes in their kindness upon that excellent lady, his mother, and upon himself. In return, to show proper gratitude for this rare favour, it was now his task to work singlemindedly for three years in classics, under the tuition of Mr Vaughan Wilkes, in order finally to pass a scholarship examination to one of the half-dozen leading public schools, as was expected of him.

Shaken by this revelation of being not only an imagined but an actual outsider in the school, yet being only an inner rebel, Orwell did in fact usually work quite hard with a sense of threat hanging over him. As he says, 'Over a period of two years, I do not think there was ever a day when "the exam", as I called it, was quite out of my waking thoughts. In my prayers it featured invariably.' But he also tells how he was tormented by the occasional impulse not to work, to slack off. At such times he was subjected to formalized scoldings by Mr and Mrs Vaughan Wilkes which seemed to be directed right at his guilt feelings. Mrs Vaughan Wilkes, Orwell said, took the lead in this attack in her experienced manner of getting through a small boy's guard.

Was it awfully decent of him, she would say, was it playing the game by his parents – did he *want* to throw all his chances away? He must know that his people weren't rich like other parents, and could not afford to send him to a public school if he didn't win a scholarship. His mother was so proud of him. Did he *want* to let her down?

At this point her husband would say that Orwell had clearly given up the idea of going to a public school. 'He wants to be a little office boy at £40 a year.'

Orwell relates that at this point, as he stood there already assailed by the sensation of tears held back, Mrs Vaughan Wilkes would play her trump card. Did he think it was quite fair to *them*, the proprietors of the school, to behave in such an idle way after all they had done for him? They had kept him at the school for years, they had even let him stay for a week in the holidays for extra tuition, they did not *want* to send him away; but did he think it was very straight, the way he did not work as hard as he should?

He never had any answer, Orwell says, except a guilty 'No, Mum,' or 'Yes, Mum,' as the case might be, and a surreptitious tear.

Previously he had partly come to terms with the fact that he could not, as he says other boys did, boast about his parents' assets and did not have as much pocket money as many other boys. But the revelation of the secret of his 'reduced fees' status and the subtle playing by the Vaughan Wilkeses upon his sense of guilt – these things, as he later suggested, caused his guilt to congeal into a fixed, negative view of the accepted social order and his lowly place within it. He concluded that in the society into which he had been harshly thrown, it was not what one *did* that mattered but what one unchangeably *was*. To succeed, to be in favour with Mrs Vaughan Wilkes, one had to be handsome or athletic and above all rich, enjoying privileges as by right. He recollected that he thought obsessively as a boy that he was none of these things: 'I had no money, I was weak, I was ugly, I was unpopular, I had a chronic cough, I was cowardly, I smelt. This picture, I should add, was not altogether fanciful. I was an unattractive boy.' If by the evidence of others (Connolly, for example) even this qualified judgement was a fancy, deep in Orwell's mind there was the picture of an impregnable social system into which rich boys were born, while there were the born outsiders like himself who were victims.

This negative view of society as an institution whose ruling caste had no real place for him was a pattern which Orwell long kept in his mind. His main fictional characters, Flory in

Burmese Days, Gordon in *Keep the Aspidistra Flying* and Winston Smith in *Nineteen Eighty-Four* were all outsiders and failed rebels in their societies. If one takes it that he half accepted Mrs Vaughan Wilkes's view of himself, one can understand how, in saying good-bye to her in 1916, Orwell could feel deep in his mind that in spite of his public school scholarship, like his past, so his future would be marked only by failure. What sort of failure? That was not so easy to say: it might be largely a mood of failure, but failure it would be. His friend Cyril Connolly has written that as a schoolboy he himself was a stage rebel, Orwell a real rebel, but this was also not quite exact. Orwell's actual rebellion against society still lay a full twelve years ahead. When parting from Mrs Vaughan Wilkes he was still only a defiant inner rebel against those right social values which she had tried her hardest to instil in him and, as she saw it, had failed to do. Writing thirty years later about that moment of parting, Orwell said that he knew that the headmistress was well aware of this inner defiance of his.

What emerges from this account is simply Orwell's special sensibility. There have been suggestions that the picture he drew of St Cyprian's is much overwritten. Orwell's early biographers, Stansky and Abrahams, visited Mrs Vaughan Wilkes many years later in her retirement. They encountered a friendly, pleasant old lady, sitting in a room filled with photographs from grateful former pupils, some become quite prominent men, sent to their much appreciated 'Mum'. She remembered Orwell, she said, recalling him as one of the rare boys in whose case, whenever she tried to show her affection, she just could not get past his resistance.

Bernard Crick interviewed some of Orwell's surviving contemporaries at St Cyprian's (including the eminent golf correspondent, Henry Longhurst). Some of the tougher-minded evidently thought that Mr and Mrs Vaughan Wilkes were good heads of a good prep school, that after the initial homesickness life at St Cyprian's was quite reasonable, that the boys weren't snobbish, that young Blair was all right and his later picture of the school one drawn by an embittered adult.

One can only say about this that such views of St Cyprian's were different from those of Orwell (and Connolly and others), the difference deriving from the character of the boy concerned. Secondly of course, as Orwell wrote in 'Such, Such Were the Joys', no one's schooldays could be all unhappy and he himself had good memories of the school among the bad ones. For instance, the secret of his reduced-fees status which he thought so shameful was decently kept secret by the Vaughan Wilkeses. (Connolly said he learned of it only when reading Orwell's memoir.) Among the good memories Orwell recalled as a country-lover was that the situation of the school on the south coast permitted 'wonderful expeditions across the Downs'. There were midsummer evenings when 'as a special treat, we were not driven to bed as usual, but allowed to wander about the grounds in the long twilight, ending up with a plunge in the swimming bath'. Led by a master he liked, there were exciting butterfly-hunting excursions. There was cricket with which he conducted 'a hopeless love-affair'. There were the marvellous pleasures of reading. He recalled stealing into the silent dormitory one summer's dawn and making off with Connolly's copy of Wells's *The Country of the Blind*. Again, the tensions of boarding-school life were broken by the relaxation of long holidays at home. As recalled by Orwell's younger sister Avril and one close childhood friend, his early life at home or on family holidays appeared one of active normality.

This normality is also reflected in his letters of the time. The point about his letters to his 'darling mother' of which unfortunately only the first two years of correspondence have survived, is that they could be the ordinary letters of any small boy. In the letters, Orwell writes in a typical small boy's brief style about sometimes getting good marks in class, about his collection of caterpillars, about games, victories in school matches, about end-of-term celebrations in fancy dress. He asks his mother for news of the family pets and for a birthday present of a gun-metal watch. In all these letters there is no mention whatever of those harrowing sufferings at the school which he so vividly wrote about in 1947.

Some critics have tried to make much of the apparent contrast between this normality and Orwell's later recollections of deep unhappiness, but I think to do so is to ignore basic child psychology. Orwell would never have confided his

peculiar torments to any schoolfellows. As he said, boys are apt
to think that if they are unhappy at school the fault is theirs and
that misfortune is a disgrace to be concealed. He said that the
last people to whom he could have written about his unhappiness in an apparently hostile St Cyprian's were his parents,
whom he regarded as being under an obligation to the
Vaughan Wilkeses for accepting him. It is a common fact that
parents are often the last to hear of their children's sufferings at
school.

No, the striking impression, as one reads Orwell's reconstruc-
tion of his childhood griefs and pleasures in 'Such, Such Were
the Joys', is how much of Orwell the adult writer was already
there in the solitary small boy he depicted.

There was the nightmarish fixed memory of the bed-wetting
and guilt, and there was his early love of the countryside. There
was his love of reading. Among the books which he and
Connolly read avidly at St Cyprian's, Orwell says that the
favourite authors he remembers were Swift, Thackeray,
Kipling, Wodehouse and Wells. All of these except for
Thackeray were to become subjects of his adult critical essays,
some of them published in Connolly's *Horizon*. He tells how,
receiving *Gulliver's Travels* on his eighth birthday, he read it over
and over again – one can see the link to *Animal Farm*.

While Orwell was at St Cyprian's and aged eleven, the First
World War, then called 'the Great War' broke out. In an initial
flush of warlike enthusiasm, in a school competition, Orwell
wrote a prize poem called 'Awake, Young Men of England'
which ended:

> 'Awake, oh you young men of England,
> For if, when your Country's in need,
> You do not enlist in your thousands
> You truly are cowards indeed.'

His proud mother had the poem printed in the local Henley
newspaper. Bernard Crick quotes it in his biography and also a
poem Orwell wrote a year later to commemorate the death of
Lord Kitchener, also published in the Henley press. Orwell's
sentiments as a small boy towards the war being fought over in
France were no doubt of the most conventional kind (at first,

that is) but I like to think that his early English patriotism was genuine; and that, when abandoning some Left-wing senti-ments and rallying to the call in September 1939, he was returning to his early love for England.

Again, one notes how early in life he showed his quite unusual sensitivity towards ugly or hostile environments. This emerges in his description of the repellent sides of life at St Cyprian's (after all, a private school run for profit). As he recalls his impressions of the sour porridge constantly served up on unclean plates, the slimy water in the plunge baths, the hard, lumpy beds, the sweaty smell of the changing room, the lack of all privacy, the rows of filthy lavatories without locks, and the constant noise of the banging of lavatory doors and the echoing sound of chamber-pots in the dormitories – as he recalls this with that peculiar sensitivity of his, one can almost see Orwell using his description of St Cyprian's as a trial run for the shabbiness of *Nineteen Eighty-Four*.

Against this were contrary memories. Connolly much later (in a review of *Animal Farm*) called Orwell a revolutionary in love with the year 1910 and the quip had its truth. When Orwell arrived at St Cyprian's, England had been largely at peace for a hundred years. Even in a melancholy memoir like 'Such, Such Were the Joys' one can catch a few glimpses of Orwell's vision of the secure England of his childhood, a largely rural England plunged into deep peace, where every person had his assured place. The vision of this peaceful England recurred in his writings all the way to *Nineteen Eighty-Four*.

And all this, both the anguished sense of guilt and the awareness of the hostile side of school life, together with the contrary pleasures of his childhood, he said he began to record at St Cyprian's with his inner voice. As he wrote in 1946 in 'Why I Write', in an attempt at retrospective self-definition, he had the lonely child's habit of making up stories:

> 'I think from the very start my literary ambitions were mixed up with the feeling of being isolated and undervalued. I knew that I had a facility with words and a power of facing unpleasant facts and I felt that this created a private world in which I could get my own back for my failure in everyday life.

... For fifteen years or more I was carrying out a literary exercise: this was the making up of a continuous "story" about myself, a sort of diary existing only in the mind.'[7]

In short, the child is father of the man. So clear is the retrospect that, if one likes, one can already see in the small boy at St Cyprian's all the traits of the essential writer to come.

THREE

Eton – and then Burma

A T ETON things were different. There, the future Orwell as writer seemed to vanish, to re-emerge only in his later years in Burma. At Eton, one is left with Eric Blair who arrived at Eton as a King's Scholar in January 1917 and stayed there for four and a half years until the summer of 1921, when he was eighteen.

The fact which stands out in Orwell's Etonian years is that his adolescence was quite different from his childhood at St Cyprian's. He was no longer deeply troubled. That can be said with certainty, but in the end not very much more. Conversations conducted many years later with his contemporaries at Eton about Eric Blair have unearthed relatively little about his feelings while he was a schoolboy there. He himself gave readers the precise account of his childhood sufferings at St Cyprian's, but about his time at Eton we have only a few brief generalizations. From *Wigan Pier* in 1936 onwards, he advocated the abolition of Eton, as of other leading public schools, in their socially exclusive form; but this was simply part of the general socialist philosophy he had by then adopted. About his actual life and individual thoughts at Eton, as opposed to the analysis of his life before at prep school and afterwards in Burma, he remained resolutely silent. It is almost as if at Eton 'the real Orwell' went underground.

One can guess at reasons. Eton in his time was a unique English institution, an exclusive school designed automatically to perpetuate a system of aristocratic rule in England and at the same time offering the best of liberal education to those who wanted it. Arriving there, Orwell faced a contradiction. He had left St Cyprian's, as he said, with a sense of failure behind and ahead, but here he was at Eton, England's topmost school, a pupil alongside upper-class boys who would after leaving go out to dominate English country life and the City, the best regiments and the Empire. He mingled with such boys within socially restricted limits, to be sure, but still he rubbed shoulders with them, as one of them. Being unchallenged in its aristocratic assumptions, Eton could also afford to be liberal and tolerant towards intellectual nonconformity and oddity. It was before and during Orwell's time a school harbouring not only future guards officers, but Maynard Keynes, Osbert Sitwell, Aldous Huxley, Richard Rees, Anthony Powell, Cyril Connolly and Orwell himself. There is no evidence that Eton's literary liberalism shaped Orwell's character in a major way – that character was set; but the tolerant upper-class environment around him from the age of thirteen to eighteen had, I think, an obvious influence on him.

It is clear that after the awful treadmill of working for his scholarship at St Cyprian's, Eton gave him four and a half years of welcome social respite. As a school Eton was divided into two sections. There was the College with some seventy to eighty King's Scholars, supported by generous scholarships. Each year an 'Election' of thirteen to fifteen boys was chosen by competitive entrance examination. Orwell had his place in the particularly bright Election of 1916. Then there were 900 or so Oppidans, living in masters' houses in the town, belonging to families which were eligible to obtain a place at Eton and rich enough to pay the high fees. If the Collegers might occasionally be looked down upon by more élitist Oppidans, their contribution in intelligence and hard work was appreciated in the school. The institution of King's Scholars at Eton, after all, went right back to the fifteenth century.

Again, most of Orwell's fellow-Collegers came from good upper-middle and professional class families. Even if it was on the lower edge, his own Anglo-Indian family could be said to belong to the same background. Orwell's overall fees at Eton took a fair slice out of his father's pension, but they were bearable. In other words, while not affluent, Orwell at Eton had what was most important to young people – he had a reasonably secure place within a respected social group. It looks as if, in this position, the sense of guilt and of being a

victim with which Orwell had arrived, became pushed back
into his subconscious by the normality of his Eton life.

Yet one point stands out. Orwell at Eton did not, as a
reasonably ambitious boy might have done, make use of the
advantages of his situation. He did not sit down to work for the
next expected stage, a scholarship to Oxford or Cambridge
which as a clever boy at Eton he could readily have obtained.
Such an Oxbridge scholarship might, for instance, have led to a
Civil Service career as Sir Eric Blair, KCMG; or it might have led
him straight into the world of English literature, like his friend
Cyril Connolly. He himself said that he felt early on that he had
a facility with words.

So why did he not apply himself to this next stage in his
career? Well, gaining such a scholarship, say in classics, would
have meant some years of fairly consistent work; and, according to the sketchy recollections of his teachers, Orwell at no
time applied himself to this task. Quite the contrary, he gave no
sign of wanting such a prize. One can only speculate about this.
Was it that working hard for successive steps in a proper career
would have meant following the instruction of Mrs Vaughan
Wilkes at St Cyprian's that he must always slave away so as not
to fall by the wayside? Was a sense of personal inadequacy still
there at the back of his mind?

This is mere surmise. In the end we are left not with the
motivations but only the shadowy outline of the schoolboy Eric
Blair.

He has been described as cool, cynical, and in some ways
mature at an early age. There is his much-quoted remark to
Cyril Connolly when he was fourteen: that whoever wins this
war, we shall emerge from it as a second-class power. Socially
he was seemingly somewhat diffident, restricting his contacts
mainly to the members of his Election and the adjoining ones at
the College. He was sometimes a welcome conversational
partner on the long walks that were an Eton habit, but he had
acquaintances rather than friends. Cyril Connolly has written
that at Eton, he and Orwell as friends drifted apart, as they did
in their reading. Orwell read authors of social significance such
as Wells, Shaw, Samuel Butler and Jack London (whose study
of East End squalor, *The People of the Abyss*, made a deep

impression on him) while Connolly, as he has said, became immersed in the Moderns and the Celtic twilight.

As Orwell grew tall, he became prominent in the annual Wall Game peculiar to Eton and was awarded his College Colours. He became a member, although never prominent, of the College Debating Society. He belonged to the Officers' Training Corps and seemed to enjoy the annual camp, while remaining completely cynical about the militarism involved. As he later recollected, in the reaction after the end of the war in 1918, a brief revolutionary tremor passed through Eton in which some boys were considered 'bolshie'. Orwell sympathized with their ideas but was never a systematic rebel. When his Election reached sixth form status, it did indeed stage an actual revolt against the Eton system of fagging and caning – in his time, the caning of junior boys by their seniors on their bare buttocks was still the accepted practice. Orwell openly despised caning and there is no evidence that as a sixth former he ever caned anyone, but again he was no active insider in the revolt.

He kept more or less out of sight. Among the Oppidans in his Eton days there was, contemporary with him, a remarkable literary and aesthetic circle, including Brian Howard, Harold Acton, Anthony Powell and Henry York (the novelist Henry Green), together with Collegers like Connolly and Alan Clutton-Brock. The group produced a one-issue magazine, *The Eton Candle*, with contributions by older Etonians like the Sitwell brothers and Aldous Huxley. There is no evidence that Orwell had anything to do with these Etonian literary aesthetes.

Did his silent Eton years then have no influence on him, as he himself, I think, rather liked to suggest? On the contrary, I think they did have a considerable influence, subtle perhaps but always there. Somebody has said that throughout his varied career, Orwell was recognizable as an Etonian – well, maybe. At any rate, for five years Orwell had been part of an upper-class group of adolescents in which snobbery was not so much internal, as directed against all the benighted people outside the school. Some of the social confidence this experience had engendered remained with him. Even when ordered around as a junior police officer in Burma or when he went slumming, some of that confidence was still there in his mind, alongside all his innate shyness and awkwardness. When he became a Left-wing socialist, he was never worried when meeting leading members of the Establishment. Finally, when he wrote his mature essays telling his readers how to use the English language and what to think of their literary heroes, one can catch hints of upper-class social assurance.

Eton also gave him a sharp idea of how the English class system worked and who was truly of the English upper class and who was not. One can see traces of his absorption of this fact in his writings. (Even in 'Such, Such Were the Joys', he described the majority of his boastful schoolfellows as coming not from the true upper class who lived on country estates but from the rich middle class who owned large suburban houses with large gardens and shrubberies.) In his time at Eton during the First World War, Orwell was also made intimately aware of how many older boys went without question into the forces and how many became casualties. Every ruling class must have a creed for which its members were ready to fight and die. What Orwell learned was that, whatever else might be said against them, the British ruling classes were still patriotically willing to do this; and he emphasized this later in 1940–1, in *The Lion and the Unicorn.*

Lastly, whether he wanted this or not, Eton provided him with a network of fellow-Etonians who gave him help at crucial stages of his literary career. It was a slightly older Etonian, Richard Rees, who became a close friend and published his first essays and criticism in the *Adelphi.* John Lehmann published 'Shooting an Elephant' in *Penguin New Writing.* Cyril Connolly favourably reviewed his early novels and praised him as a young English novelist in *Enemies of Promise* and after 1940 provided a place for Orwell's writing in *Horizon,* as David Astor did a little later in the *Observer.* In his last years, for all that they were completely opposed in their political views, his Eton contemporary, Anthony Powell, became his firm friend. The Eton network was always there for the author of *Nineteen Eighty-Four.*

On his leaving in 1921, one comes on something of a puzzle. According to the literary chronology he presented in 'Why I

Write', it was in his last year at Eton, and with much
heartache, that he temporarily gave up the idea of becoming a
writer. Why? One does not know. So what next? He told me
once that he had not wanted to go on to Oxford or Cambridge
as there he would still have been in the undesirable position of
being among people richer than himself, but this sounded not
very convincing. In any case, as he had not worked for a
scholarship, financially the idea of Oxford or Cambridge (other
universities hardly counted at Eton) was not on. Whether he
had any alternative ideas about his future we do not know, but
it could have seemed the simplest thing to follow in the family
tradition and go into the Colonial Service in Burma where his
mother's family had connections. His father, that shadowy
figure Richard Blair, was said to have played a role in
influencing him to take this decision. But why did Orwell enrol
as a police officer charged with what he later described as the
'dirty work' of upholding British imperial rule by force? This
seemed a strange choice for an aloof and at times rebellious
adolescent, who had stigmatized caning at Eton as 'disgusting
and barbarous'.

Perhaps Orwell was ambivalent about the role in life he saw
for himself at the time. His second wife Sonia told me that not
long before his death she asked him: 'George, why not
Oxbridge? Why the Burma police?' Orwell replied that this
was a long and complicated story and he would tell her some
time. But he never got around to it.

So one is left with the puzzle. But the point is also that after
his restful interlude at Eton, by entering the Indian police
service in Burma, he became once more a young man filled with
an increasing sense of rebellion, once more characteristically
George Orwell, starting out on the decade of his wandering
years in Burma, Paris, London, Wigan and Spain.

The contrast between the relaxed upper-class atmosphere of
Eton and the life of a very junior Assistant Superintendent of
Police plunged into the problems of Burmese colonial life of the
twenties must have been a striking one for Orwell. In the
British colonial police Etonians were few and far between.

In his career as a writer, however, it may have been highly
valuable to Orwell that he went as a police officer to Burma

instead of proceeding conventionally from Eton to Oxbridge and on into literary London. There he would have been immediately exposed to *received* English high-cultural opinions; as it was, in the Indian police service in Burma he saw life in the raw. He observed all the glaring foreignness of Asian culture and the fact that British rule with all its benignity rested ultimately on the application of brute force, a decisive lesson for him as a writer. He also learned about the way people complied with a government machine they hated, another lesson he noted for life.

It is already difficult to visualize the Burma to which Orwell came in 1922. Shortly after his arrival the so-called Montagu-Chelmsford reforms, already in force in India, were applied to Burma, too. This meant the grant of an elected Burmese legislature with limited powers and other small advances in self-government as a concession to sporadically militant Burmese nationalism. But at the same time the British still ruled Burma at the top; British troops and police remained responsible for law and order and British interests ruled the country's economic heights. British imperial rule over Burma – that is, white European rule over Asians – was still regarded by the Europeans in Burma as a permanency, as simply the natural order of things.

It was into a divided society that Orwell was plunged. There was the small insulated world of the British military and civilians with its officers and clubs, its newspapers and magazines from home, its functions and very British class distinctions; and there was the sprawling world of the Buddhist Burmese, with little meeting between the two. Orwell's writings suggest an awareness of this sharp division from the beginning of his training as Assistant Superintendent of Police in the fort at Mandalay, the chief city of Upper Burma. There, alongside the British enclave, he observed the native Burmese life of crowded, noisy streets and teeming bazaars, of priests and pagodas. As he later wrote, his first impression was that beside the fine-boned golden-skinned Asians, Europeans looked uncouth.

His first two postings were in the Irrawaddi Delta, the next in the capital, Rangoon. The advantage of the Delta posts was that from there he could also visit Rangoon for brief snatches of a civilized European life of meeting his acquaintances in clubs, shopping and above all browsing in Rangoon's handful of bookshops for his favourite pastime – voracious reading. Disadvantages were the repellent landscape of the Delta and the hot, oppressive climate. Sensitive as he was to hostile environments, Orwell later wrote that for years afterwards his dreams were troubled by nightmarish visions of Burmese scenery.

In 1926 Orwell was transferred to police headquarters in Moulmein, a largish coastal city with a fair-sized European community, its own racecourse and so forth. Orwell's Limouzin grandmother was a prominent local citizen of Moulmein and was by now an eccentric old lady who liked to dress in native Burmese garb. Orwell must have visited her, although, like so many other facets of his life, he never mentioned her in his writings.

His last assignment, early in 1927, was to a more remote station in Katha, in Upper Burma. Here the landscape was garishly colourful, the vegetation lush; Katha was situated among dense riverside jungles, where an extensive timber trade was conducted. It was Katha with its small European community and club which was to be the model for the 'Kyauktada' whose Burmese and British inhabitants he was later on to satirize so fiercely in his novel *Burmese Days* (1935). In Katha he also fell very seriously ill with chest troubles. This was the first of several collapses in his life. It was not yet diagnosed as TB, but was enough to make him apply for home leave. He was granted leave of eight months and in July 1927 embarked for England, not to return. He had served as a police officer in Burma for five years.

Directly and autobiographically Orwell only wrote about his Burmese experience ten years later, in *The Road to Wigan Pier* (1937). There he said definitely that, 'I was in the Indian Police in Burma for five years and by the end of the time I hated the imperialism I was serving with a bitterness which I probably cannot make clear.'[1] This retrospective declaration of hatred for the Empire, however, does not quite tally with the evidence of others about his outward attitudes while actually in Burma, nor indeed with all of his own recollections.

His fellow-Etonian, Christopher Hollis, who visited Orwell in Burma in 1925, claimed that he found him transformed into a Kiplingesque empire-builder, intolerant of those Burmese, the Buddhist monks in particular, who made nuisances of themselves. His Etonian theory of no punishments and no beatings, Orwell apparently said to him, did not work in Burma. Hollis said that he heard no liberal opinions expressed by Orwell nor complaints about the unpleasantness of a police officer's life.[2] Stansky and Abrahams, who were able to interview some of Orwell's Burma colleagues in the early sixties, found some of them very surprised that the ordinary Assistant Superintendent of Police, Eric Blair, whom they knew as performing his duties as conscientiously as the next man, should have become the great critic, George Orwell.[3]

The explanation seems fairly simple. Orwell was only an ex-schoolboy of nineteen when he arrived in Burma. In the group photograph of new police officers taken in 1922 at training school in Mandalay, he seems to stare impassively ahead, a tall youth smartly turned out in his British uniform, looking like a fully integrated member of his group. Conscientious? Orwell was conscientious in all he undertook in life, and so he must have been in carrying out his police duties in Burma. If he was a rebel against the Empire, it was only at decisive moments and then only as an inner rebel. Most of the time he must have looked at the Burmese colonial scene through the same eyes as his colleagues, seeing the Burmese as people to be kept in order. As he himself recalled in *Wigan Pier*, he had his moments of suppressed violence when he would have liked to plunge his bayonet into a jeering Buddhist priest: Asians could be very provocative. Also, he said, he shared the European view of regarding Asians as quite different humans, as when he let his Burmese servant undress him, which he would never have let a European do.

He also tells how on one occasion when travelling with a colleague in a train, they sat up into the night damning the British Empire from the inside. But they had been speaking forbidden things and in the morning, Orwell reported, they parted 'as guiltily as any adulterous couple'.

So what did Orwell as a future writer carry away from his Burmese experience? First, in Burma he began to read some of the Moderns; he tried his hand at writing some poetry. In his decision to listen to his inner voice again and to devote his life to becoming a writer lay his primary rebellion.

This must have told him plainly that whatever his outward conformism, he was deeply opposed to the British Empire which he regarded as by now running down. He made the shrewd secondary observation that it was not the British ruling classes whom one found in the colonies. In *Burmese Days* it is with almost Etonian social disdain that he satirizes his little group of Burma British, intent on keeping the natives out of their precious European club. (In *Wigan Pier* he stated that most of the white men in Burma were not of the type who in England would be called gentlemen.)

Thirdly, from his experience as a colonial officer he carried away with him a sense of revulsion against the brutality involved in any maintenance of law and order. Four years after his return to England, in his essay 'A Hanging' (1931) he described his revulsion over an execution:

> 'I watched the bare brown back of the prisoner marching in front of me. He walked clumsily with his bound arms, but quite steadily . . . and once, in spite of the men who gripped him by each shoulder he stepped slightly aside to avoid a puddle on the path. It is curious, but till that moment I had never realised what it means to destroy a healthy, conscious man. When I saw the prisoner step aside to avoid the puddle, I saw the mystery, the unspeakable wrongness, of cutting a life short when it is in full tide.'[4]

Fiction or stylized autobiography: the essay makes its point. Five years later in *Wigan Pier* he tried again to sum up what he felt, or thought he should have felt, in Burma about the 'dirty work' he had to carry out as a police officer:

> 'Say what you will, our criminal law (far more humane, by the way, in India than in England) is a horrible thing. It needs very insensitive people to administer it. The wretched prisoners squatting in the reeking cages of the lock-ups, the grey cowed faces of the long-term convicts, the scarred buttocks of the men who had been flogged with bamboos,

the women and children howling ... things like these are beyond bearing when you are in any way directly responsible for them. I watched a man hanged once; it seemed to me worse than a thousand murders. I never went into a jail without feeling (most visitors to jails feel the same) that my place was on the other side of the bars.'[5]

Finally, in one of his best-known essays 'Shooting an Elephant' (1936), he tried once more to indicate his ideas about the impending end of the British Empire in describing his feelings during an incident when he was forced by a Burmese crowd to shoot an elephant, even though he knew that the runaway beast had turned harmless and he did not want to kill it:

'It was at this moment, as I stood there with my rifle in my hands, that I first grasped the hollowness, the futility of the white man's dominion in the East. Here was I, the white man with the gun, standing in front of the unarmed native crowd – seemingly the leading actor of the piece; but in reality I was only an absurd puppet pushed to and fro by the will of those yellow faces behind. I perceived in this moment that when the white man turns tyrant it is his own freedom that he destroys. He becomes a sort of hollow, posing dummy, the conventionalized figure of a *Sahib*.'[6]

I have cited these definitions of Orwell's about himself in Burma because in their mood they suggest that some of the imagery Orwell was to incorporate in *Nineteen Eighty-Four* was already in Burma vaguely in his mind. At any rate, it was with the notion that the British Empire should be wound up forthwith and with the reawakened idea of becoming a writer that he returned in 1927 from Burma to England.

One last point. Amid the glaring heat and colours of Burma, he realized that faraway Britain with her grey skies was only one fragment of the global scene. I have a feeling that from then on, with all his emotional involvement, he looked on Britain at times as if through the eyes of an outside observer.

FOUR

Down and Out?

O RWELL'S parents with whom he went to stay in Southwold on his return to England must have been bewildered that their son had thrown up a promising career in Burma with no prospects other than that he wanted to write – but write what? A writer he did become, but it took five years of painful setbacks before his first book was published. This was *Down and Out in Paris and London* (1933), a portrait of the sordid undersides of British and French societies.

Why did he choose this theme? Looking back a decade later in *Wigan Pier*, Orwell wrote that his motive for plunging into the social depths arose from feelings of guilt because of the punitive role he had played for five years as a colonial policeman. He was conscious of an enormous weight of guilt he had to expiate, so he wrote, and therefore, being politically inexperienced, he wanted to make contact with social outcasts, with tramps, criminals and prostitutes, the lowest of the low in society. Indeed, his serious aim was 'to get out of the respectable world altogether'.

In this self-definition he was, I think, rationalizing somewhat. He may have felt pangs of political guilt over his job in Burma, but the emotions which prompted him in 1927 to try to drop out of respectable society altogether were surely much deeper and went further back – right back to the sense of guilt and isolation he had felt as a small boy at St Cyprian's. At the same time, of course, these psychological reasons for seeking to drop out of society merged more and more with his search for specific material for the writing he had in mind – this was where he followed his inner voice.

The search quite evidently did not start at all well. A family acquaintance, the writer and artist Ruth Pitter, remembered him at the start of his literary career as a tall, awkward young man who seemed to her far from well, who talked wildly about the need to end British rule in Burma and saved money by warming his hands above a candle flame. Taking as model one of his favourite books, Jack London's *The People of the Abyss*, he roamed the slums of the East End for material. Ruth Pitter thought that at the start he wrote badly, but seemed determined to go on.[1]

Orwell was to need all his determination to become a writer during the next four years of setbacks, of rejections and of enduring spells of poverty. Considering his later facility in turning out journalistic pieces by the score plus essays and books, one may wonder why it took him such a painfully long period to get started, as opposed to other young writers of the time who sat down to turn out novel after novel. My guess is that he just could not write well in any received or imitative way. He had to listen to his own voice, and deciphering just what this voice wanted him to say was a task he at first found excruciatingly difficult.

Early in the winter of 1928 he took himself off like so many other would-be writers and artists of the time to Paris, where he was to stay for twenty months. Looking back on it, this was a fortunate move, because in the cosmopolitan Paris of the day he was ultimately to discover the eccentric human scenes whose description would give him his literary start. This Parisian material makes up the first part of his book of autobiographical reportage, *Down and Out in Paris and London* which he was to complete four years later but only after agonizing effort. In the event the book opened with a sprightly account of morning in a Parisian working-class street:

'The rue du Coq d'Or, Paris, seven in the morning. A succession of furious, choking yells from the street. Madame Monce, who kept the little hotel opposite mine, had come out on to the pavement to address a lodger on the third floor. Her bare feet were stuck into *sabots* and her grey hair was streaming down.

Madame Monce: *"Salope! Salope!* How many times have I told you not to squash bugs on the wallpaper? Do you think you've bought the hotel, eh? Why can't you throw them out of the window like everyone else? *Putain! Salope!"*

The woman on the third floor: *"Vache!"*

Thereupon a whole variegated chorus of yells, as windows were flung open on every side and half the street joined in the quarrel. They shut up abruptly ten minutes later, when a squadron of cavalry rode past and people stopped shouting to look at them.'[2]

From this account of early morning life he went on to give a general description of the street in which he lived.

'It was a very narrow street – a ravine of tall, leprous houses, lurching towards one another in queer attitudes, as though they had all been frozen in the act of collapse. All the houses were hotels and packed to the tiles with lodgers, mostly Poles, Arabs and Italians. At the foot of the hotels were tiny *bistros*, where you could be drunk for the equivalent of a shilling. On Saturday nights about a third of the male population of the quarter was drunk. There was fighting over women, and Arab navvies who lived in the cheapest hotels used to conduct mysterious feuds. . . . And yet, amid the noise and dirt lived the usual respectable French shopkeepers, bakers, laundresses and the like, keeping themselves to themselves and quietly piling up small fortunes. It was quite a representative Paris slum.'[3]

The description is witty and economical, already revealing that spare style of the clear-eyed and dispassionate observer which Orwell was later so effectively to develop. The book is also deceptive in the suggestion that Orwell was autobiographically presenting a picture of how he had lived for twenty months in Paris. He reports for instance how in the autumn of 1929 – that is, towards the end of his stay in Paris – he was robbed of the small savings he possessed. For a month or so he was really poverty stricken, living as he said on a shilling a day and observing himself suffering the pangs and lassitude of hunger. How far his Russian friend 'Boris', who promised him a job in a restaurant which he optimistically hoped would open soon, is a fictionalized figure we do not know. What is a fact is that in late 1929 Orwell worked for some weeks in a smart Paris hotel in one of the lowest-paid and most back-breaking jobs going, namely as a *plongeur* or dishwasher.

Orwell presents a solemnly objective description of this occupation – the crushing monotony of the job, the total exhaustion and getting drunk after work, the bedlam that broke out daily in the kitchen behind the scenes at dinner time when the customers gave their orders, bedlam of which the diners sitting a few yards away amidst spotless table-cloths and bowls of flowers knew nothing as the waiters stuffed the food on to the plates with their thumbs and then glided swanlike into the dining room.

All this Orwell wittily described. What he does not make clear, however, is that the spell of extreme poverty of which he tells in *Down and Out* and his life as *plongeur* occupied only a relatively short part of his stay in Paris. About the major part of this stay, as Richard Mayne has said in a perceptive essay, 'A Note on Orwell's Paris',[4] we know next to nothing. We know that he supported himself precariously in Paris mainly by giving English lessons and that he lived in a cheap hotel through whose thin walls he was made witness to the quarrels and sex life of his neighbours. In the middle of his Paris stay, in February 1929, with his troubled lungs affected by the winter cold and perhaps by overwork and lack of proper food, he had another of his physical breakdowns. He caught pneumonia badly and spent some weeks in a public Paris hospital, an experience whose shattering sights he later recollected in a memorable essay, 'How the Poor Die'.

During all this time, as he later wrote (in an essay on Henry Miller), multitudes of foreign artists and writers were living in Paris, but one can guess that his own social life was probably very limited. As Mr Mayne has said, the Scott Fitzgeralds lived not far from Orwell at the time, Hemingway passed through, although Orwell got to know neither. There is only a brief later reference that he thought he once saw James Joyce in the *Deux Magots*.

About his spare time, about his serious acquaintances, about his contact with other writers and about his sex life Orwell has said nothing, as about other phases of his life. One knows that his favourite aunt, Nellie Limouzin, was at the time living in Paris with her husband, a professor of Esperanto. Orwell must have seen her, and she could have helped him financially, but of this he makes no mention.

One obvious fact, to judge from his actual output, is that apart from keeping himself by English lessons he must have spent most of his time in his room in the solitary and depressing act of writing – depressing because it brought so little result. During his stay in Paris he wrote two whole novels which came to nothing plus short stories which he sent to an agency, only to have them rejected. As a work-load, Mr Mayne has said, this certainly suggests a young man determined to become a writer rather than courting failure – only the results remained absent. When Orwell finally called it a day in Paris, half a dozen journalistic pieces were all he had to show for his twenty months of living in the city and writing. The end came when in December 1929 he accepted a small sum of money from a friend to see him back to England and went home to spend Christmas with his parents in Southwold. Then he took a temporary job nearby as tutor to a backward boy.

If he had the Parisian material for *Down and Out* with him, it was surely still only in rough notes. Being unshakably determined to become a writer was one thing; actually becoming one still looked far off. I think that his next two years in London and elsewhere, in 1930–2, were the hardest in his life as he gradually fought his way towards completing his first book. (These were also the years of the most acute economic depression England had known, following on the Wall Street crash, although Orwell makes no mention of this.) They were his make-or-break years.

By now the intended outline of *Down and Out* would have been taking shape in his mind. The slum life of the rue du Coq d'Or and his experience as *plongeur* would provide the Parisian part. For the English part he would report on the life of English tramps, that odd band of ragged vagabonds who in the nineteen-thirties still shuffled along the roads of England as they were by tradition moved on by the authorities from one 'spike' or overnight resting place to the next.

Perhaps he still thought that he had to expiate some guilt by plunging into the lower depths, but by now his main aim surely was to gather literary material. A new friend he had made was Mrs Mabel Fierz, a lady with literary connections some years older than himself. Her house in the Hampstead Garden

Suburb was one of the places where he would change into the ragged dirty outfit worn by a tramp and with very little money in his pocket set out to explore the life of tramps and their 'kips' and 'spikes'. He would then return to change back into his normal garb (pretty rough, too) and sit down to write up the experience. He did this a number of times. A dispassionate observer, he wandered with tramps through London and on the road through Kent, Essex and Suffolk; with one special companion, one Ginger, he tramped in tandem for a fortnight. He also met more ordinary members of the working class when he joined the traditional hop-picking in Kent.

How was he to accomplish this research without money? At times it was as if, like his anti-hero Gordon in *Keep the Aspidistra Flying* (1936), he wanted to live without the constraint of money – a friend remembered how he exhausted her by making her walk through London to save bus fares. He earned small sums through tutoring. For two summers he tutored three boys from a family near Southwold called Peters. One of them, today a professor, has in a broadcast recalled Orwell as a tall, spindly young man with a gift for entering into boys' minds and discussing any subject objectively with them. He also had recourse to that way out for the educated jobless of the time, spells of ill-paid private schoolmastering. More important, the Eton network came back into his life.

He made contact with the liberal monthly, the *Adelphi*, and made a few pounds by writing occasional book reviews and some descriptive poems for it under his own name, A.E. Blair. The *Adelphi*, founded by Middleton Murry, had been taken over by Sir Richard Rees, that well-to-do mild-mannered idealist who had been slightly senior to Orwell at Eton. Orwell had come across the *Adelphi* while in Burma where (so he once said) its anarchic anti-imperialist views had so angered him that he used it as a shooting target. Now he was pleased enough to be an occasional contributor. Richard Rees, patient man that he was, became an immediate friend of his erratic young schoolfellow. (It was Rees who after Orwell's death called him a 'saint' – but it is Rees himself who lingers in one's memory as saintly, a tall awkward gentle man and friend.)

These small earnings were only intermittent and Orwell in these two years obviously lived through spells of acute poverty. He had after all to find time for work on the book instead of earning. He once told me that he typed our the full manuscript of *Down and Out* five times. Many years later I was given an insight into Orwell's life at the time in talking to his brother-in-law, Humphry Dakin. To make progress with the book, Orwell had come to stay with him and his wife Marjorie at the height of the financial crisis in 1931, when Dakin himself had lost his livelihood and found a temporary home near Leeds. There Orwell arrived:

> 'He looked to me long, lanky, and ill, and he had no money at all apart from what his mother and aunt could send him. With my wife ill, we were in no position to do much for him, but at least we could give him a well-heated room. He remained with us for at least three months and I remember the impression he made on his sister Marjorie and myself – that he was determined to be a writer, come what may. I must admit that I thought the chance of his making a living from writing was hopeless and I used to urge him to get out and get a job.'[5]

After leaving the Dakins, Orwell did in fact get one of his temporary schoolmastering jobs. But to Dakin it seemed that at the time he led a dreary life. At the local pub he sat silent in a corner in his threadbare overcoat. The landlord told Dakin that Orwell gave him the willies. And then, Dakin said, half the night he would hear his typewriter going tap, tap, tap.

To stay with his brother-in-law was one of the humiliations Orwell evidently accepted. But in thinking about this period I feel that for Orwell his crucial experience lay not in his work as *plongeur* or his wanderings with English tramps, perhaps not even in his poverty: the crucial sweat and agony was not in the slum life but in the effort to turn the experience into literature.

When at last he had the hang of it and by mid-1932 finished the book, it did not reflect this struggle. If the Parisian part of *Down and Out* was written in a style that was both colourful and dispassionate, so is the English part. On re-reading the book, one is struck by the fact that as Orwell reported on the various 'spikes' as seen through tramps' eyes, those with dirty mattresses, those without, those offering cups of tea and those only water and oatmeal, much of the description reads like an excellent piece of one-man sociological research. Only, being presented by a major novelist, it remains entertaining reading for today when the professional social studies of the time are long dead and gone.

There is a touch of Hogarth in Orwell's portrait of the repellent look of the tramps as they stood, pot-bellied and bow-legged, naked for inspection in a 'spike'; or as they were forced to sing hymns for their tea or, being bone-lazy, wriggled out of doing any work. He also classified the various types of English beggars of the thirties together with the organ-grinders and pavement artists, the hymn-singers and sellers of matches and bootlaces, with the precision of Thomas Dekker's catalogue of Jacobean rogues. Altogether he tried hard to achieve a style that should be at once vivid and spare, and objective:

> 'We stayed talking for an hour or two. The Irishman was a friendly old man, but he smelt very unpleasant, which was not surprising when one learned how many diseases he suffered from. It appeared (he described his symptoms fully) that taking him from top to bottom he had the following things wrong with him: on his crown, which was bald, he had eczema; he was short-sighted, and had no glasses; he had chronic bronchitis; he had some undiagnosed pain in the back; he had urethritis; he had varicose veins, bunions and flat feet. With his assemblage of diseases, he had tramped the roads for fifteen years.
>
> At about five the Irishman said, "Could do wid a cup o' tay. De spike don't open till six."'[6]

Moralizing a little at the end, Orwell put in the thought that the beggars he had met were honest compared with the sellers of patent medicines and more highminded than the proprietors of some Sunday newspapers. But this was detail; it was the descriptive passages that stood out.

Down and Out did not have an easy journey into print. Orwell first sent the manuscript to Jonathan Cape who suggested changes. He made some changes; the MS came back a second time, rejected. Next, through a friend, he submitted it to T.S. Eliot, as a director of Faber's. After a long time it came back with a note of rejection from Eliot himself. The book was too short, too loosely constructed, the French and English episodes did not hang together, perhaps Mr Orwell could develop one or the other, with many thanks, sincerely, T.S. Eliot.

Eliot, apart from being a great poet, could be very blinkered. Not only did he reject *Down and Out* which developed into a little classic; he was later with equal lack of logic to reject *Animal Farm*. Yet Orwell bore him no personal rancour. Perhaps he saw Eliot, a major poet, as a justified figure of authority, another Mrs Vaughan Wilkes? All the same, in 1932 the rejection by Eliot threw Orwell into one of those fits of angry despair which he described the heroes of his fiction as undergoing. Here his friend Mrs Mabel Fierz came into the picture.

Mabel Fierz had not only her literary connections but a remarkable memory. At the unveiling of a plaque to Orwell in 1980 she told me that she remembered clearly how Orwell and her husband, both Dickens-lovers, would talk for hours about his characters. She has also recalled that when the manuscript came back from T.S. Eliot, Orwell brought it to her and told her to destroy it and keep the paper clips. She, sensible woman, did nothing of the kind. As she told me, she knew he had another copy of the manuscript, but she took the copy he gave her to a literary agent of her acquaintance, Leonard Moore, of Christie & Moore. Moore read *Down and Out*, liked it, and thought it a suitable book for the up-and-coming radical publisher, Victor Gollancz. Gollancz received enthusiastic reports from his readers and accepted the book. After some delay over the choice of title and pseudonym, the book would soon be published.

The pseudonym: as a journalist Orwell was still writing under his name of A.E. Blair, but the book was to be by 'George Orwell'. I had long thought his choice of a pseudonym symbolically important for him. Since then it has become

known that Orwell wanted his book to appear under a
pseudonym to spare what he thought would be embarrassment
to his family. Also, the name 'George Orwell' was actually
picked by his publisher, Gollancz, from a list of four names he
submitted. But 'Orwell' was the name he himself favoured and
I still think that psychologically his choice of pseudonym
marked a new phase in his life. As he had perforce taken on the
personality of a Sahib in Burma, so now by choice he took on
that of an incisive writer and critic under a new name.

In January 1933 *Down and Out in Paris and London* by George
Orwell was successfully published. Two further printings
followed quickly and the book also achieved a fair critical
success. It was recommended by the Book Society. Mabel Fierz
told me that as Orwell had strongly criticized J.B. Priestley's
Angel Pavement in the *Adelphi*, he was particularly pleased by
Priestley's generous praise of his own book in the *Evening
Standard*. Compton Mackenzie was perhaps the most prescient
critic to greet the new writer. He wrote that in spite of the
squalor and degradation unfolded in Orwell's book, the result
was curiously beautiful, with the beauty of an accomplished
etching on copper.

Passing reviewer's praise, no doubt: but the point is that after
five long years of struggle since he left Burma, he had created
the writer 'George Orwell' who had successfully arrived on the
scene

FIVE

Orwell as a Young Novelist

THE YEAR, 1933: the decisive step had been taken, Orwell was a writer with a reasonably publicized book to his credit. For the next three years, having himself turned thirty, I think that he more or less coasted. Setting himself the task of producing a book a year, he wrote his three angry youthful novels, *A Clergyman's Daughter*, *Burmese Days* and *Keep the Aspidistra Flying*, all published by Victor Gollancz, whom he kept on the hop about dangers of libel.

The evidence presents a curiously fragmented picture of Orwell as a young novelist (I wish I had known him at the time). He was a young man ineradicably public school in appearance and manners, who expressed his undoubted anger very much in his writings and talk rather than in any direct action, not an unusual pattern. But he was pleasant enough company to friends like Mabel Fierz and her husband. He was often hard up, but liked public houses and going fishing. He had some unimportant affairs with young women; his feelings might have been more seriously engaged with a young woman back in Suffolk, but she married a friend of his instead. Mabel Fierz remembered him as a young man who was always writing and smoking; she warned him seriously against the smoking, but alas without success.

During part of this period he worked as a bookshop assistant. This came about through an introduction from his aunt Nellie Limouzin to an elderly couple, the Westropes, who ran a well-known bookshop in Hampstead. The Westropes were enthusiasts for both Esperanto and the Independent Labour Party, the ILP, that small, very Left-wing offshoot of the British Labour Party whose outlook has been described as like that of a nonconformist parson who tries to be a Marxist. Orwell had been preceded as assistant in the bookshop by Jon Kimche, a young Jewish intellectual and ILP member, who years later as wartime acting editor of *Tribune* was to take on Orwell as literary editor. In the bookshop in 1934–5, Kimche worked mornings while Orwell wrote, handing over to him in the afternoons. In return both received board and lodgings above the shop. Kimche (a long-standing friend of mine) told me that for him the bookshop was a welcome forward step towards the world of writing. For Orwell, twelve years after leaving Eton, it was no great advance. Kimche remembers how in their sitting room in the evenings Orwell would at times hold forth in long harangues against the smooth literary young men from Cambridge who had everything going for them, or else against the British Empire, the Catholic Church, or the filthy rich.

He no doubt had his grievances. Still, he was now writing reviews for the *Adelphi* and elsewhere as well as his novels and making a small literary name for himself – he *was* a writer. When he had to leave his bookshop lodgings, Mabel Fierz found him a pleasant room in Hampstead of which, she told me, she secretly paid part of the rent. She introduced him to another of her literary protégés, the young writer and critic Rayner Heppenstall. With him and a third young writer Orwell for a time shared a small house in Kentish Town. The arrangement broke up after a notorious occasion when Orwell in a fit of puritanism allegedly beat up Heppenstall for coming home drunk – Heppenstall made much of the incident.

During those years of the early thirties, Britain remained caught in the grip of harsh economic crisis and of mass unemployment. Previously Stanley Baldwin and Ramsay Macdonald had alternated as Prime Ministers; now both were included in a National Government in office at Westminster. In the US, Roosevelt had launched his New Deal. Over in Germany, Hitler had seized power and was fast rearming. The international picture looked distinctly ominous. Of this one finds no direct reflection in Orwell's work – he was still largely unpolitical. If he wrote egocentric novels disguising his own life in fiction, he was merely following the literary fashion of the day – which Orwell's friend Cyril Connolly described as one of novels about a sensitive young man and the dirty deal life gave him.

But had he a novelist's gifts? What emerged, I think, was that because he always looked at the world from the perspective of his personal situation, he could basically write only about himself and his own experiences and predicaments.

This shows itself in all three novels. In the least successful, *A Clergyman's Daughter* (1934), he has Dorothy, the spinster daughter and unpaid housekeeper of her clerical father, lose her memory after a sexual assault and walk out of her home in a small Suffolk town which seems not unlike his parents' Southwold. Orwell sets her among proletarian hop-pickers in Kent, here drawing on the memory of his own exploits. After a nocturnal interlude in Trafalgar Square written unsuccessfully in the manner of James Joyce, Orwell lets Dorothy become an ill-paid teacher in a wretched little private school, again drawing on his own experience of such teaching. Finally, Dorothy returns home to resume her status as her father's drudge.

In the climax to the novel, Orwell has Dorothy ponder over her lost faith – one can see what sombre thoughts were whirling through his own mind:

> 'Life, if the grave really ends it, is monstrous and dreadful. No use trying to argue it away. Think of life as it really is, think of the *details* of life; and then think that there is no meaning in it, no purpose, no goal except the grave. Surely, only fools and self-deceivers, or those whose lives are exceptionally fortunate, can face that thought without flinching.'[1]

In his second novel, *Burmese Days* (1935), Orwell drew equally on memories. Its hero is Flory, a melancholy young man who is a timber agent at a small station in Upper Burma. Orwell fiercely caricatures the fairly low-class local British planters and officials as they try to resist a Government suggestion to admit one or two native members to the European club. Poor Flory – *Burmese Days* is the one novel where Orwell could be accused of some self-pity. Orwell endows him with a disfiguring birthmark which he tries to hide by turning his head away. Flory is also a divided soul, as Orwell presumably was in Burma. He is inevitably part of the local

European society, part of the club life, but secretly he despises it. He is also the friend of an Indian doctor in love with the British *Raj*, whom he proposes for club membership in opposition to an intriguing local Burmese magistrate. It is the latter who encompasses Flory's downfall and disgrace. This leads to his rejection by Elizabeth, a commonplace English girl with whom poor Flory fancies himself in love. Rejected, alone, Flory shoots himself.

Burmese Days was presumably intended as Orwell's farewell to his Burmese memories. They must have been vivid; what stands out in the book, as he himself reluctantly admitted is his descriptions of the lush Burmese landscape in the fierce heat and sun.

Orwell's third novel *Keep the Aspidistra Flying* (1936) was most directly autobiographical – one almost feels that in its writing he was beginning to run out of personal material to put into fictional form.

His hero in the novel, Gordon Comstock ('twenty-nine and moth-eaten already'), comes from a shabby-genteel family and like Orwell had suffered from going to school with boys much richer than himself. To become a writer, Gordon has abandoned a promising career as an advertising copywriter and when we meet him is working as Orwell had done as assistant in a bookshop. Here Orwell lets him rail against the customers, the whole book trade, successful young writers as well as established authors. 'Gordon knocked down reputation after reputation. Shaw, Yeats, Eliot, Joyce, Huxley, Hemingway – each with a careless phrase was shovelled into the dustbin.' (In actual life Orwell could be very different. A solicitor of my acquaintance told me that in his youth he often visited the Westropes' bookshop to build up his personal library and always found Orwell politely helpful and informative.)

Gordon has a friend, Ravelston of 'Antichrist' – modelled on Rees of the *Adelphi*? – who tries in vain to help him. Orwell lets Gordon lose his job, to end his subservience to the Money-God; he lives in total poverty as he carries with him the hopelessly criss-crossed manuscript of a poem called 'London Pleasures'. (This became an actual poem Orwell wrote for the *Adelphi*.) Gordon's state of poverty is clearly based on Orwell's own

memories of his times of such poverty as he struggled with the
MS of *Down and Out* four years earlier. Finally, Gordon is
rescued by his girl Rosemary whom he marries while also
returning to his job as copywriter in his advertising agency and
buying an aspidistra to signal his return to bourgeois respectability.

Some interesting points about the novel: Orwell reluctantly
lets Gordon admit that he has a facility with words and slogans
– was he beginning to feel more confident about his own
facility? Again, more love out of doors: Orwell has Gordon take
Rosemary for a walk in the countryside, where he finds himself
unable to make love to her because he has only sixpence in his
pocket. Also in *Aspidistra* Orwell through Gordon expressed a
violent dislike of London's crowded life and mass advertising –
a foretaste here of *Nineteen Eighty-Four*. He has Gordon reacting
to a poster saying 'Corner Table Enjoys His Meal With Bovex'
in a manner already suggesting that of the later novel:

> 'Gordon examined the thing with the intimacy of hatred . . .
> Corner Table, heir of the ages, victor of Waterloo, Corner
> Table, modern man as his masters wanted him to be.
> A docile little porker, sitting in the money-sty, drinking
> Bovex . . .
>
> Corner Table grins at you, seemingly optimistic, with a
> flash of false teeth. But what is behind the grin? Desolation,
> emptiness, prophecies of doom. For can you not see, if you
> know how to look, that behind that slick self-satisfaction,
> that tittering fat-bellied triviality, there is nothing but a
> frightful emptiness, a secret despair? The great death-wish of
> the modern world. Suicide pacts. Heads stuck in gas-ovens
> in lonely maisonettes. French letters and Amen pills. And
> the reverberations of future wars.'[2]

Although none of the three novels sold as well as *Down and
Out*, they brought Orwell appreciative reviews and a growing if
still limited reputation as a young writer and critic. Some
Etonian contacts were re-established. Cyril Connolly, who was
by now literary editor of the *New Statesman*, praised *Burmese Days*
in a review as an admirable novel, an almost boisterous attack
on both the Anglo-Indians and the Burmese. In 1935, after not

having seen each other for a full thirteen years, the two writers met. Looking at his former companion from St Cyprian's and Eton, Orwell – according to Connolly – gave him a long but not unfriendly stare and broke into his characteristic wheezy laugh. 'Well, Connolly, I can see that you have worn a good deal better than I have.' Connolly related that he himself could say nothing, for he was appalled by the ravaged grooves that ran down from cheek to chin in Orwell's face. Orwell's illnesses in Burma and Paris as well as his spells of poverty must have taken their toll.

In 1936 another Etonian, John Lehmann, wrote to Orwell to ask him to contribute to a volume of anti-Fascist literature to be called *New Writing*. Orwell replied that all he could offer was a piece about Burma called 'Shooting an Elephant' and he did not know how far this qualified as anti-Fascism. Fortunately Lehmann took a positive view and the essay was printed.

The year 1936 saw two other important changes in his life. He had long claimed that he detested London and early in the year he took over (for 7/6 a week) a neglected small house known as The Stores in the small, isolated village of Wallington (population around 200) near Baldock in rural Hertfordshire. The house had a downstairs room which had been the village shop, a function Orwell proposed to renew, and two smaller rooms above it. No gas or electricity were laid on and there was an outside privy and a small garden with roses and fruit trees. Across the road, Orwell rented a tiny smallholding on which to keep geese and two goats.

The Stores was no picturesque country cottage to which he could retreat. Moving there from London was a deliberate attempt to change his whole way of life. I think he had long cherished a somewhat fanciful picture of himself as not just a writer but also a self-sufficient smallholder, growing his own vegetables, keeping chickens, geese and perhaps goats, fishing, shooting rabbits and doing his own carpentry as he worked productively with his own hands. If I think this aim fanciful, it is only because I think he was not very good at working with his hands, and his writer's destiny was to shape his life quite otherwise. Still, in 1936 he was evidently set on leaving London literary life for the bare rural isolation of Wallington.

His second major step in 1936 was that he got married. When Orwell first met Eileen O'Shaughnessy, he told Mabel Fierz the next day that she was the girl he wanted to marry. Eileen came of safe upper-middle-class background. At thirty she was two years younger than Orwell; she had read English at Oxford and since held various jobs. When Orwell met her she was studying for a higher degree in Educational Psychology at University College, London. She was living in Greenwich with her brother Lawrence, a consultant surgeon, and his wife Gwen, also a doctor. Her brother was the love of her life; she was also close to her sister-in-law. As seen by her friends, she was a vivacious young woman, at times looking pretty, at times a little eccentric. She was more cautious than Orwell in contemplating marriage. As a husband and provider this erratic young novelist with his odd ideas about leading a simple life could not have looked much of a catch. Even so, they were in love and in June 1936, roughly a year after they first met, they were married in Wallington in a simple family wedding.

Eileen must indeed have been very much in love with Orwell, for while he gained the companionship he wanted, marriage involved her in immediate sacrifice. Life in Wallington meant that she had to break off her university studies. Instead she now looked after Orwell, and had to get used to being hard up and to sharing his views on a spartan life-style. Since she was as reticent about personal things as Orwell himself, it is hard to know how Eileen felt, but outwardly her friends saw her settling down contentedly in Wallington, sharing her husband's sense of humour and his odd ideas, feeding the chickens, giving the goats comic names and running the miniature village shop on the ground floor which Orwell had reopened. This was also partly a fantasy, because by now the Wallington housewives went by bus to shop in the nearby small town of Baldock. Almost the only customers were children asking for penny-worths of sweets – a small substitute for Eileen's university studies. A later acquaintance said that their life at The Stores must have been like that in a wendyhouse. Still, Orwell's friends regarded his first months at Wallington with Eileen as the happiest period they had seen in his life.

In the autumn he sat up in his room typing away, for in

addition to his marriage another great change had taken place in his life. His period of coasting along as just another angry young novelist was over. In the spring his publisher Victor Gollancz had sent him on a trip to the depressed north of England and he was writing up his findings – as the result showed, with excitement. He had been to Wigan Pier and politically he had become an ardent socialist.

SIX

Becoming a Socialist

A FEW WEEKS after Orwell's quiet wedding at Wallington, General Franco and some of his fellow-generals staged a coup against the legal Spanish Republican Government. The Spanish workers, organized in their Anarchist and Socialist unions, resisted fiercely, foiling the coup in Madrid, Barcelona and other cities. The Spanish civil war began which was to be so long drawn out and so costly in Spanish and other lives.

Already, earlier on, all the rearmament, the militarism and the violent threats emanating from Hitler's Nazi Germany and Mussolini's Fascist Italy had led to an 'anti-Fascist' reaction in intellectual and literary circles in Britain and elsewhere, all increasingly politicized. The Communists under Moscow's orders, that is Stalin's orders, had launched their concept of a 'United Front' of all progressive people against Fascism, a front especially of writers and artists; and this led to an approach to Orwell from his publisher.

Victor Gollancz, in the thirties something of a mixture between an idealistic Jewish rabbi and an enterprising businessman, had early in 1936 started a publishing venture called the Left Book Club. His fellow-selectors in choosing books for the club were the eminent political pundit, Harold Laski, and the then very Left-wing writer (although later to become a very moderate Labour Minister), John Strachey, Orwell's contemporary at Eton although they did not know each other at school. Each month the Left Book Club issued one or two anti-Fascist books, mostly written along orthodox pro-Communist lines, which the club distributed through its members in a large cheap edition of 50,000 copies.

In the spring of 1936 Gollancz proposed to his novelist author George Orwell that he should visit the badly depressed

areas of heavy industry up in the north of England and report
on the hardships he saw there, offering Orwell an advance of
£500, unusually large for the time. Orwell eagerly accepted and
Gollancz decided to commission his report for the Left Book
Club. He little knew what an extraordinary literary career he
was to launch through this idea, or perhaps he suspected it but
thought he could manage Orwell like his other Left-wing
authors – why not?

In this he was wrong, for the outcome of Orwell's journey
was to be that much-debated Left Book Club choice, *The Road to
Wigan Pier* (1937), a landmark in Orwell's career. (It was the
first of Orwell's books which I myself read; I did so while
abroad and went on to read all his others.)

The memorable title referred to an old music-hall joke about
a pier in the grimy canal in the run-down Lancashire mill town
of Wigan. The book was to be controversial in a number of
ways. For one thing, in the spring of 1936 Orwell spent less than
eight weeks in the north and even this period was interrupted
by a stay with the Dakins in Leeds to type out his notes. During
these few weeks he covered the ground on which a more
professional social researcher might have spent a year, yet he
wrote with remarkable assurance about the decayed industrial
scene which had opened itself to his gaze. By 1936 the very
worst of the Great Depression had abated somewhat in London
and the more modern south of England; but up in the harsher
north, the older industrial areas based on coal, steel and
engineering remained inertly in the grip of recession and mass
unemployment. Here he was in another world from that of the
sleek English south, as Orwell was swift to notice.

He travelled north with some introductions to members of
Richard Rees's *Adelphi* circle and others to very Left-wing
contacts among members of the Independent Labour Party;
one or two of his guides in the north turned out to be
Communists. He almost went wrong at the very beginning. In
Wigan, his starting point, he had been provided with a
reasonable room, but he soon moved to grotesquely poor
lodgings above a notorious tripe shop. These he immortalized
in his opening chapter about the filthy lodging house of that
frightful couple, the Brookers. Still, he did quickly realize that

he had not come north to continue writing *Down and Out*.
Instead, being a hard worker, he did his homework thoroughly.

Wigan, an industrial and mining town, was suffering
particularly from unemployment. From Orwell's typed notes
one can see that his investigation, if impressionistic, was very
much to the point. It has to be borne in mind that compared to
life on social security in the slump in the British consumer society
of the seventies and eighties, living conditions in the crisis of
mass unemployment in England during the thirties were
incomparably harsher. As Orwell found, workers' families
living on unemployment benefit, the dole, lived on the barest
minimum. Up in the north it was also clear how far England
remained a class-ridden capitalist society. Apart from a few
activists, the poor and the unemployed, remembering the failure
of the General Strike of ten years earlier, endured their plight
passively – they saw no alternative.

I think that Orwell saw this whole picture in a flash. In Wigan
he was shown round jerry-built, overcrowded working-class
homes. He talked to unemployed miners. He spent some busy
days in the Wigan Public Library, reading up the facts and
figures about local health and employment which shocked him.

Then came a traumatic experience. Orwell had already
discovered what he saw as the dramatic nature of the coalminers'
work deep under ground, and he reflected that the whole of
English daily life depended on the continuity of their exhausting
work. He decided to see all this for himself and went down the
elderly Cribbens pit near Wigan. There he had to walk a quite
unusually long distance from the shaft to reach the coalface, bent
double, tall as he was. Not surprisingly, in view of his lung
troubles, he collapsed completely as he started out on the return
journey and had to be carried out of the pit in a state of total
exhaustion. The experience and his discovery of the arduous
conditions in which the miners worked made a profound
impression on him. On recovery he felt an attack of bronchitis
coming on and took refuge for some days with a middle-class
family, a contact of the *Adelphi*, in Liverpool. In that city, forcing
himself to get up, he saw unemployed dockers compelled to
compete viciously for the odd day's job, one of the industrial
disgraces of the time, and noted the picture.

He went back to Wigan and from there he took a train to Sheffield. By this time he had decided that the partly derelict northern industrial scene was like a nightmarish blight on the countryside. In Sheffield, he lodged in a miner's back-to-back house. His guide here was a Communist and occasional contributor to the *Adelphi*, who introduced him to various local Communists, Trotskyists and ILP members. It is clear that Orwell saw them all as working-class activists, their differing political theories being very immaterial to him.

From Sheffield he went to stay for a week with his sister in Leeds, to type his notes. He next went to Barnsley, a Yorkshire town affected less by unemployment than by conditions of acute poverty. Here he went down the pit again to see miners at work, but this time under much easier conditions in a modern colliery which was electrified and had pithead baths, which he noted as being much appreciated.

In Barnsley he also went with some Communist miners to hear Oswald Mosley address a mass meeting and remained unimpressed. He wrote that Mosley held forth with the usual claptrap: Empire free trade, down with the Jew and the foreigner, higher wages all round, etc. He wondered how Mosley as an educated man could possibly be sincere. Interestingly he took no special notice of the dynamics of Mosley's anti-Semitic message. By the end of April he was back in London with Eileen and his friends and after his wedding he sat down at The Stores to turn his notes of what he had seen into the expected book for Gollancz's Left Book Club.

The Road to Wigan Pier is clearly an angry book, unique in English political writing of the time. It stands out because Orwell wrote both as an objective social observer and as a gifted novelist. At the start, we are, in his usual style, plunged straight into the action as, lying in bed, he found himself awakened in Wigan by the clatter of the mill girls' clogs as they walked past the appalling dosshouse run by the Brookers – his distasteful description of this establishment reads as though he had stayed there for months instead of days. All in all, what he saw as a repellent industrial landscape of pits and slag-heaps, of deserted factories and sprawling stretches of back-to-back terrace houses confirmed his dislike of modern industrialism.

In detail, he wrote with a fascination of discovery about the physically demanding work done by miners and the remarkable comradeship and cultural cohesion he found within the mining community. He noted the long distances which the miners had to walk – unpaid – to their work at the coalface. He calculated miners' wages and household budgets; he went into the question why the older pits had not got the elementary amenity of pithead baths. He discussed the problems of the frequent illnesses and enforced early retirement of so many miners who seemed simply to accept being thrown on the scrap-heap, a fact he again thought shocking.

In other chapters he noted the acute housing shortage in areas he visited. He emphasized how the gross overcrowding in working-class dwellings which he came across made it impossible to keep the houses clean. He described the squalor of jerry-built back-to-back terrace housing, which involved the inhabitants of the front houses in long walks in health or sickness to the rear toilets in the backyards – should this be the rule in the twentieth century?

Above all he wrote about the obvious effect of long-term mass unemployment in sapping the men concerned of their self-respect. He calculated the budgets of families living on the dole and he drew a memorable picture of unemployed miners whom he watched as, followed by their wives, they scrabbled for odd lumps of coal high up on slag-heaps. He castigated the capitalist rulers of England for the degradation into which they had forced so many of the men from whom their wealth had been derived; and he made two special points.

He thought that working-class families coped with the disasters of unemployment, poverty and ill health better than most middle-class families would have done in their place. Where the latter would have gone to pieces, the working-class families endured, they scraped and saved and above all they clung together socially and so survived. The firm faith in the common people he subsequently expressed must have sprung from that conclusion.

Secondly, through observing the spectacle of industrial capitalism in decline, he had become a convinced socialist, openly advocating socialist solutions to current problems.

Up to this point one would have thought that the book was precisely, indeed triumphantly, what Gollancz and the Left Book Club readers wanted: but now came a snag, for *The Road to Wigan Pier* also contained a description of Orwell's lifetime journey to that destination and that was something else again. He had not only discovered the need for socialism, he also had some harsh things to say about middle-class socialists whom he did not care for. If he was now one of their number, he felt that he had to add a long piece of his habitual self-definition to the book.

This is where, as if to exaggerate the effect of English class distinctions, he wrote how as a child he had been taught that the working classes smelt – one can see how this remark would outrage the mainly middle-class readers of the Left Book Club. He told how he had served as a policeman in Burma and had hated it. He said that when in reacting against his past he had associated with tramps and beggars, this was because the frightful doom of decent working men suddenly thrown on the streets by economic laws they did not understand had been outside the range of his experience. Now he understood this, now he was a socialist, but as he had to emphasize, a socialist with a difference.

He claimed that the middle-class opposition in England was directed not so much against socialism as an ideal, as against the character of individual socialists which left a good deal to be desired. He sweepingly denounced various people he had met in the socialist ranks – feminists, pacifists, bearded vegetarians, birth-control fanatics, and polysyllabic Marxists with fuzzy hair, with a sideswipe at working-class intellectuals who had become Labour MPs or high-up trade union officials – 'one of the most desolating spectacles the world contains'. Perhaps Orwell had to get this ranting denunciation, which at times reads as though uttered by a middle-class Colonel Blimp, off his chest. More seriously, aware of the difference between his own education and that of the working class, he attacked the sincerity of English middle-class Left-wingers (who of course included himself) at its most vulnerable point: 'It is strange how easily almost any Socialist writer can lash himself into frenzies of rage against the class to which, by birth or by adoption, he himself invariably belongs.'[1]

He also criticized his fellow-socialists for their uncritical belief in universal industrial progress, which, as he saw it, *could* lead not to socialism, but to a slave state. He further attacked them for their naive acceptance of the blatantly dishonest Communist propaganda in praise of the Soviet Five Year Plans. He described Stalin's commissars as 'half gramophones, half gangsters' – a very telling phrase. In the eyes of the British Communists and fellow-travellers advocating a 'United Front', this phrase alone was enough to turn him into a potential enemy to be carefully watched.

Orwell's positive aims for socialists as he set them out in *Wigan Pier* remained vague enough. Behind all the ranting, there lay, I think, a basic plea that the values of his native upper-middle class – the values of rural life, of patriotism, religion and a sense of service – should somehow be absorbed into the whole socialist movement, not just rejected. But writing hurriedly as he did, Orwell did not really think out this theme.

His attacks on socialists and especially on Communists in the latter part of *Wigan Pier* threw the selectors of the Left Book Club who had admired the earlier descriptive passages into a quandary. To publish or not? Orwell characteristically refused to change a word. It speaks much for Victor Gollancz that he insisted on *Wigan Pier* being selected and published early in 1937 – with a preface by himself which he hoped would be disarming.

In this preface Gollancz said that surely Mr Orwell was exceptional in being told as a child that the working classes smelt. As for his attacks on fellow-socialists, surely there was nothing wrong with being a feminist, a vegetarian or an advocate of birth control. As for his dislike of industrialism as such, surely the essential difference lay between chaotic capitalist industrialism and planned and therefore beneficial industrialism, as shown to a great extent by the Soviet example. And so forth: in the outcome, *The Road to Wigan Pier* created more stir and interest and debate among Left Book Club readers than any choice that had come before. Gollancz decided to reprint its early descriptive sections in a cheap edition at one shilling.

But Orwell did not know about this, nor did he voice any particular objection to Gollancz's preface. By the time Gollancz sent him a copy of *The Road to Wigan Pier*, in March 1937, his feelings were quite otherwise involved. He was in the front line in the mountains of Aragon as a soldier in the Spanish civil war.

SEVEN

The Spanish War and Truth

I MYSELF still well remember watching the development of the Spanish civil war with agonized attention, especially in its early stages.

By the autumn of 1936 the battle lines were clearly drawn. Right across the Peninsula, General Franco with his battalions of colonial and regular troops was locked in civil war with the forces of the legal Republican Government, a bourgeois government but whose strength was now based on the socialist and communist workers in Madrid and the even more militant Anarchist workers in Barcelona. Meanwhile Hitler and Mussolini openly supported Franco as a fellow-Fascist with all the military aid he could use. The faraway Soviet Union helped the Republicans, to a lesser extent. But Britain and France, to whom the Republicans appealed for armaments as the legal Spanish Government, instead declared their notorious policy of 'Non-Intervention' towards the civil war. Basically, this policy denied Western arms only to the Republicans, because Franco could obtain whatever arms he needed from Nazi Germany and Fascist Italy.

Although this unevenness was plain, the British and French Governments looked resolved *not* to side with any Left-wing Spanish Government against European Nazism and Fascism. But the hypocritical unfairness of 'Non-Intervention' led to some growing intellectual anti-Fascist protests in the West. For years democracy had appeared to be in retreat before dictators. Now, so it seemed, one could fight for it in Spain. Some thousands of volunteers flocked into the International Brigades, set up under Communist control, which helped to stop Franco and his Italian allies at the very gates of Madrid.

During this time, at The Stores in Wallington, Orwell sat writing *The Road to Wigan Pier*, while Eileen looked after him and ran the miniature shop and sometimes took refuge with her beloved brother in Greenwich. Orwell took his new socialism seriously. Reviewing his friend Cyril Connolly's novel about Riviera Bohemians, *The Rock Pool*, he said sternly – it was to be his habit to be stern with friends' books: 'Even to want to write about so-called artists who spend on sodomy what they have gained by sponging betrays a kind of spiritual inadequacy.'[1]

Committed to his ideals as he was, Orwell had early on decided to make for Spain, there to write or fight as he saw the situation; Eileen wanted to follow him. On 15 December 1936 he handed in the manuscript of *Wigan Pier* to Gollancz. Thinking that he needed Left-wing credentials to enter Republican Spain, he asked Gollancz to introduce him to John Strachey, at the time still virtually, if cautiously not in fact, a Communist. It would have been interesting to know what exactly passed between these two very different Etonian Left-wingers, but Strachey sent Orwell to see Harry Pollitt, the ebullient secretary of the British Communist Party and here occurred one of those accidents that shaped Orwell's career. The details are again not known, but Pollitt must have been alerted about the anti-Communist statements in *Wigan Pier*, while it seemed that Orwell for his part was not ready to place himself under Communist authority in Spain before seeing things for himself. In the outcome Pollitt would not give him special help.

Orwell therefore turned instead to his contacts in the Independent Labour Party, and as a result, instead of going to the International Brigade in Madrid, he arranged to travel under ILP auspices to Anarchist-ruled Barcelona. Jon Kimche, who had meanwhile opened a political bookshop of his own off Fleet Street underneath the ILP head office, remembers how just before Christmas there was commotion overhead over the problem of finding size twelve boots, large enough for his friend Orwell to wear in Spain.

Orwell broke his journey for a day in Paris to visit the American novelist Henry Miller, with whom he had corresponded. He found Miller friendly but quite sceptical about there being any value in a writer's volunteering for the Spanish civil war; he was all for ignoring politics and violence and passively letting life flow by. That Orwell had some sympathy with this attitude, he later made plain in *Inside the Whale* (1940). But at the moment it was not for him, and on the last day of the year he presented himself to John McNair, an experienced political organizer and linguist who had opened an ILP office in Barcelona. McNair introduced this curious tall Etonian into the militia of the 'Workers' Party of Marxist Unification', known as the POUM, a small Spanish revolutionary party whom the ILP regarded as a sister organization.

After a short spell with teenage Catalan recruits among whom Orwell with his Burma police training stood out as almost a professional soldier, he found himself in a POUM militia division on the Aragon front, together with thirty other ILP volunteers who had come from England a little after him. They were stationed high up in the wintry mountains opposite Huesca, a town the Republicans attacked but were never to take. Orwell remained in the front line for 115 days, an exceptionally long spell, demonstrating a victory of his disciplined will over his uncertain health.

In his first-person documentary account of his Spanish war experience, *Homage to Catalonia* (1938), Orwell wrote with exemplary objectivity about those 115 days in the Republican front line – about the appallingly few modern rifles, not to speak of artillery, possessed by the young POUM militiamen, about their lack of military training, all the boredom and quarrelling, the dirt and lice and the occasional casualties through sniper fire.

Homage to Catalonia was to be the first of his three major books. It has with hindsight attracted some professional criticism. Thus Professor Hugh Thomas, who is certainly an authority on the conflict, has described it as a book about war rather than the Spanish civil war. This seems a cryptic comment. To be sure, Orwell in 1937 wrote *Homage to Catalonia* with immediacy in mind rather than lengthy research. Neither did he have a personal overview of the whole conflict, seeing only Barcelona and the rest of Catalonia and the Aragon front; he did not witness the defence of Madrid by the International Brigades. Yet in fact the book is presented precisely as one man's experience of the Spanish civil war, no more; and just because he was attacking what he saw as a distressingly wrongful Communist policy in Spain, he tried to be at all costs fair in his political conclusions.

This quality of dedicated fairness is remarkable in any autobiographical writing and it is this quality which comes across even in some of the book's lyrical passages. In *Wigan Pier* he had first discovered the ideals of socialism. In his first sight of revolutionary Barcelona he seemed to glimpse an enthusiastically classless society. He saw that shops and cafés had been collectivized; tipping was abolished; there were no more private cars; Anarchist flags and posters were everywhere. Most remarkable of all were the people:

'Down the Ramblas, the wide central artery of the town, where crowds of people streamed constantly to and fro, the loudspeakers were bellowing revolutionary songs all day and far into the night. And it was the aspect of the crowds that was the queerest thing of all. In outward appearance, it was a town in which the wealthy classes had practically ceased to exist. Except for a small number of women and foreigners, there were no "well-dressed" people at all. Practically everyone wore rough working class clothes, or blue overalls or some variant of militia uniform. All this was queer and moving. There was much in it that I did not understand, in some ways I did not even like it, but I recognized it immediately as a state of affairs worth fighting for.'[2]

Only considerably later, so Orwell wrote, did he realize that in what had looked like a workers' metropolis, the local Barcelona bourgeoisie was merely lying low. Yet already at the start of his long spell at the front in the Aragon mountains, everything had begun to look different to him. As he took stock of the ill-trained and ill-equipped Catalan forces among whom he found himself, he quickly decided that, sniping apart, there could be no major action in his sector of the civil war. Serious warfare was evidently being waged only on the Madrid front. Like other foreigners in the war he developed an immediate affection for the ordinary Spanish people, and he was only too pleased to serve in the POUM militia together with the thirty other ILP volunteers who appeared as committed to the anti-Fascist cause as he was.

This sense of commitment comes out in his convincing picture of life at the front. He realistically described the shambles of a nocturnal raid on the enemy lines, in which his unit temporarily captured an enemy trench, his only piece of real action during the period. He wrote about the biting cold of winter in the mountains, the acute lack of firewood, and about the growing indifference of everyone towards living with dirt and darkness and spells of hunger. He reflected that the soldiers at Verdun, Waterloo and Thermopylae were probably, like himself and his companions, overrun by lice. He remarked on the strange absence of birds which he noted in Aragon, and on the friendliness of the Spanish villagers towards foreigners, which surprised him. He also noted how his company commander, Georges Kopp, a Belgian soldier of fortune who became a close friend, described the current warfare in the sector as 'comic opera with an occasional death'.

In February, Eileen arrived in Spain to work as assistant to John McNair in the ILP office in Barcelona. Orwell's one surviving letter of the time to her, his 'dearest', is infused with love. While on guard duty, he wrote to her, it had occurred to him how in his ILP and POUM unit, chance had dropped him into an environment where the ordinary class divisions of society had disappeared to an extent that was almost unthinkable in the money-tainted air of England.

As Orwell recollected it, the group of ILP volunteers were continuously arguing among themselves about the course the civil war should take: was it to be a revolution or not? The answer was not easy. As Orwell and the other ILP volunteers soon realized, it was not the liberal Spanish Government which had stopped Franco and his fellow-generals in their tracks, but the revolutionary workers, such as the Anarchists in Barcelona, who had taken over urban areas and factories, together with peasants who had seized their land (and burned churches). As a result two distinct groupings had arisen in the Republican camp. On one side was the Republican Government now in Valencia: still with a bougeois, liberal, capitalist façade but supported largely by the militant Socialist and Communist

Party machines. The Communists, few at first, had rapidly expanded their power thanks to the Soviet Union's supply of arms to the Republic.

As Orwell saw it, at Stalin's orders the Communists appeared charged with creating a seemingly moderate Spanish Republican 'united front against Fascism and Nazism' which would not antagonize the British and French Governments. This meant giving military measures for the war against Franco complete priority over revolutionary aims. It meant a strong central government and a single, properly officered army; it meant not antagonizing the Catholic peasantry or frightening the Spanish progressive middle classes with talk of a dictatorship of the proletariat.

Opposed to this Communist policy of compromise, in Orwell's view, stood the militant Anarchists, now the rulers of industrial Catalonia, who with their lesser allies, the POUM, on the contrary saw the outbreak of civil war as the start of a Spanish revolution. The POUM was a small, very Left-wing party which had been founded by Andres Nin, who at one time had been Trotsky's secretary, but had broken with him. The Communists had been angered by the POUM because its newspaper attacked Stalin for his notorious Moscow treason trials even while Soviet arms were helping to sustain the Republic. The firm view of the Anarchists and the POUM was that the workers were not fighting for any liberal Spanish capitalism. On the contrary, they had to resist all attempts by the central government to take back the factories they had nationalized. They had especially to resist any steps to break up their party militia units; for, as the POUM said quite correctly, if the workers did not control the Republican armed forces the latter would control them.

Thus the debate: weighing up these rival notions for conducting the civil war against the Fascist generals, Orwell, as he wrote, personally inclined to take the Communist view. True, he felt that the Spanish workers must be given a better war aim than preserving the democratic capitalist status quo and he had no hope of British and French support for the Republic. Even so, as a practical man he thought the Communists were right in making the efficient waging of the war the overriding short-term policy.

Indeed, when in mid-May he went on two weeks' leave to join Eileen in her Barcelona hotel, one of his first actions was to contact a Communist acquaintance to ask about his chances of transfer to the International Brigade in Madrid where the real fighting was going on. One can speculate what might have happened had he as a loyal soldier joined a Communist-officered unit in Madrid and made friends there – there would have been no *Homage to Catalonia*, and *Animal Farm* and *Nineteen Eighty-Four* might well have been different. But it was not to be. The Communist-inspired coup against the Anarchists and the POUM in Barcelona came first.

It is all so long ago; revolutionaries always quarrel; as Auden said, history has little pardon for losers. The conflicts in the Republican camp between the Spanish Communists on the one hand and the Anarchists and the POUM on the other in a war which they collectively all lost to General Franco have passed into the dimness of history. Yet Orwell in his story has captured a vital political moment in this war in very human and personal terms.

Orwell recounted how from the moment of his return to Barcelona he felt politically uneasy and saw his experience of Catalonia at war, which had given him some magic moments of comradeship, turning into nightmare. After his long spell at the front he suffered the shock of finding Barcelona transformed. Gone was the revolutionary enthusiasm. It seemed to him that class distinctions had returned and people appeared almost uninterested in the war. Then came the great shock of an actual armed clash in the city. The Republican Government in Valencia, and the Socialist and Communist Parties, had been steadily chipping away at the Anarchists' control of the administration of Barcelona. When in mid-May some police-men tried to expel the Anarchist workers from the central telephone exchange by force, the Anarchists fired back. As if by a signal, barricades went up in the streets and confused firing broke out all over the city.

Orwell described how as one of a dozen available militia members of the POUM, with not quite that many rifles between them, he was enrolled to guard the Party headquarters and sat for some days on a flat roof overlooking the broad avenue of the

Ramblas, not far from the Hotel Continental where Eileen and some friends had their rooms. During those days he never fired at anyone but sat passively on the roof, reading Penguin paperbacks, unsure of what the conflict was about but 'marvelling at the folly of it all'. He described how John McNair at some personal risk brought him cigarettes from the Hotel Continental and how his Belgian friend, Georges Kopp, at even greater risk, indeed quite heroically, established a pact of peace between the POUM members and a group of frightened Civil Guards who had barricaded themselves in a café opposite.

After five days, by official agreement and through evident exhaustion, the firing between the Anarchists and their opponents suddenly ceased. Orwell watched the barricades go down and saw the streets of Barcelona cautiously patrolled by the new 'Assault Guards' which had been sent by the Republican Government by sea from Valencia. They were tall men in clean uniforms carrying modern sub-machine guns, whom Orwell thought a great contrast to the ragged soldiers of the POUM at the front. But their coming did not bring peace.

Instead, Orwell and his POUM comrades, including the ILP volunteers, found themselves suddenly attacked by the Communists in the press and on the radio on a charge of treachery to the Republic. The attackers said that the POUM had not only instigated the street fighting in Barcelona against the Republican Government. They had done so in company with Trotskyist traitors as the direct hirelings of General Franco. It was a piece of typical Stalinist topsy-turvy slander: the POUM as the most revolutionary party of all was accused by the Communists of being in the pay of the Fascist Right. And this Stalinist accusation put forward without any evidence was being spread not only in Spain but internationally: Orwell saw it quoted in the liberal *News Chronicle* in London.

Now, Orwell in his account said that he understood how the POUM with its doctrinaire Marxism was a nuisance to the Communist strategy of a united front and how they might therefore oppose the POUM politically. What utterly shocked him, however, was the mendacious totalitarian tactic under which leaders of the POUM were now flung into Republican prisons. To accuse the POUM of actually being in the pay of

Franco, as the Communists did – that Orwell recognized as the Big Lie in the style of Hitler and Goebbels. What shocked him most, he wrote in *Homage to Catalonia*, was that this character-assassination was conducted even as 15,000 under-equipped and hungry POUM militiamen were fighting against Franco on the Aragon front.

The totalitarian character of Soviet Communism had re-vealed itself to Orwell and this clear recognition of an enemy force was to remain with him for life. For some days Orwell, Eileen and their friends found life difficult in Barcelona as wildly disturbing reports succeeded each other. It was in a subdued mood that Orwell – now promoted to lieutenant – left the fears and suspicions now ruling Barcelona behind him to return to his POUM military unit on the Aragon front.

There, shortly after his arrival, through not keeping his head down in the trench, he was shot by a sniper through the neck – one millimetre to the side, the doctors later said, and the main artery would have been severed. For a few moments Orwell thought himself at the point of death. He reported how he thought first of Eileen and secondly how stupid it was to have sacrificed all his efforts in Spain through a moment's careless-ness. But surprisingly his injury was not fatal. Instead, he was moved to the rear by a series of acutely painful bumpy journeys, ending up in a military hospital in Tarragona, where Eileen joined him and doctors attended to his injury which, surpris-ingly again, left him upright and mobile except for an intermittent loss of voice.

From there he was moved to the POUM's Maurin Sanatorium on the outskirts of Barcelona. He found this institution filled with wounded POUM militiamen who were now desperately anxious about their future in view of the constant Communist propaganda against them. Orwell himself, suffering from his wound and even more from the shock of the political turn of events, felt that his usefulness to the Spanish Republican cause was at an end. As he wrote, his only desire was to get away from the atmosphere of political suspicion and hatred which by now horrified him; indeed from his whole association with Spain.

But to get his discharge from the army, he had to be declared unfit by a specific medical board back at the front. It took

Orwell five exhausting days of journeys to and fro, which he endured with his usual stoicism, to find the right board and obtain his clearance. Back in Barcelona, even as he entered the Hotel Continental, he found himself hustled out of the hotel lounge by Eileen who explained the new situation to him. What he had not known was that while he was away at the front, the POUM had been officially suppressed by the authorities as pro-Fascist; its executive members were arrested or in hiding and its assets confiscated. Some ILP volunteers had already left Spain; others were detained. They themselves, like the other foreigners associated with the POUM, were now suspects. The police had in fact already been to search the Orwells' room in the hotel, taking away all Orwell's papers. Fortunately, they had not taken their passports which were hidden under the mattress of the bed on which Eileen was left lying undisturbed during the entire search. (Orwell observed ironically that the Spanish police were still gallant, as their Soviet counterparts would certainly not have been.)

There followed a few days of farce mingled with nightmare, during which Orwell and Eileen, joined by John McNair, for whom a warrant was out, and Stafford Cottman, the youngest ILP volunteer, moved in apparent safety through the street crowds and cafés in the daytime, while at night they slept in hiding to avoid arrest.

Since they fortunately still possessed their passports, Orwell and Eileen had them stamped by the British Consul for crossing into France. Orwell recalled that all this time, even while he knew it to be an illusion, he could not rid himself of the Englishman's innate assumption that just because he had done nothing illegal, he could not possibly be arrested.

This illusion of being safe showed itself when he and Eileen took the risk of visiting Georges Kopp in prison. As a POUM officer Kopp had been arrested although carrying an important letter from the Government in Valencia. In the overcrowded prison Orwell noticed wounded POUM militiamen: the Communists were doing their job of suppression thoroughly. In spite of this, Orwell dutifully took the fearful risk of actually going to the police to retrieve Kopp's Government letter for him. The letter did not do Kopp much good. He languished in a

Republican jail for eighteen months, as Orwell might easily
have done. Instead, Orwell, Eileen, McNair and Cottman
travelled untroubled by train to the French frontier where the
Spanish police who searched them evidently did not know that
the '29th Division' stamped on Orwell's discharge paper was
the POUM unit and let them through.

Orwell spent a few days with Eileen in France – personally
safe but, he reported, with an overwhelming sense of anti-
climax.

In Orwell's life, his six months' experience in revolutionary
Spain with its initial idealism and its traumatic change of
fortune proved crucial. The memory for long remained a fixed
point in his thinking. In Wigan he had become a socialist. In
Barcelona he had seen his brief glimpse of a classless socialist
society crushed by the Communists with the use of the Big Lie.
He had recognized the nature of totalitarian Communism. As
he observed, from then on every serious piece of his writing was
in some way directed against totalitarianism and in favour of
the democratic socialism he believed in.

I think that his Spanish experience perhaps also subtly
changed his view of England. In the concluding paragraph of
Homage to Catalonia he described how on his return home he felt
that as he looked at the soothing landscape of southern
England, it was already hard to imagine anything violent
happening anywhere:

'Earthquakes in Japan, famines in China, revolutions in
Mexico? Don't worry, the milk will be on the doorstep
tomorrow morning, the *New Statesman* will come out on
Friday. The industrial towns were far away, a smudge of
smoke and misery hidden by the curve of the earth's surface.
Down here it was still the England I had known in my
childhood: the railway-cuttings smothered in wild flowers,
the deep meadows where the great shining horses browse
and meditate, the slow-moving streams bordered by willows,
the green bosoms of the elms, the larkspurs in the cottage
gardens; and then, the huge peaceful wilderness of outer
London, the barges on the miry river, the familiar streets, the
posters telling of cricket matches and Royal weddings, the

men in bowler hats, the pigeons in Trafalgar Square, the red buses, the blue policemen – all sleeping the deep, deep sleep of England, from which I sometimes fear that we shall never wake till we are jerked out of it by the roar of bombs.'[3]

The passage seems to express what some of Orwell's early writings suggested to me: that ever since his return from Burma, with all his love for it he could not but look at England at times with the eyes of an outsider. There was yet a further step waiting for him to take in his political pilgrim's progress.

EIGHT

The Detour

THE TWO YEARS from his return from Spain in 1937 to the outbreak of world war in 1939 were for Orwell by and large a period of political detour.

When in July 1937 he and Eileen were back with their chickens and geese in Wallington he found that arguments within Left-wing circles about the publication of *The Road to Wigan Pier* were still going on. Harold Laski had given high praise to the descriptive first part of the book, while simply dismissing part two. Victor Gollancz was still pleased with the stir the book had caused. But there had also been a concerted attack on *Wigan Pier* and on Orwell himself by the Communists and their sympathizers entrenched in English literary circles. In the Communist *Daily Worker*, Harry Pollitt said in a vituperative review that Orwell was a disillusioned middle-class boy and an ex-imperial policeman who was looking for socialism but was worried chiefly by the smell of the working class. This slander caused Orwell to write an angry letter to Gollancz who seems to have intervened on his behalf.

More seriously Orwell found himself in conflict with the Communists and their United Front allies over his champion-ship of the POUM in Spain. Among Orwell's Independent Labour Party friends there was now acute anxiety over the fate of their arrested POUM comrades. An international delegation to Spain was told by the Republican Government that enquiries had disclosed no evidence whatever of any 'Fascist putsch' by the POUM. But the Communist attack branding the POUM as traitors in General Franco's pay did not let up and as in Spain, so now in England, Orwell found himself at the receiving end.

First, Victor Gollancz turned down *Homage to Catalonia* on merely hearing of its theme. Orwell thereupon offered the book to the smaller independent Left-wing publisher, Fred Warburg of Secker & Warburg (about whom more later). Next, Orwell's article on his Spanish experiences submitted to the *New Statesman* was rejected outright by its editor, Kingsley Martin, and he had to be content with publication in the much less prominent *New English Weekly*. The rejection was not surprising since in the article Orwell stated that while it was doubtful whether the Republican Government still aimed at military victory over General Franco, its jails when Orwell left were bulging, not with Fascists but with imprisoned revolutionaries and that Spanish Communists were the jailers.

Orwell might have expected such views not to be welcomed in the by now pretty pro-Communist *New Statesman*, but he did burst out in an angry letter when Kingsley Martin equally rejected his review of *The Spanish Cockpit* by Franz Borkenau, a disillusioned ex-Communist in Spain, not because he thought Orwell's review factually wrong but because again it con- travened the *New Statesman*'s line. When Orwell in the autumn of 1937 settled down to write *Homage to Catalonia*, it must have been with a strengthened sense of belonging to a beleaguered minority.

Presumably these feelings were responsible for his support of the Independent Labour Party's revolutionary political line on the international class struggle. He did not support it in *Homage to Catalonia*. There he held back; but for the next two years he espoused the ILP line in all his articles, reviews and letters – and with the ILP he went wrong in his idea of how history would proceed.

Briefly, the ILP line was that Fascism was only a late stage of capitalism, leading inexorably to inter-capitalist wars. The workers and all truly progressive people must therefore reject every alliance with capitalist forces and aim only at inter- national socialism. The error in this argument lay in its equating Chamberlain's democratic Britain with Nazi Germany and seeing them as merely two rival capitalist states, presumably both equally aggressive. It followed from this argument that the United Front call to 'stand up to Hitler', initiated to be sure by the Communists but now backed from Left to Right by the Communists, Labour, Liberals and in a different form by such anti-Chamberlain Conservatives as Winston Churchill – that this call was a mere disguise for preparing for a British capitalist war against Germany.

The fallacy of course was that this argument ignored the essence of what was clearly going on in Nazi Germany – the crazed nationalist streak and the racialism in Hitler's dictatorship which were to lead to war and genocide. But as he took up the ILP line, Orwell's ideas were not shaped by the preparations for aggression in Nazi Germany, a country of which he knew little, but by what he had personally experienced in Spain. It was there that he had become convinced that any alliance of revolutionary workers with a capitalist middle class offered no feasible framework for resisting Fascism. Thus in a book review in August 1937 he wrote that two facts were self-evident:

> 'War against a foreign country only happens when the moneyed classes think they are going to profit from it.
>
> Every war when it comes, or before it comes, is represented not as a war but as an act of self-defence against a homicidal maniac ("militarist" Germany in 1914, "Fascist" Germany next year or the year after).'[1]

It is interesting that he wrote of 'Fascist Germany', the abstraction, not 'Nazi Germany', the reality. A month later he wrote in a letter to his friend, the sociologist Geoffrey Gorer, that the Popular Front talk was a mere trick to get the Labour Party to line up behind a British capitalist war. But as Spain had shown, if one collaborated with a capitalist-imperialist power in a struggle against Fascism, one simply let in Fascism by the back door. Indeed, the general fear that even so mild and democratic a country as Britain would become a Fascist police state if it went to war against Germany (as he thought it would) clearly troubled Orwell at this time acutely. It is interesting, however, that he did not include such fears in *Homage to Catalonia* – this remained simply the objective recollection of his Spanish experience.

Being a methodical hard worker, he handed in the manuscript of the book to Fred Warburg in late January 1938, but then came a reaction. His health, which had so surprisingly stood up to the ravages of his frontline service and being wounded in Spain, gave way. In March 1938, a few days before

Hitler sent a shudder through the world by his seizure of Austria, Orwell fell gravely ill with a tubercular lesion in one lung and under the care of his brother-in-law, Lawrence O'Shaughnessy, was rushed to a sanatorium, Preston Hall, in Kent. There he remained for nearly six months, for a good part of the time bedridden and compelled under doctor's orders to rest and do no writing except the odd book review.

In April 1938 while Orwell lay ill, *Homage to Catalonia* was published by Secker & Warburg – considering the book's later popularity, the impact at the time was very muted. Orwell's friend Geoffrey Gorer paid the book its deserved tribute in *Time and Tide*, but pro-Communist reviewers in various journals (including the B B C's *The Listener*) condemned it as a defence of treacherous Spanish Trotskyists. Some other reviewers who felt that in their difficult situation the Spanish Republicans should not be attacked at all were doubtful about the justification of Orwell's criticisms, even though he had ended the book by wishing the Republican cause well. I remember a particularly damp comment in the *New Statesman*. As a result of this hostile or tepid reception, the first sales of *Homage to Catalonia* were disappointing in the extreme. Orwell, aware how strong Communist influence was in English reviewers' circles, may not have been surprised.

A minor but interesting event during his illness was a visit to the sanatorium by the poet, Stephen Spender, who had been briefly – very briefly – a Communist, and whom Orwell in his writings had attacked if not by name, then as a member of the parlour Bolsheviks, 'Auden & Co'. One remembers Spender in the thirties as a gentle, reflective, handsome young poet and Orwell of course immediately took to him. Explaining this in a letter to Spender, Orwell wrote that he had been hostile towards him as a fashionably successful writer and a Communist, but this had merely been an abstract attitude:

'Even if when I met you I had not happened to like you, I should still have been bound to change my attitude, because when you meet anyone in the flesh you realize immediately that he is a human being and not a sort of caricature embodying certain ideas.'[2]

(This distinction by Orwell between his personal and

political life was characteristic. Some years later he eventually made friends with pacifists whose views he had strongly attacked during the war.)

After his run of ill luck, Orwell had some better fortune. An anonymous donor (later revealed as the novelist L.H. Myers) gave him a loan to enable him to convalesce from his illness during the winter in a warmer climate. In September 1938, just as Hitler prepared with Chamberlain's help to carve up Czechoslovakia, Orwell and Eileen sailed for Morocco.

There they were to stay for six months, mostly in Marrakesh, where Orwell again fell ill for some weeks. He wrote little about his Moroccan surroundings, really only one piece, but in that he did make the interesting point that as he looked at the swarming Arab crowds in the street, he tended to regard them not as individuals but as part of the scenery, as invisible. (When I passed through North Africa with the Anglo-American forces four years later, our attitude towards the indigenous Arab seemed similar; our contacts were only with the French minority; how quickly viewpoints have changed since then.)

While in Morocco, Orwell still seemed to be firmly of the belief that a war against Hitler's Germany would lead to Fascism in Britain. In letters to Herbert Read he discussed the chance of setting up secret printing presses to provide a wartime voice for a British underground. But by and large during his Moroccan winter, Orwell took a holiday away from the tense rumours of war of the day, a trip back into his childhood past, in writing his fourth novel, *Coming Up For Air*.

Some critics have regarded this as his best-constructed novel. To my mind its themes are a little too schematically hammered home. In the main these were his intense dislike of London as a nightmarish metropolis, his pervasive fear of impending war and his nostalgia for the imagined safety of his childhood past.

He expounded these themes through the thoughts of another typically Orwellian hero, even though this time he tried to draw him deliberately as unlike himself. George Bowling, a short, stout, garrulous, middle-aged suburban insurance agent, seems more a portrait of his brother-in-law Humphry Dakin than of himself, but Orwell's intellectual outlook all the same comes through. Thus he has Bowling reflect that in his pre-1914 childhood people did not yet know that their whole familiar world would slide away from them; or he has him conclude about a Left Book Club lecturer that 'what he's saying is that Hitler is after us and we must all get together and have a good hate'.

Orwell's Bowling was born and spent his childhood in a Home Counties village called Lower Binfield and as he drives through the London of 1939 which seems to be waiting for enemy bombers, he recalls what seems the safety and peace of his lower-middle-class origins at the turn of the century. There are echoes here of H.G. Wells's *Mr Polly*. In that safe childhood world – so Orwell let Bowling remember – one could buy sweets for a farthing! And oh, the peace of being a boy and lying on one's belly and reading an always reassuring boys' magazine like *Chums*. Or the peacefulness of fishing in a local pool; Orwell devoted some quite lyrical passages, lovingly detailed, to describe a boy idling an afternoon away in fishing, with instructions as to the different kinds of bait.

Orwell has Bowling on impulse go back to look at Lower Binfield, only to find his childhood scenery inevitably all changed. The pool where he had fished is drained, the fields have become part of a 'rash' of new housing estates. There is no going back in time. (Already in *Wigan Pier* one could note Orwell's unwillingness to be shown new housing estates. Was he more concerned with castigating slum life than with slum clearance? Perhaps.)

In March 1939, a few days after Hitler had marched into Prague (with Jews and Czechs flung into concentration camps) Orwell and Eileen returned to England. In May they were back in Wallington. In June, Gollancz, still the publisher of Orwell's novels, brought out *Coming Up For Air*. This time sales were good; reviewers were appreciative; comparisons were drawn with the early novels of H.G. Wells. But among the prevailing expectations of war with Hitler, Orwell brooded about other things.

With both Soviet Russia and Nazi Germany in mind, for instance, he thought about the question whether their control of radio, the press and the secret police had not made modern tyrannies quite unprecedented in history, perhaps not removable. I well remember a fierce review he wrote in the *Adelphi* of July 1939 which I read after my return to England. It was entitled 'Not Counting Niggers'.[3] He was writing a propos of a (now long forgotten) book called *Union Now*. He magisterially took to task the American author, Clarence Streit, and writers and journalists like him, for talking of Britain, France and other West European countries as 'the peace bloc' or 'the democracies' opposing Hitler. Did such writers not realize, he asked, that these so-called democracies ruled over vast empires which were nothing more than autocratic arrangements for exploiting cheap coloured labour? As I read this passage, I recall, I felt that I was with Orwell – imperialism had to go! But I had my doubts when, referring to British rule in India, he went on to ask what value there was 'in bringing down Hitler in order to stabilize something that is far bigger and in its different way just as bad'. Bigger than Hitler and just as bad? I could not see the final phase of British rule in India in that light. And I parted company from Orwell when he went on to refer to Winston Churchill as 'posing as a democrat' and claimed that through the current British war preparations 'we may sink almost unresisting into some local variant of Austro-Fascism'.

I have often felt that had I met Orwell earlier, in 1939, I might have argued strongly with him. I had returned to England in late 1938 with my own eyes firmly fixed on the, to me, uncanny rise of Hitler. I had watched Hitler's systematic use of the weapon of demonic anti-Semitism to build his Gestapo police state and to bedazzle the German people into carrying out his aggressive nationalist designs. I was convinced that all European history depended on whether Britain would find the resolution to resist him and not for a moment did I believe as Orwell did that Britain by going to war would also turn to Fascism.

On the other hand, as I look at Orwell's writing in the two years before the war, it is perfectly evident that it was his own Spanish experience which shaped his thinking and not the build-up of Hitler's Germany of which he knew little, about which, indeed, I think he had something of a blind spot. Since he placed so much stress on the precise use of words, one should mention again that quite remarkably not once in his writings of these two years did he refer to Nazism or Nazi Germany. Instead he spoke only in ILP revolutionary language of 'Fascist Germany' thereby turning Hitler into an abstraction.

But I did not have to argue with Orwell, because by the time we met the war had broken out and he had entirely changed his political viewpoint. A year later he wrote that during the night of 25 August 1939 something crucial happened to him:

'The night before the Russo-German pact was announced I dreamed that the war had started. It was one of those dreams which, whatever Freudian inner meaning they may have, do sometimes reveal to you the real state of your feelings. It taught me two things, first, that I should be simply relieved when the long-dreaded war started, secondly, that I was patriotic at heart, would not sabotage or act against my own side, would support the war, would fight in it if possible. I came downstairs to find the newspaper announcing Ribbentrop's flight to Moscow. So war was coming, and the Government, even the Chamberlain Government, was assured of my loyalty.'[4]

I think that in effect he had taken the fourth major step in his career. First he had become a writer, then he had become a socialist; in Spain he had recognized the Communist enemy and now he had returned to his special socialist English patriotism. It was at this point that I met him in January 1940 to become his admirer and (I hope) a friend. The story of his dramatic life up to this point, as I have tried to relate it, is one I have traced mainly from his own writings in which he continuously defined his attitude to his surroundings and from my own memories of him; and to a lesser extent from what people have said or written about him.

PART TWO

In Orwell's Company

NINE

Meeting Orwell

M Y FIRST MEETING with Orwell was in January 1940, in the despondent blackout days of the 'phoney war' in the West which had followed Hitler's swift destruction of Poland in September 1939. Half a year later, during the glorious summer of 1940, which saw the dramas of the fall of France, the evacuation at Dunkirk and the heroism of the British fighter pilots in the Battle of Britain, through accident I had a brief share in the events which led to his writing *The Lion and the Unicorn*. If I here bring myself into the story, it is not to lend any special value to my conventional war and post-war experiences, but because by doing so I can better recall an extraordinary period of history; and so may see Orwell's unique role more clearly in the context of his time.

The helpless sense of utter uncertainty about the future which from 1936 onwards began to oppress so many people in Britain is already hard to convey to today's younger readers. It may by now linger only as an uneasy memory even in the minds of people who lived through this period. But the causes of the uncertainty were real enough. In the late thirties, as one watched Hitler's relentless advance in the face of supine British and French Governments, suddenly no assumption about the stability of European democracy seemed any longer safe. Hitler's domination of Europe, which only a few years previously had seemed a fantasy, was suddenly a possibility.

I remember how early in 1938 I read a review by Orwell of Arthur Koestler's Spanish war book, *Spanish Testament*, in which he drew attention to one passage where Koestler said that if the European press remained uncommitted about the hell created in Madrid under Fascist bombardment, then Europe was lost. Orwell wrote:

'I quite agree. You cannot be objective about an aerial

torpedo. And the horror we feel of these things has led to this conclusion. If someone drops a bomb on your mother, go and drop two bombs on his mother. The only apparent alternatives are to smash dwelling houses to powder, blow out human entrails and burn holes in children with lumps of thermite, or to be enslaved by people who are more ready to do these things than you are yourself; as yet no one has suggested a practical way out.'[1]

Precisely so, I thought. I read those lines of Orwell's while staying in Jerusalem, the holy city, in the then British Mandated Territory of Palestine.

I was born in 1907, the son of an early Zionist leader who as a young student in Vienna had in 1897 joined the founder of Zionism, Theodor Herzl. I first went to a Swiss-German state school whose classless, disciplined, puritan atmosphere, as I remember it, had as lasting an impact upon me as the snobberies of St Cyprian's had on Orwell; and then continued my education at a minor English public school and Cambridge University.

Compared to Orwell's sharp vision of the world my own Left-wing views were both wavering and much more conventional. In 1935, before going abroad, I went with a Communist friend, Tom Wintringham (who was later to command the British battalion in the International Brigade in Spain), to attend the Founders' meeting of a body called 'Writers and Artists Against Fascism', presided over by John Strachey. I recognized the occasion as a Communist Party manoeuvre to line up writers according to the new Soviet policy in a 'Popular Front' ranging from Communists to Liberals, but at the time I regarded the Communist domination within the British intelligentsia as just one current fact one had to accept.

During my travels I stayed for a time in Tel Aviv and Jerusalem, in the then small Jewish sector of British Mandated Palestine. From there I also visited the neighbouring Arab countries and then settled down to write a book about the triangular Zionist-Arab-British conflict over Palestine. Yet during all my time in that disputed small country I read the British press with increasing anxiety in following the course of the Spanish civil war. Again, it is hard to explain now how agonizingly my friends and I mentally identified ourselves with the Republican cause in the Spanish war, how I had a war map of Spain covered with pins on my wall, as it were willing the Republicans to hold on. I shared the general Left-wing view that Britain and France by their policy of Non-Intervention were effectively supporting a Fascist government, and believed that without a change in this Anglo-French attitude the Spanish Republic was ultimately doomed.

Meanwhile in Palestine one had the Jewish-Arab conflict in which the British Government, with its strategic interests in the Arab countries in mind, was moving steadily towards cutting all British support for Zionism, just as the flow of Jewish refugees from Germany increased to a minor flood. But this small conflict in Palestine and even the Fascist advances in the Spanish civil war were for me overshadowed by the spectacle of Hitler's swift conquest of Central Europe. From the small confines of Palestine one could only powerlessly watch this Nazi advance, with ominous fears for the future of the European Jews – was there any future? I still remember how on the day of Hitler's triumphant march into Austria in March 1938, Reuter's first 'newsflash' said that 'in the streets of Vienna, Jews are being rounded up like cattle'.

At that time, and here I come to a circumstance which was to have a passing effect – via myself – on Orwell, I came under the influence of a unique friend I made in Palestine. This was Captain Orde Wingate, a young, very pro-Zionist Intelligence Officer in the British forces in Palestine, who was later in the war, as General Wingate, to become the famous Chindit Commander who so spectacularly led his forces into the Burmese jungles behind the Japanese lines. At this earlier stage, in Palestine, Wingate was preparing to lead his 'night squads' of British and Jewish soldiers against Arab rebels. Like Orwell, though in a totally different way, Wingate was a self-taught individualist, I think of genius. He was also a born leader of men. Sceptical intellectual though I was, in ways and for reasons too complicated to tell here I fell under Wingate's spell (as many people were to do subsequently), and as a result returned to England with instructions to concern myself as a writer with British war aims.

I remember an occasion when on our return from a trip to Transjordan we walked along the tall sedge by the banks of the Jordan river and Wingate outlined his three personal aims in the war he saw as looming inevitably ahead: to lead Palestine-Jewish soldiers, to help liberate Ethiopia from Mussolini and to fight with the Chinese against the invading Japanese – and he, Captain O.C. Wingate, would try to fulfil all three aims.

Which in different ways he did. As for the course the coming war against Hitler would take, so Wingate informed me, the German armies would sweep round the Maginot Line at Sedan any time they chose; France would collapse; Britain alone must then hold the line against Hitler and Mussolini in her island and the Middle East until the Russians and the rearmed Americans could pile in. There would be a British-American alliance and probably a British-Russian alliance. But while resisting alone, Wingate added, Britain must at all costs declare that she was fighting against the dictators in the name of international justice and decency – for the safety of the threatened Jews, for the freedom of the Ethiopians and the Chinese and the oppressed everywhere. It was vital for Britain to fight the war for true democracy, true Christian ideals. If I wanted to go back to England and write, Wingate said, let me return to London and write about decent, idealistic British war aims.

I remember how in that strange and confused pre-war climate, Wingate's certainties inspired me with a kind of certainty of my own in which I was to bring his ideas about decent British war aims to the attention of my publisher, Fred Warburg, and of George Orwell. Only after two years or so did the spell fade amid the realities of the actual war. But this came later. First of all, in the autumn of 1938, I was back in London with my book about the Palestine conflict being published by Secker & Warburg. In this book I had strenuously and equally criticized the policies of the British, the Zionists and the Arab leaders. It brought me fair reviews, but few friends, but this hardly mattered for the book was published the day after Chamberlain had returned from Munich waving his piece of paper with Hitler's signature promising peace in our time. In the subsequent turmoil over Chamberlain's consent to Hitler's dismemberment of democratic Czechoslovakia, which to those who had eyes to see made war between Britain and Nazi Germany look inevitable, the small conflict in Palestine and with it my book were to me as if blotted out.

What now?

Enquiring about Orwell, I learnt from Warburg that following his collapse, he was wintering in Morocco. I was sorry to miss him. I had avidly read *Homage to Catalonia.*

During the year 1939 I began to see a good deal of Fred Warburg, who deserves more notice than is usually given him in Orwell's story because he became not only his publisher but his good friend and a constant if often frustrated giver of sensible advice to Orwell.

Just old enough to have fought at Passchendaele, Warburg was almost the least Jewish Jew I had met, but even so Hitler had now reawakened his Jewish feelings. He told me that he had had some strong arguments about this with Orwell. Warburg felt quite simply that everybody should line up behind Churchill in opposition to Hitler and therefore to Chamberlain and the appeasers. While himself firmly opposed to Communism, he now did not even mind Communists in such an alliance. In turn, I told Warburg about Orde Wingate's ideas on the need for Britain to put forward decent, progressive, idealistic war aims in the conflict to come. Warburg appeared interested. At that time part-publisher, part-politician, he said that he had played with the idea of forming a group of likeminded writers to support social-democratic ideals.

I often felt about Fred Warburg that with a few additional qualities in his make-up – greater ambition, greater persistence – he might have become a significant politician: as it was, he remained a rather highbrow publisher. Still, in 1939 he was also very much an embattled figure in British intellectual life. Three years earlier he had set out with limited capital to become an independent 'political' publisher. In addition to his general publishing (of Thomas Mann and H.G. Wells, among others), he aimed to bring out successive books to propagate his own ideal of a democratic, humanist socialism, free from the false dogmas of Stalin's Communism. In this task Warburg felt opposed not only by the inertia of English conservative tradition but on the Left by the big battalions of a publisher like Victor Gollancz, with his Left Book Club bringing out vast editions of largely uncritical pro-Soviet books. In these circumstances Warburg's venture looked to me financially precarious.

Still, Warburg had published *World Revolution*, a weighty treatise by the leading West Indian Trotskyist, C.L.R. James, and Jomo Kenyatta's *Facing Mount Kenya*. He had published André Gide's *Return From the USSR*. Gide, previously highly courted by the Communists, had wildly infuriated them when on his return from Soviet Russia he asserted that the stifling Soviet censorship of thought was even greater than that in Nazi Germany. Warburg had also published *Homage to Catalonia* which Victor Gollancz had turned down, and, because of bad reviews, in the year since publication he had sold less than 700 copies. (Jon Kimche told me later that in 1945, after the war, he remaindered the rest of the first edition of *Homage to Catalonia* in his bookshop, together with my book on the Palestine conflict – what an honour for me!)

If the struggle in 1938–9 between pro-Communists and anti-Communists within the small British progressive intelligentsia aroused such violent emotions, this was because it seemed fraught with a significance which may already be hard to explain in the very different Britain of today. In Britain there was somehow an ever-increasing awareness that perhaps for the last time, Britain, still an imperial power, was playing a pivotal role in human history. Everything in Europe and beyond depended on whether Britain would resist Hitler and stop him, or would seek agreement with him – in vain, as many people thought – to share the spoils with his barbarian European empire, in return for his recognition of the safety of Britain's own imperial position.

That was Britain's pivotal choice: and as more and more ordinary people came to understand it, one saw a rising tide of anti-Nazi popular opinion which finally swept away Chamberlain and the appeasers and brought into office Churchill and his Coalition Government pledged to resist Hitler. It was a public opinion based in part no doubt on insular patriotism and ignorance of the military odds against England, but based also on a support of democratic freedoms, and on a spreading belief in social progress. In trying to give a sense of national purpose to this public opinion, the members of the Left-wing intelligentsia felt they had a special role to play, and they did have some role, through their positions in newspapers and periodicals. Only their ranks were divided. The Communists and their various supporters were in the majority within this intelligentsia and controlled institutions like the Left Book Club – they were really quite influential in shaping public opinion. They held that nothing whatever critical of Stalin's régime, which could harm the prospect of a Soviet alliance with the West against Hitler, should be written. At the same time a much smaller minority of writers on the Left (some of them ex-Communists) maintained that in order that British readers might see clearly what lay ahead, they should be told the full facts about Stalin's own gigantically despotic rule and the destructive character of Communist policy in the Spanish civil war.

The struggle between the two groups within the intelligentsia was fought out with such special bitterness first of all, of course, because the issues involved appeared as so large, but also for another reason. Compared with today, the British intelligentsia of 1938–9 was very small indeed – an enclosed little society. There were as yet no television commentators, no Sunday newspaper supplements; radio, still called 'the wireless', had little influence; there were as yet no new universities or polytechnics; studies like the social sciences were only fringe subjects. Everyone on the Left religiously read the weekly *New Statesman* and that was that. When the views of its gifted but politically slippery editor, Kingsley Martin, appeared to veer closer to the Communist party line, as they often did, this therefore mattered in a major way. When Kingsley Martin refused to print Orwell's despatches from Spain and Victor Gollancz turned down the very idea of *Homage to Catalonia*, this too mattered. Warburg certainly thought that this political bias mattered profoundly, and so above all, he told me, did Orwell, out of action for a year in his sanatorium and in Morocco.

The fateful year 1939 has become dreamlike in my memory. In March Hitler took over Prague; Gestapo rule was imposed on all Czechoslovakia; first reports stated that many Jews trapped in Prague committed suicide. I remember an editorial in the early edition of the *Evening Standard*, then still a politically influential newspaper in a capital city which mattered, which was headed 'A Ramshackle State' – good that it was got rid of. The proprietor, Lord Beaverbrook, must have telephoned his minions. The later edition carried a slashing anti-Hitler editorial written by Michael Foot, headed 'Attila!'. The so-called Fleet Street revolution had begun.

At the end of August came the shock of Stalin's pact with Hitler. I heard Chamberlain's croaking voice on the radio saying: 'Now this country is at war with Germany.' As Hitler's armies in their Blitzkrieg, the new cliché, destroyed Poland and Soviet armies marched in from their side, the Anglo-French forces in the West remained inactive in their lines. The phoney war had begun.

After two absurd days of queueing with many others at the War Office, I told Warburg that I was moving with my family to near Hastings, there to write a book for him about the war and British war aims, roughly on Wingate's formula. The first war winter was severe; above Hastings we were heavily snowed under. In January 1940, Warburg asked me to meet him in London and there at last I also met George Orwell as I had so much wanted to do.

Our meeting took place at the St John's Wood home of Hans Lothar, a German-Jewish exile who in pre-Hitler days had been deputy editor of Germany's leading liberal newspaper, the *Frankfurter Zeitung*. I remember how in the complete London blackout, I walked through the empty nocturnal streets of St John's Wood. In a bright room I met Warburg, Lothar and Orwell – three tall, thin men, all well over six foot. Introducing me, Warburg told Orwell that he was one of my literary heroes. Gaunt faced, Orwell gave me an awkward though not unfriendly smile.

Warburg said he had invited us because with British policy apparently paralysed in this phoney war, he wanted to found a group of writers to discuss issues. For instance, Hans Lothar

wanted to start a German-language anti-Nazi weekly newspaper in London to be called *Die Zeitung*, as a small sign that
this war was against Nazism, not just a repetition of the first
war against Germany. This idea should be supported.

Secondly, Warburg spoke about the case of Sebastian
Haffner, a young anti-Nazi German refugee, who had come to
London with his Jewish wife and written a brilliant analysis of
Nazism, *Germany – Jekyll and Hyde*, which Secker & Warburg
had published. Now, under the prevailing wartime stupidity,
Haffner had as an 'Aryan' German been interned as an enemy
alien – an outrage, said Warburg, which must be rectified.

Thirdly, there was the suggestion that I had made to him of
a discussion group on war aims.

While the talk went on, I looked with curiosity at Orwell,
whose appearance very much surprised me: it was so unlike
what I had expected. He was a very tall, thin man, with a
long, thin, haggard face, with deep-set blue eyes, a poor skin, a
poor, small moustache and deep lines etched in grooves down
his cheeks. Lines of suffering? He wore a shabby sports jacket
with worn leather patches at the elbows and frayed corduroy
trousers. In spite of this obvious external neglect, he reminded
me of British colonial officials I had met in the Middle East.
His social background was still recognizable; he looked like a
seedy Sahib. (John Beavan, a north country miner's son, who
as news editor of the *Observer* met Orwell a little later, told me
that to his working-class eyes, Orwell seemed like 'a broken-
down officer of the First World War selling insurance from
door to door – there was something vaguely military about
him'.)

This aspect derived presumably from his past as Eric Blair;
as Orwell, so it seemed to me, he also wore the typical French
working man's dark blue shirt, something still unusual in
those more formal days, and he incessantly rolled his own
cigarettes out of blackish, acrid tobacco, two things which
reminded me of the Parisian characters in his first book, *Down
and Out in Paris and London*. A unique appearance, fitting the
man and his style, I thought.

I can remember the main themes of our talk because at the
time they appeared important to me.

I told him how much I had liked his *Homage to Catalonia*, especially his picture of early revolutionary Barcelona. He appeared pleased – but as if Spain now lay in the past.

I mentioned how in one piece by him I had read in early 1939, he had said that the British Labour Party, by calling for armed resistance to Nazism and Fascism, was lining up with the British capitalist rulers against the interests of the British workers, and how this trend should be resisted.

Orwell said that since he wrote this article he had changed his views. He told me the story (one I think he often told) of his dream the night before Ribbentrop's journey to Moscow and how on waking in the morning he had decided that he was now a simple British patriot: when his age-group was called up, he intended to enlist and fight. He no longer thought there was any danger of British Fascism; but he said that what was so oppressive was the way in which, the moment war was declared, the British military, whose closed minds he knew well, had taken complete charge of the country in First War style, with old hacks like Hilaire Belloc and the novelist Ian Hay dug up to make national propaganda again. There was no sign as yet that the war was leading Britain towards any social breakthrough.

I mentioned the Fleet Street revolution, which made the Conservative Beaverbrook press sound at times like the Left-wing *News Chronicle* and *New Statesman*. Orwell was sceptical – he thought this 'revolution' largely a ploy by the Government to enlist Left-wing support for a united war against Germany.

War against Germany? I remember asking. Surely Britain's declaration of war had been mainly defensive. It was Hitler who for years had been engaging in aggression on all sides, as he extended the German Gestapo state. Orwell agreed that of course Hitler was the aggressor and everyone must resist him, but he had doubts about the direction in which the present British resistance was being exerted. The British capitalist rulers had suddenly discovered the well-known facts of Nazi atrocities, such as the persecution of the Jews. They were now making the most of these facts because it temporarily suited their book. But Chamberlain and his colleagues were still not seriously opposed to Nazism as such. They could drop their concern over its atrocities as soon as this was no longer useful – as soon, for instance, as they had guarantees from Hitler that their own imperial rule in India could look safe again.

I told Orwell that I had also read his recent outspoken article 'Not Counting Niggers' and agreed with him that so many English people who now newly protested against Hitler's racial policies still remained content with the racial oppression practised – well, among other policies – by the British rulers in India. Orwell repeated that there was no point in getting rid of Hitler merely to leave autocratic white rule in the British Empire intact. Here we were evidently of one mind, yet I was aware of an emotional difference. To me, resistance to Hitler came first and foremost, while freedom for India was somehow an abstract idea for the future. In Orwell's conscience, on the other hand, the two themes were indissolubly linked; indeed, new progress towards Indian freedom might be the more urgent need.

I next mentioned Orde Wingate's forecast of the course of the war: how the French would collapse when attacked by Hitler, a notion which very much interested Orwell, and how Britain would then have to hold the line, proclaiming decent idealistic war aims, 'until the Americans and Russians could pile in'. I told how Wingate had said that one should expect not only a British-American but a British-Soviet alliance against Hitler.

Orwell appeared interested in the question of war aims but expressed his doubts whether there could be any common Anglo-Soviet aims whatever for the future, even if Britain and Soviet Russia were to fight against Hitler side by side. Although, he said, one could now read about the unspeakable Nazi atrocities in all the British newspapers, there was an enduring silence on the progressive Left about the mass purges and the atrocities perpetrated by Stalin and his henchmen in Soviet Russia. Indeed, these atrocities were now again being denied or disregarded by British Communists. Even if, after making his pact with Stalin, Hitler were to attack Soviet Russia – with that dry chuckle of his Orwell thought this perfectly possible, even probable – how could a struggle for a socialist Britain be squared with the aims of Stalin? The last thing Stalin wanted was to see any strong and independent socialist movement in Europe.

Here I had no immediate answer. As a Jew I felt ready to compromise with all who opposed Hitler, Stalin or anyone else. Orwell by contrast seemed incorruptible in sensing the threat to civilized and democratic values from whatever quarter it came, Nazi Germany or Soviet Russia. I could feel that he also never ceased to recognize war itself as a terrible human catastrophe.

So there we stood in our views. During that whole evening Orwell seemed to me somewhat sad; not at all bitter, as a common friend had suggested I should find him, just sad; gentle in his personal manner however sharp his political views, with a straightforward and sad charm. I felt enormously drawn towards him. To be sure, as a Jew, partly Continental and with a Zionist background of which he disapproved, I had to be something of a stranger to him, but the fact that we agreed in nearly all our political opinions made up for this.

We parted; I had a blacked-out train to catch back to Hastings. During the next few weeks, Warburg's little group, enlarged by some other people, met a few more times, surprisingly enough not unproductively. After a while, Hans Lothar received official permission to launch his anti-Nazi German weekly, *Die Zeitung* – a tiny step in the transformation of the war into an anti-Nazi struggle. As for his author, Sebastian Haffner, Warburg actually had him freed almost immediately from internment. This at the time was a unique feat. It spoke much for the firmly authoritative manner in which Warburg demanded Haffner's release in telephoning his contacts in the Home Office.

As for myself, I remember how during the train journey back to Hastings I reflected on Orwell's fear of the threats for the future which would lie buried in any British-Soviet alliance against Hitler. This appeared true enough. Should I therefore perhaps say in my book that in such a case the Western allies should give priority to the rescue of Soviet Russia from the worst results of the tragic Bolshevik revolution?

Delusions, naive delusions, but in those dull, blackout days before the storm such delusions were not too surprising.

TEN

Searchlights

A CHANGE OF SCENE. From the winter of the dull discontent of the phoney war, one moved to the astonishing events of the glorious summer of 1940. During the winter, above Hastings, I began to write my book on the causes and outbreak of the war and war aims. In this book, blithely ignoring the Stalin-Hitler pact, I followed Wingate's prediction in assuming that there would be a certain alliance against Hitler between the Soviet Union and the West. I suggested that within such an alliance the Western powers should urge Stalin to grant his subjects greater democratic freedoms (vain hope!). I also urged that before winding up the Empire, Britain should enact sweeping land reforms, thus freeing the indebted peasants in India and elsewhere (not much hope of that, either).

I read Orwell's latest book of essays, *Inside the Whale*. Among the contents I was specially interested by the long and lovingly defensive essay on Dickens with its ringing peroration. I also read his period-piece essay on 'Boys' Weeklies', which I thought a delightful study of English popular culture – I had been a reader of the *Gem* and *Magnet* myself – in which his nostalgia for his own boyhood reading showed through.

I remember that in the early spring my wife and I met Orwell and Eileen somewhere amid the blackout gloom of London. We thought Eileen an attractive woman in her thirties, if looking a little tired, both rather echoing· Orwell and remaining a personality in her own right with a nice feminine vivacity. She was then working in the Censorship Department and talked wittily about all the weird characters collected in this as yet amateurish wartime institution and the gossip in the squalid canteen. She also talked about Spain, recalling humorous incidents during her and Orwell's traumatic experience there.

Recalling the occasion, I am put in mind of a rather cryptic remark once made by Orwell that Eileen herself could have been a writer. How serious was he? One cannot know.

Orwell by contrast seemed on the gloomy side. I remember that I wanted all the time to talk about the war but he did not. Instead he held forth about the English novel having become a purely upper-middle-class art form analysing purely upper-middle-class characters. There could not be aristocratic characters because most novelists didn't know any. As for lower-class characters, after the era of Wells, Bennett and Lawrence English novelists, themselves upper-middle class, had abandoned them to write again about individuals of their own class. Orwell saw no great prospects for the English novel because whatever the outcome of the war, it must mean a vast increase in the power of the state and this meant that the decline of the independent upper-middle class would be accelerated. Under strict state control the novel as an essentially individualistic art form could not flourish. His argument went something like that: like most thinking people during the phoney war, Orwell appeared pessimistic. Like many people he had as yet found no war work and he was writing very little. He talked about his hens and goats at Wallington and suggested that he might grow potatoes there against an impending food shortage – the German U-Boats, he foresaw, were pretty certain to sink British merchantmen.

Then suddenly it was the summer of 1940 and all our lives were changed in a gigantic upheaval.

In his concluding sentence in *Homage to Catalonia*, Orwell had said that the British people would only awaken from their sleep when the bombs fell on them. Now this was happening and Chamberlain was gone and Winston Churchill stood at the helm, voicing defiance like the very embodiment of British upper-class history and courage.

As Hitler struck in' the West, his tanks swept round the Maginot line north of Sedan, precisely as Orde Wingate had predicted and the Anglo-French lines crumbled. I can still recall the voice of Duff Cooper saying manfully on the radio: 'The German salient has become a bulge.' Fatal words. In the German Blitzkrieg, all seemed over within days, but large

British forces were evacuated from Dunkirk and propaganda somehow turned this defeat into victory. Paris fell; France surrendered at once, as Wingate had prophesied. Hitler was triumphant. At Westminster, Churchill proclaimed that the British would fight on the beaches, in the streets, they would never surrender.

While Hitler's forces raced through France, I myself in Hastings frantically incorporated the new situation of the French defeat into the last chapters of my war book which for reasons I cannot recall I named *The Malady and the Vision*, ending with proposals for a saner post-war world. I took the finished typescript to Fred Warburg, who with few enough books coming in sent it straight to the printers. Meanwhile my wife and I with our small daughter moved from Hastings to share a house near London with Fred and Pamela Warburg. This was Scarlett's Farm, a converted farmhouse standing in lush meadows near Twyford in Berkshire, set conveniently not far from a Green Line bus stop on what was then the Great West Road from London.

In my memory the summer of 1940 is a time and Scarlett's Farm is a place of which I have fond and enduring memories, particularly because throughout that summer Orwell came on many weekends to visit the Warburgs and ourselves. Scarlett's Farm was also the place where we brought to fruition our joint project of the Searchlight Books.

Orwell told me that he and Eileen were now staying in London and he was thinking of closing his retreat at The Stores in Wallington for the duration: that was the end of a dream. On the first few occasions, Eileen accompanied him on his visits to us, but we all noticed a profound change in her. She seemed to sit in the garden sunk in unmoving silence while we talked. Mary, my wife, observed that Eileen not only looked tired and drawn but was drably and untidily dressed. Trying in vain to involve Eileen in conversation, Mary said that she seemed to have become completely withdrawn. Since both Orwell and Eileen were reticent to a degree, it was only after her second or third visit that we learned that her brother Lawrence, who was serving as a doctor with the British forces, had been killed while attending to the wounded on the beaches at Dunkirk. As far as I recall, after a few visits in June Eileen went to stay with her now widowed sister-in-law and no longer came to Scarlett's Farm. Did we think sufficiently about her? Perhaps not as much as we should have done, but it was wartime with people frequently disappearing from view; and the débâcle in France had brought news of a number of casualties.

Orwell of course suffered on Eileen's behalf and he saw her during the week but he was stoically silent about her and continued to come at weekends. In my memory, indeed, the whole fateful summer of 1940 reduces itself to a tableau of cloudless, sunny days during which Warburg, Orwell and I sat and talked in the lush garden of Scarlett's Farm. In what could seem an unreal present, while around us England, half armed or quarter armed, held its breath, waiting for the heavily armed German invaders; while German bombs, at first only a few, began to fall on London; and while above our heads – we only saw the constant vapour trails in the clear sky – the Spitfires and Hurricanes of the RAF accomplished their decisive defensive air victory of the war, we talked about the future.

As Fred Warburg recalled it in his memoirs, we discussed how the slovenly Tory England could be transformed into an up-to-date socialist community which could inspire the world.

I thought this was going a bit far; but still, with Britain standing alone and defeat not impossible, it seemed a time for Utopian talk. With my book finished I again felt unoccupied. I had actually had my army medical test in Reading and passed A1; but I suspected that little would in the short run come of this, as in my folder on the counter which I surreptitiously opened, I had seen that my birthplace in Germany (although neither of my parents was German) was heavily underlined in blue pencil and an acquaintance in the know assured me this meant that my call-up would be deferred (which is what happened). Most days I therefore travelled with Warburg up to London, to help him in his office in his task, which could seem highly theoretical, of setting up a future publication list, at a time when a German invasion might well be expected.

In London I had a brief meeting with Orde Wingate, the unheeded prophet of the fall of France. For his pro-Zionist exploits in Palestine he had been barred from the Middle East but he sounded sardonic, purposeful and confident as he was off to an undisclosed destination. A year later I was to learn that it was to lead Ethiopian guerrilla forces in a brilliant campaign against the Italian Fascist occupiers.

Perhaps because of my renewed encounter with the hero, or my itch at being unemployed, I developed an idea which I put to Warburg and Orwell. Why not publish a series of short books on war aims for a better future, called 'Searchlight Books'? Orwell could start off the series, setting the tone with an optimistic book about the future of a democratic socialist Britain. Sebastian Haffner could write about the right way to treat a post-Nazi Germany. In London I had seen William Connor, who under the pseudonym 'Cassandra' in the *Daily Mirror* was the most popular newspaper columnist in the country. He was professionally gruff, sceptical and patriotic, out to puncture authority, with a gift for the striking journalistic phrase. I had sounded him out – he could write about shortcomings in the British popular war effort. And so on: one could readily think of half a dozen further titles.

Warburg who was generally cautious was for once quite keen on the idea, but Orwell initially demurred about writing the first book. He wanted not to write but to join the forces, he said; if he could not join the forces he might grow potatoes at Wallington. He knew what he could say in such a book, but in his present mood he would work at anything with his hands rather than write. I could see that he was all the same quite keen on the idea; Warburg added his persuasions and in the end Orwell agreed grudgingly to produce a 'positive' book. Warburg in his publisher's style immediately wrote out the text of an announcement for the 'Searchlight Books'. The series, he wrote 'will stress Britain's international and imperial responsibilities and the aim of a planned Britain at the head of a greater and freer British Commonwealth, linked with the United States of America and other countries, as a framework of world order . . .'.[1]

For my taste, that again went rather far, but we worked quite successfully at launching the series. I can remember listening to a lengthy conversation between Orwell and William Connor, that professionally cynical Fleet Street professional, and noting that the two did not really communicate at all as Orwell tried to persuade Connor to write a Searchlight book. This was not surprising. Connor seemed to have the egocentric fixed views of a star Fleet Street commentator who is accustomed to lay down the law in short paragraphs rather than to discuss things. Orwell also had his firm views but was always ready to discuss them; but then in spite of the efficient journalistic work he came to perform, he was never remotely a Fleet Street professional. However, Connor in the end wrote his Searchlight book which proved to be a bestseller. T.C. Worsley, literary editor of the *New Statesman*, the distinguished Spanish writer in exile, Arturo Barea, and Orwell's fellow-novelist, Joyce Cary, definitely promised to write for us. Arthur Koestler, Stephen Spender and Cyril Connolly told Orwell they might let us have short books. Of the last three, only Spender actually found time to write his book (*Life and the Poet*), but the series was a reality.

So I had my temporary occupation. This time at Scarlett's Farm seems in retrospect a leisurely time although it could not have been that. I have a visual memory of Orwell in a very frayed shirt and ragged trousers sitting patiently in a chair while being painted by Pamela Warburg, with his drawn features for once relaxed. The portrait was a good likeness, although like many of the artist's works, never quite completed.

I have another image of Orwell lying on his back on the grass, the full length of him, and chuckling as he held up my small daughter above his head. He was quite obviously devoted to small children. Pamela Warburg, who had a way of finding out about such things, told me that it was one of his sorrows that he was, or believed himself to be, sterile. True? Perhaps. I never knew.

I can remember listening to lighthearted conversations between Orwell and my wife. I had noted that he was reponsive to goodlooking young women (he had responded at his first meeting to Eileen). I recall listening to him talking to Mary in a half-teasing way about devious ideas for getting into the army past a second medical test. He had been rejected the first time, to his indignation: surely he could do clerical army jobs. He said that the next time he would arrange to come before a tired, overburdened hack of a doctor late in the day and would then fake his way through the test. We thought this was a vain dream: one application of the stethoscope to his chest and he would be out.

I heard him talk with his dry humour about life at The Stores. Mary was interested in his shopkeeping which she thought a quite unsuitable occupation for Eileen and him. He denied this. But had they made a profit, Mary asked. He laughed: at the best of times the profit had been about £1 a week and he added that since they lived on the premises, keeping up the shop meant a seven-day week. When he and Eileen tried to lie in on a Sunday morning there might be a customer banging on the door and what did he want? Most likely a sixpenny mousetrap.

Once Mary thought that Orwell looked more harassed than usual and when she dared to ask why, he answered: 'It's these buff envelopes that keep arriving,' and he pulled one from his pocket, an obvious Income Tax demand, unopened, adding, 'Of course, I never open these things.' When Mary expressed amazement that one could ignore the Inland Revenue, he sadly shook his head. 'What's the good? You can't get blood from a stone.'

I can also remember his talking to Mary about the time he and Eileen spent in Morocco. He said that he found himself increasingly attracted by the young Arab girls and the moment came when he told Eileen that he had to have one of these girls, on just one occasion. Eileen agreed and so he had his Arab girl. True or imagined? It did not matter.

Orwell also brought us his serious news from London at war, where while Eileen worked at the Censorship Department he spent much time in his own one-man social research.

He studied the popular newspapers, now drastically reduced to six pages, observing how much space they devoted to war news and how much to advertisements of patent medicines. He told us that he had long looked on advertising posters carrying insidious slogans for patent medicines as an obscenity and had hoped that with the war they would disappear, but they were still there. Putting himself into the mind of the man below the £5-a-week level, he wondered how much he understood of official war speeches; he thought that Churchill conveyed his

defiant message even to people who did not understand all his
words. He jotted down new words in the language, such as the
German word 'Blitz' for bombing.

As the bombs increasingly fell on London, he observed
Londoners sheltering on Underground platforms. (I think out
of respect for me he did not say that an undue proportion of
these shelterers were Jewish families from the East End.) In
looking at bomb damage he noticed how people displaced stood
about aimlessly, with their personal world shattered, while not
far away life and traffic and shopping proceeded normally.

I thought that he had material here for another report in
Wigan Pier style, but he was against this. In London he had been
seeing a good deal of his friend Cyril Connolly who was
unexpectedly keeping *Horizon* going, and had asked him to
write about the German bombing but he had decided not to do
so. He and Eileen were now definitely living in London. He did
not know whether to close down The Stores at Wallington and
turn the garden into a potato patch; I think he later did so.

As the next best thing to being in the army, he had joined the
Home Guard serving in a unit near Regent's Park, an area
which my wife and I knew well. His good news was that with his
Spanish experience he had immediately been made a sergeant.
His bad news was the lack of rifles for the unit and its small
proportion of working-class members. Considering the middle-
class character of the Regent's Park area, my wife and I thought
this natural, but no, Orwell said, it was important for
working-class men to join the Home Guard so that it could be
the nucleus of a citizens' army, especially as the Communists,
then opposing what they called the imperialist war, were
urging the workers not to join.

Also, my old acquaintance, that amiable ex-Communist
Tom Wintringham, formerly of the International Brigade in
Spain, had opened a training school for guerrillas in South
London. Orwell told me that he and Wintringham had
discussed making use of his notes on the workers' militias in
Catalonia. It was something to do.

Something to do: that was the problem for many people in
England in 1940. In October and November, as the nocturnal
German bombing of London rose to its full climax, Warburg

and I firewatched for two nights a week at his offices near the Temple, a much-bombed area. This was to be my closest exposure to danger during the war. There were some tricky nights when one heard the constant 'tearing-silk' sound of descending bombs and the Temple seemed engulfed in flames. I noticed that Fred Warburg as an old warrior from Passchendaele was imperturbable.

These were also stirring times. With Mussolini's entry, the war had spread to the Middle East and for a short spell I suddenly seemed to be writing everywhere. I wrote features for the *Evening Standard*, I wrote for the *New Statesman*. After an article on Middle East strategy outlining Wingate's blueprint, I was even invited on one occasion to give the BBC's military commentary (which I had the decency to give anonymously).

In November, too, my war aims book, *The Malady and the Vision*, was published, with considerable response. The *Times Literary Supplement*, by now very small, gave me a respectful full-page review; other journals followed suit. Looking back, I see now that through my contact with Orde Wingate I was, in that difficult early phase of the war, a year ahead of most people. At a time when the US was stolidly neutral and the USSR surlily hostile, I took for granted an Anglo-American and Anglo-Soviet alliance; I also took for granted the post-war disbanding of the British Empire. At any rate, this was my own brief flourish as a wartime writer. More important was the fact that – also in November – Orwell brought us his opening book for the Searchlight series which he had written very quickly and called *The Lion and the Unicorn*. Warburg was delighted with it.

I have over the years found it interesting to look at this short book which differs from all Orwell's other writings in its expression of optimism about England's future. But then it was Orwell's way to catch and reflect a moment of history. In *Homage to Catalonia* he had caught a revolutionary socialist moment. In *The Lion and the Unicorn*, in a larger war, he caught a patriotic English socialist moment – a moment in that dramatic year when England gathered herself from what seemed imminent defeat by Hitler.

For a start, as usual, Orwell defined his personal situation: sitting on the grass at Scarlett's Farm with the Battle of Britain in progress above him. 'As I write, highly civilized human beings are flying overhead, trying to kill me.' These enemies had nothing personal against him. They were simply serving their country, impelled by nationalism, the strongest force in the world. The thought brought him to the counter-force of English nationalism and so to an attempted definition of English culture (or British, since he included the Scots, Welsh and Northern Irish).

He wrote that one only had to arrive from the Continent and to mingle with the English crowds 'with their mild, nobbly faces, their bad teeth and gentle manners' in order to realize that a distinct English national character did exist: to define it was not easy but one could venture some observations.

The English were not gifted artistically, he wrote. They lacked the French or German capacity for systematic thought. One might deem them hypocritical in professing democracy at home while maintaining autocratic rule in the Empire. But before discussing this he wanted to single out a marked English trait, namely a love of gardening and flowers. This trait led him to stress another thing, the essential 'privateness' of English life. The English were not only a nation of flower lovers; they were a nation of pigeon fanciers, amateur carpenters, darts players and the like. The best of English life centred on unofficial things – the pub, the back garden, the cup of tea. It was for many people a contented private life.

To be sure, the English common people also had to live to some extent *against* the ruling social system. They were, many of them, heavy drinkers, inveterate gamblers, addicted to bawdiness. But their share in the English trait of gentleness was seen in their anti-militarism. True, there was the far-flung Empire but this had been created by the British navy and a navy, being away at sea, could not impose jingoism on the nation. Again, the English of all classes were essentially law abiding (in 1940 this was still largely true). England was a country where captured burglars admitted a fair cop and Marxist professors protested against 'miscarriages of British justice'.

In short, he wrote, England was like a family with the wrong members, namely the rich and the aristocracy, in control. But of late something had gone badly wrong with these controllers. A dominant aspect of recent English life had been the accelerating decay in ability in the ruling class, shown both at home and in the unending errors in foreign politics, as in the appeasement of Hitler, Mussolini and Franco.

For Orwell the reason was that the position of the English ruling class had ceased to be justifiable. If England was beset by slums and unemployment and large sections of the Empire slept in the Middle Ages, the ruling class knew no answer. Yet their loss of function had not as in other countries led to revolution, Fascism or corruption. Here Orwell, as it were, took a look at the Etonians among whom he had been educated: if he had long shed their class outlook, he could still understand its ethos, as he showed in a much-quoted passage:

'The British ruling class obviously could not admit to themselves that their usefulness was at an end. Had they done that they would have had to abdicate.

For it was not possible for them to turn themselves into mere bandits, like the American millionaires, consciously clinging to unjust privileges and beating down opposition by bribery and tear-gas bombs. After all, they belonged to a class with a certain tradition, they had been to public schools where the duty of dying for your country, if necessary, is laid down as the first and greatest of the Commandments. They had to feel themselves true patriots, even while they plundered their countrymen. Clearly, there was only one escape for them – into stupidity. They could keep society in its existing shape only by being *unable* to grasp that any improvement was possible. Difficult though this was, they achieved it.'[2]

Orwell saw this flight into stupidity as setting off the chain of events which had led England to the brink of disaster in war with Nazi Germany. But the war could also become a great awakening in which he believed England must change while remaining true to her gentle self. The intellectuals who hoped to see England Russianized or Germanized would be disappointed. In a later chapter where he urged the British Labour movement to transcend its insularity, he put forward a

six-point programme for a wartime approach towards socialism:

'I.   Nationalization of land, mines, railways, banks and
major industries.
II.   Limitation of incomes, on such a scale that the highest
tax-free income in Britain does not exceed the lowest by more
than ten to one.
III.   Reform of the educational system along democratic
lines.
IV.   Immediate Dominion status for India, with power to
secede when the war is over.
V.   Formation of an Imperial General Council on which the
coloured peoples are to be represented.
VI.   Declaration of formal alliance with China, Abyssinia
and other victims of the Fascist powers.'[3]

Of Orwell's last three points, land reform for the subject
peoples of the Empire had been sketchily discussed among us;
the idea of a British alliance with China and Ethiopia came
from Orde Wingate via myself; Indian independence had long
been Orwell's own demand. His idea for ending private
education in England by flooding the public schools with
state-aided pupils – that he was not to see. But concerning his
first two major points, namely large-scale nationalization and a
certain equalization of incomes through high taxation – these
were measures which before his death he saw carried out to
some extent by Attlee's post-war Labour Government. By that
time he was not against these measures – he remained to the
end a democratic socialist – only he had become profoundly
suspicious of any extension of state power. But at this earlier
date, in 1940, he momentarily put aside his fears of such
extension of power. He had his vision of a socialist England and
he ended *The Lion and the Unicorn* by saying that he believed in
England 'and I believe that we shall go forward'.

A very different ending from, say, that of *Nineteen Eighty-Four*.

I like looking at *The Lion and the Unicorn* not only because it
brings back memories of the eventful time of the Battle of
Britain and the German bombing of London: it shows Orwell
too in the spirit of that time letting himself be the patriotic

Englishman he always was in part of his make-up, seeing an optimistic vision of an England which was partly the nostalgic image of the England of his boyhood carried on into the future.

To be sure the euphoria could not last. Still, Orwell's definition of both the variety and the essence of English culture was written with such a moving turn of phrase that it has found its way forty years on into school curricula. Fred Warburg has said somewhere that Orwell's exposition of an English social-ism free of jargon made many recruits for the Labour Party's electoral victory of 1945. Well, perhaps it made some. Louis Heren, who was to become deputy editor of *The Times*, told me that the book so impressed him when he first read it as a young soldier in Italy that he kept a battered copy which he used as a basis for a journey through England in 1980 about which he wrote his own book, *Alas, Alas for England* (published by Hamish Hamilton in 1981).

The Lion and the Unicorn was published in February 1941 at the height of the German bombing of London and the first two editions rapidly sold out. The other Searchlight books followed quickly. In *Offensive Against Germany*, Sebastian Haffner drew his distinctions between Germany and Nazism. In *The English At War*, William Connor spoke out in the most ringing of journalistic phrases for the common man. In *The End of the Old School Tie*, T.C. Worsley looked to a British state education system incorporating the public schools. In *The Lesson of London*, Ritchie Calder wrote of the comradeship among ordinary Londoners under German bombing. Arturo Barea in *Struggle for the Spanish Soul* looked towards the deliverance of Spain from the yoke of Franco, while in *The Case for African Freedom* which he had discussed at length with Orwell, Joyce Cary wrote with insight about the vast problems lying in wait for self-governing African states. Orwell had conscientiously done his work in talking to the various authors, but I had seen that he did so with reluctance. His heart was not really in being concerned with the work of others. He had to go his own way.

For a moment in the increasingly harsh course of the war, the Searchlight books were much discussed and Warburg could regard them as a success. However, they were mostly published in the earlier part of 1941 and by the end of that same year of

1941, the optimistic era of the Searchlight books was in a sense already over. Our little group had broken up, we had all left Scarlett's Farm and Orwell wrote sadly in his war diary: 'Now I am definitely in the employment of the BBC.' That is, he had, like myself, become a professional wartime propagandist, something which even at the outbreak of war he had been determined to avoid.

ELEVEN

Anticlimax

THE REASON WHY our little group broke up was not
that Warburg's London office suffered bomb
damage and, at his printer's, stocks of the Searchlight
books (and *The Malady and the Vision*) were largely destroyed by
enemy action, though this played its part. The reason was
simply that we adjusted ourselves to the reality of a long-
drawn-out war.

In May 1941 the German bombing of London ceased, and
between the first day of 1941 and the last day of that year the
war was quite transformed. In one of his letters to *Partisan
Review*, Orwell wrote that at the outbreak of the Second World
War, some English intellectuals imagined that it would be like
an enlarged version of the Spanish civil war in which intellectuals could freely voice their views, but it was not at all like that:
the war was being fought by technical experts and conducted
by people who were patriotic while reactionary in outlook. In
June 1941 Hitler attacked Soviet Russia. Welcomed by Churchill as allies, the Russians piled in, as Wingate had predicted.
In December 1941 the Japanese attacked Pearl Harbor and
the Americans piled in. By the beginning of 1942, it had become
fairly clear that Hitler and his Italian and Japanese allies would
in the end be defeated, although not by the power of ideas but
by the superior manpower and material of the new West-East
alliance. Under Churchill, Roosevelt and Stalin, the politi-
cians, the military and the bureaucrats were running the war,
including its official ideas. The intellectuals had little role
except as subordinate technicians, or so it seemed at the start of
1942.

Everything told us that the Searchlight books phase had
made its point, but it was over. In London after the German
bombing stopped, the worst damage was being boarded up;

people settled down rather wearily to the road ahead, of war and blackout, call-up and uniforms, of fairly stringent rationing and news of military setbacks. Fred Warburg, facing severe paper rationing, returned to London to busy himself with survival as a publisher. Orwell, who could not be called up on medical grounds, began again to feel unemployed. In *The Lion and the Unicorn* he had had his say. Now he looked for a wartime occupation.

I recall that late in 1941 I met Orwell and Eileen a few times in pubs in Fitzroy Square. He had acquired some minor literary hangers-on with whom I thought him too patient. Eileen generally accompanied him. I was glad to see her recovered from the blow of her brother's death, outwardly anyway. I had a strong feeling, however, that she did not really like pubs but she loyally sat alongside Orwell, sipping her beer. I thought him lucky to have a wife who looked after him so well.

He had done much reconnoitring of bombed areas, but when I asked whether he planned to write about this he repeated that he would not. He only made notes. He and Eileen had themselves been stoical under the bombing.

An incident. In July 1941, three weeks or so after Hitler invaded the Soviet Union, Stalin made what I thought from his viewpoint an admirably emotional rallying speech to all Soviet citizens. One could hope that aided by the Russian winter, the Soviet armies would in the end stop the Nazis. I remember how to my surprise I found Orwell sharing this positive view of Stalin. He always liked to say that he had known about the beastly nature of the Bolshevik régime from the very start, but now Stalin, the chief murderer, had called for resistance to the Nazis in a tremendous fighting speech which to Orwell sounded quite right for the occasion. But he also saw it as a sign of the current moral deterioration that Stalin was now a canonized friend on our side, hailed as such even by British Conservatives.

Towards the end of 1941 Orwell joined the BBC as a talks producer in its Indian and Burmese service, with offices at Oxford Circus. I understood that the job meant projecting British democratic values, for what that was worth, at Indian listeners. I myself had moved my family to Buckinghamshire,

taken a room in London and joined the Political Intelligence
Department of the Foreign Office, which was to furnish
personnel for the British section of the Anglo-American
Psychological Warfare Branch. My chief – a very brilliant
propagandist, I thought – was Richard Crossman (later to
become a prominent Minister in Harold Wilson's Labour
Government). Each day I assiduously read the intelligence
reports on Nazi Germany. I soon felt that I knew it better than I
knew Britain. Yet having nothing to do but read, I walked two
floors down from our office in Bush House to join in the work of
the BBC's broadcasts to Nazi Germany, directed by Hugh
Greene (later to become Director-General of the BBC). My
closest co-worker there, arranging broadcasts to German
workers, was Patrick Gordon-Walker (later also to become a
Labour Government Minister). From the first day in the job
until the end of the war, my work was determined: with my eyes
fixed on Nazi Germany, I lived for psychological warfare.

Only on a single occasion was I drawn again into public
affairs, and then briefly. There had been a flurry of enthusiastic
publicity about Orde Wingate as he rode into Addis Ababa at
the head of his victorious Ethiopian guerrilla forces, having
taken large numbers of Italian prisoners. Some weeks later for
reasons not relevant here he tried unsuccessfully to commit
suicide in Cairo. He was shipped home by slow convoy; the
many enemies he had made thought they had him in their
power. But back in England, Wingate, fit again, launched a
counter-offensive to demand that he be given an appropriate
new command. As always when I was in touch with Wingate,
my own life seemed momentarily transformed. No possibility of
advocacy for him was left untouched. Among many others I,
too, was enrolled in his campaign and through my colleague
Patrick Gordon-Walker I got a message on Wingate's behalf
through to the Labour Deputy-Premier, Clement Attlee, who
replied testily to Patrick that Harold Laski had already told
him all about Wingate's ideas. Wingate himself was fully back
in his role as a prophet of the course of the war. In my mind's
eye I can see him now as, smartly uniformed, with his piercing
blue eyes, he stood before a large globe. This was some three
weeks or so after the Japanese had struck in South East Asia.

They had sunk two British battleships and were advancing through Malaya.

'Do you see the Malayan peninsula? It's a long sack. And do you see Singapore at the bottom? That's the tip of the sack, where the Japanese will pick up General Percival and his entire army.'

I was appalled. 'But what would you do, Orde?'

'Evacuate at once! Ship every possible man and gun by sea to Burma, which can be defended!'

Would Wingate's plans have been possible? I was in no position to know. After he left, my life resumed its humdrum course. Only later did I learn that he had been rehabilitated and flown out to India to prepare for his Chindit campaign behind the Japanese lines. I could only follow events in the press and they went as Wingate had predicted. In February 1942 the Japanese did take General Percival and his entire army prisoner in Singapore at the bottom of the sack. Burma was also lost. When I told Orwell about this, I remember his saying gloomily that from his recollection of Burma there was a lot of pent-up nationalist feeling there against the British rulers, to be tapped by the Japanese if they wanted to. They could even exploit the prevailing anti-British feelings in India if they were clever. Fortunately they seemed simply crude imperialists and politically not clever at all, but this Japanese defect was all the more reason for Britain to announce a sensible policy on India.

My work had brought me into occasional contact with David Astor who was taking over the direction of the *Observer* to turn it into an exemplary liberal Sunday newspaper. He had brought in a few Continental refugees, since they were available. They included our Searchlight author, Sebastian Haffner, Fritz Schumacher (of *Small is Beautiful* fame) and Isaac Deutscher (to become Trotsky's biographer). I remember introducing Jon Kimche as a military expert. Then Arthur Koestler introduced Orwell to David Astor who from then on became his good friend and most loyal supporter. Orwell began to write book reviews for the *Observer*. If he was never at his untrammelled best in the polite columns of the *Observer*, I was glad for his sake of this new opening for him. Although he would have disliked the idea profoundly, like many others he was benefiting from

the war; his and Eileen's income had gone up a good deal; he
was becoming an established writer and journalist.

In the war year of 1942 I saw less of Orwell than I could have
done (or looking back, would like to have done). Our viewpoints, mine trained on Nazi Germany, his on India, were
separate. In wartime life, the two-mile bus ride between my
office and his at Oxford Circus could seem a dividing distance.
We ate in different canteens, we went to different pubs with
working colleagues. By this third year of the war, the ideas
which had inspired us at the time of *The Lion and the Unicorn* were
in abeyance. I spent my moments of free time in the country
with my family; Orwell devoted much of his to his Home Guard
unit at Regent's Park. About this activity I had ironical reports
from Warburg, who had become a corporal in the unit to
Orwell's sergeant. As the young Englishmen in the unit were
being called up, Warburg told me that their places were being
taken by Jewish refugees and exiled Poles and Czechs. He
thought that this process rather puzzled Orwell. . . . Orwell and
Eileen lived in reasonable discomfort in a small flat near Maida
Vale. I learned that Eileen now worked in the Ministry of Food,
which I thought interesting in view of their own deliberately
spartan way of life.

Looking back now, I feel that during 1942, as he worked in
the BBC, Orwell as a writer was marking time. As his hopes of
1940 in a socialist breakthrough were fading, he must have
returned to the very different mood which was to produce
Animal Farm and *Nineteen Eighty-Four*. He has told how the basic
idea for *Animal Farm* came to him years earlier when he saw a
small boy lead a huge cart-horse along a narrow country lane
and wondered what would happen if the beast were to rebel.
The main pieces he wrote during this time which seemed to
develop his thinking significantly were in Cyril Connolly's
Horizon.

In 'Wells, Hitler and the World State', he took Wells severely
to task for his optimistic belief in the beneficence of science.
Earlier, during the Searchlight days, Warburg, Orwell and I
had called on Wells in search of guidance but found only a
querulous old man who was ailing. Orwell and I both felt the
loss of a boyhood hero. Orwell continued his contact with

Wells, but the acquaintance remained uneasy. While he still would not write about the bombing of working-class London, in 'The Art of Donald McGill', an essay on the comic postcards sold in small stationers, he returned to one of his favourite subjects, an analysis of what he saw as English working-class mythology.

I had thought that in the Indian service of the BBC Orwell initially quite liked his talks producer's job of projecting English democratic and literary values, and only gradually became disillusioned, but evidently this was not so. He must have felt uneasy in the job from the start. David Astor has told me that in his redesign of the *Observer*, he introduced an unsigned editorial column on international affairs called 'Forum' and that Orwell wrote several of these. As early as February 1942 after the Japanese capture of Singapore, when he was still relatively new in the BBC, Orwell wrote in one of the first of these 'Forums' that Britain must at once use the opportunity of disaster to announce that Indian independence was possible if Britain won the war and impossible if Japan won:

> 'First, let India be given immediate Dominion status, with the right to secede after the war, if she so desires. Secondly, let the leaders of the principal political parties be invited at once to form a National Government. . . . Thirdly, let India enter into formal military alliance with Britain and the countries allied to Britain. Fourthly, let a trade agreement be drawn up.'[1]

These views were hardly those of the BBC Indian service.

I remember a meeting with Orwell some time later – it must have been in the early days of 1943 – when we talked about our respective propaganda jobs. I can distinctly recall Orwell remarking: 'When I listen to the high-pitched Indian voices in the office, as I look out of the window I am surprised not to see palm trees waving.'

I told Orwell how a few days before I had sat in a room at Bush House listening to one of Hitler's ranting speeches laced with hysterical threats against world Jewry, Churchill, the Bolsheviks and his other enemies. I sat listening together with such eminent propagandists as Richard Crossman, Hugh Greene, Patrick Gordon-Walker and others, plus our young Hungarian producer, Martin Esslin (after the war to become a leading authority on modern drama). We listened calmly to Hitler's hypnotic voice in order to pick out his most vulnerable threats and to record them (still done on disc at the time, not tape) in order to play them ironically back at German listeners, say after a large-scale Allied bombing raid. I told Orwell that I found myself looking round the room and thinking how with our different backgrounds, we had all become dedicated propagandists in the same mould.

Orwell was not impressed by this picture of our professional uniformity. He was never much interested in Hitler, and *he* did not like *his* job as a propagandist BBC broadcaster to India at all. He said gloomily that it was fortunate they had so few listeners.

I said, probably rather cheerfully, that this seemed to me exaggerated and that his job did not appear to be so bad. He worked with interesting people, he had that famous critic and wit, William Empson, as his neighbour in the next cubicle. He had had the chance to bring such literary figures as T.S. Eliot and E.M. Forster to the microphone and had written some good talks himself. Relatively it appeared to me an agreeable war job.

It was quite the wrong thing to say – an agreeable job in which to endure the war was the last thing Orwell had in mind. He said that even when the BBC talks were purely cultural, in the context they were propaganda; somehow any idea that was politically unsuitable, however good it was, managed to be eliminated.

I said that I had read two of his own talks in *The Listener* on totalitarian issues in Europe and thought them excellent expositions of the Western democratic viewpoint. Evidently this was again the wrong thing to say. Orwell replied that given what reputation he had in India as an anti-imperialist writer, he was unhappy about lending his name to BBC broadcasts; to put out talks on British literary values was irrelevant at a time when Nehru and other Indian Congress leaders were being held in prison by the British Government and were in consequence refusing all cooperation against the Japanese. All he thought needed to be broadcast by the BBC was straight news and a British declaration that after the defeat of Japan, India could have immediate self-government.

Oh, I agreed, I said, but Churchill and the Government did not and broadcasters could not make policy. I mentioned how our broadcasts to Germany had also been severely handicapped by the Churchill-Roosevelt declaration demanding unconditional German surrender, but one just had to work within such limitations. But Orwell remained quite unconvinced about this. He stuck to his view that a promise of Indian independence was the only statement worth putting out. I think he also said in a throw-away remark that he would like to leave the BBC and propaganda if some alternative wartime work would offer itself.

I can remember reflecting on our conversation. In the course of two years of world war, I too had travelled a long way from the heady ideas about a better post-war world which had so filled my mind during the Searchlight Books days of 1940. I had become content to be a cog in the powerful machine of psychological warfare against Nazi Germany, and so had the people in whose company I had listened to Hitler's latest tirade. But I could see that Orwell was different. He could not adapt himself to the mere psychological warfare needs of the war machine. His view on the need for Indian independence was what he saw as the truth: he could not change from it. He could not become a spokesman for a merely cultural British viewpoint, however polite and liberal. This was so especially as he always had in mind that in fighting against Hitler and the Japanese, Britain had allied herself with the tyranny of Stalin's Soviet Union. War or no war, he was concerned with the truth as he saw it. He could not be happy in the wartime BBC.

Some time after our conversation, in the early spring of 1943 (after the battles of Stalingrad and Alamein and the Allied invasion of French North Africa), Orwell and I dropped in on Jon Kimche who was now deputy editor of the socialist weekly, *Tribune*, under the editorship of Aneurin Bevan. Orwell had begun to contribute short pieces to *Tribune*. So had I, under a pseudonym.

The attacking, independent wartime *Tribune* – it must be said that it had little connection with the tied, factional Left-wing *Tribune* of today – was a fluke that had come off. It had been started as a socialist weekly, which was to be without both the pro-Communist leanings and Mandarin high culture of the *New Statesman*, by two leading MPS, George Strauss and Aneurin Bevan. Largely financed by Strauss, it had by 1942 become an excellent platform for Bevan, that fiery offspring and representative of the Welsh miners and eloquent parliamentary orator well to the Left in the Labour Party, who had rejected any part in the Churchill administration to remain its socialist critic.

I met Bevan a few times in 1942–3 and again after 1945, although I gained most of my knowledge of him through reading his speeches; yet I always felt distinctly that he was *just* short of being a great man.

I remember his once telling me how he would take action against the men who had degraded his Welsh people – the coal owners, the jerry builders, the promoters of patent medicines. Already in 1942–3 he was intimately involved in Labour's post-war programme for the nationalization of the mines, steel and railways, for the drastic expansion of public housing and for a national health service.

With hindsight, I think where Bevan later fell short was in his failure to imbue his steelworkers and coalminers with the notion that the nationalized undertakings they worked for were their own. He also did not inspire the tenants of the new council estates with any thought that these estates were their own collective dwelling place to be treasured. With hindsight again, it was through Bevan's inability to inspire his followers with a *positive* socialist outlook, that I think he lost out in 1949 to Hugh Gaitskell in the Labour Party leadership race.

But all this is speculation, and came much later. In 1942–3, Bevan was still being swept forward by the full rhetoric of his plans for a post-war socialist Britain.

However, because his part-time editing of *Tribune* through a committee did not work, Jon Kimche was brought in as deputy editor. Under his guidance, all kinds of leading Fleet Street journalists contributed pseudonymous criticisms of Britain's war policies to *Tribune*. There seemed room for Orwell, too. Jon

Kimche remembers clearly – though I have only a vague memory of this – that on hearing that his literary editor was leaving, I urged strongly that his old bookshop colleague, Orwell, should be invited to take over.

I imagine that Orwell might well have left the BBC for *Tribune* in any case, but if I did accelerate this step, I did him a good turn. In his warm, outgoing editor Aneurin Bevan, he had the chance of working alongside one of the few Labour leaders whose imagination he could respect. (He decidedly did not respect Clement Attlee.) More than that, since Bevan and Kimche gave him full journalistic freedom, he could in his well-known 'As I Please' column give direct expression to that 'inner voice' of his in which he had since preparatory school days documented his daily outlook on life. He could hold forth in this personal voice on topics ranging from politics to the pleasures of country life, from the baseness of book reviewing to seeing a kestrel in London. He could in fact adapt his inner voice to the requirements of ephemeral weekly journalism and in the process produce short pieces of enduring literary value, something pretty rare in modern journalism.

By the time he joined *Tribune*, however, I was far from the scene. A week or so after I had talked to Jon Kimche about him, I flew out to Algiers to become a member of Richard Crossman's Anglo-American psychological warfare unit in North Africa, not to return until the end of the war.

The author as
psychological
warfare officer in
Italy, 1943

Mary Fyvel, 1945

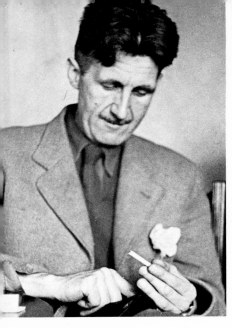

Orwell in thoughtful mood, 1945

Eileen Blair, *circa* 1941

Orwell at work in Canonbury Square, winter 1945

Orwell with a Burmese sword, souvenir of his days with the Imperial Indian Police

Taking a break from writing, winter 1945

Orwell in Canonbury Square, winter 1945

Cyril Connolly, Orwell's friend at prep school and Eton, later his editor on *Horizon*

Richard Rees, who first published Orwell in the *Adelphi*

Julian Symons, a younger writer and Fleet Street lunch companion

Malcolm
Muggeridge,
another intimate
lunchtime
companion and
appreciative critic

Arthur Koestler,
Orwell's friend
and admirer
during the war
and post-war years

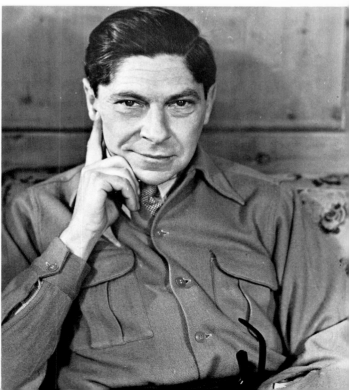

David Astor, editor of the *Observer* for which Orwell wrote, and his firm friend and supporter

Pamela de Bayou (Pamela Warburg), who painted the only portrait of Orwell in summer 1940

Fredric Warburg, Orwell's publisher, friend, adviser, sponsor and ally

John Beavan (Lord Ardwick) of the
Observer and *Manchester Guardian*, who
helped arrange Orwell's column for the
Manchester Evening News

Aneurin Bevan was in charge of *Tribune*
when Orwell was literary editor

Jon Kimche, who worked with Orwell
in the Hampstead bookshop and on
Tribune

Susan Watson, who kept house for Orwell and Richard in 1945–6

Sonia Orwell (*foreground*) in the *Horizon* office and just married, October 1949

Orwell with Richard, 1946

TWELVE

On to Animal Farm

I HAD THOUGHT I should be in Algiers for six weeks or so to set up broadcasts to the German forces from there, but instead I returned to England twenty-six months later, pretty punch-drunk, from the north of Italy. Richard Crossman, my chief, was soon invalided home. I later learned that he had asked that I should join his psychological warfare unit for the invasion of France, but I discovered that once a military command possessed one's body, it did not easily let go. I remained in Italy to the end.

I interrogated German prisoners, I arranged for leaflets to be dropped over the German lines and for frontline broadcasts. Trained in Hugh Greene's BBC German Service, I imposed its essentially factual line on our output. As I became absorbed by the military life around me, memories of London faded. After a few letters to friends, including one or two to Orwell, I stopped writing except to my family.

I suppose that in my Anglo-American psychological warfare unit I had a good war. In Italy I enjoyed the landscape and art treasures. In my unit I worked closely with an excellent Scottish poet, Norman Cameron, and a future director of Ealing film comedies, Alexander McKendrick. When I served with the US Fifth Army, a sergeant with me was Klaus Mann, the great novelist's highly gifted and unhappy son.

Yet all the time I felt under increasing pressure in my wartime role. On the seafront in Naples in 1944 I heard of the death of Orde Wingate in an air crash in Burma just when as a major-general he had been given his great chance by Churchill. I can still remember, as I heard the news, staring across the masts and funnels of the Allied invasion fleet assembled in Naples harbour. Something went out of my life. Slowly, my function of fighting the Germans with my typewriter, while ahead of me members of the poor bloody infantry were dying, became oppressive. Things I did, such as having plaintive German letters from home dropped as leaflets over German troops, I liked less and less. Nor did I like the alleged fraternization of the Anglo-American top military with formerly pro-Fascist Italian high society.

Finally in late 1944, Jewish friends from Palestine, passing through, briefed me on the full scale of the Jewish catastrophe in Nazi Europe. I heard the dreaded word 'Auschwitz'. I heard how the British navy in the Mediterranean prevented Jewish refugees from fleeing to Palestine. In my book on the Palestine conflict I had criticized Zionist policies but from now on, until the State of Israel had settled down, I became obsessive about the need for Jewish survivors to leave Europe for Palestine – by any road.

When I returned home I remember how, compared to the eventful military scene I had left, London looked to me at first like a curiously static place, crowded with tired people to whom, apart from the flying bombs, little had recently happened. The newspapers appeared parochial. Meeting Orwell again I could see at once that he had grown into a much more practised journalist. He appeared steadier, a touch more worldly. But as for his physical appearance – here I was taken aback. He looked to me gaunt, and not two but ten years older; all the lines etched on his face had deepened. He told me that as war correspondent for the *Observer*, he had gone into defeated Germany and in Cologne had fallen very ill; his wretched chest troubles again. 'I thought at one time it was all up with me,' he said.

He was so reserved – or it was so painful for him to speak of it? – that I only learned a few days later from Fred Warburg that Eileen was dead. When? 'A few weeks ago, while Orwell was in Germany.' She had died under an anaesthetic during an operation. Where? I asked. Apparently in Newcastle, staying with her sister-in-law. What sort of operation was it? Warburg did not really know. And why had Orwell not been with her? Some time later, David Astor told me that Orwell had wanted at all costs to go to Germany for the *Observer* as soon as possible after the surrender, to see a totalitarian state before it disappeared, only to find that the Nazi structure of Germany had dissolved overnight as though it had never been.

From my Italian experience I could have told Orwell that, I thought. And then, in an occupied Germany that no longer knew Nazism, he had fallen gravely ill. I also learned that a year earlier, Eileen and he had adopted a baby boy, Richard. So he was now a widower, responsible for the adopted infant. Did he feel guilt at not having been at Eileen's side for her operation? I imagined so, but when on the next occasion I tried haltingly to express my sympathy over his loss, he muttered brief thanks and then changed the subject. But I had an idea that he felt desolate without Eileen and grieved deeply.

Yet he kept his discipline. I discovered what a leading essayist and journalist he had become. In addition to his regular work for *Tribune*, he had been writing for the *Observer*, for *Horizon* and for a new quarterly, *Polemic*, brought out hopefully by his ex-Communist friend, Humphrey Slater. In 1944, John Beavan, who was now London editor of the *Manchester Guardian*, told me that after adopting the baby Richard, Orwell had told him that he wanted a further regular income and Beavan had arranged for him to write a weekly main book review for the *Manchester Evening News*, the *Guardian*'s popular companion paper. Beavan said that Orwell had immediately grasped the need for the simple journalistic style required by a popular newspaper. Whatever the state of his health, his copy arrived in time, impeccably typed and written to size. When I told Orwell that John Beavan had praised his typing, he looked melancholy. He said that in earlier days he had written out his pieces by hand up to five times but now he did many of them straight on to the typewriter: this was a deterioration. I took this merely as one of his habitual self-deprecatory remarks.

The other major news about Orwell concerned the impending publication of *Animal Farm*, about which I heard as soon as I arrived back in London. Calling on Fred Warburg, I found him in his office looking typically pleased with himself as he sat at his desk with the typescript of a short book – Orwell's latest, he said, which was at the printer's for quick publication. Warburg said that it had been turned down by Gollancz and others and that Victor Gollancz was now going round London saying that the work should not be published for fear that it would endanger Anglo-Soviet relations.

I thought this last remark somewhat far-fetched. I said : 'It's just a fable, isn't it?'

Yes, said Warburg, but it was a satire about a revolution of farm beasts, based on the Bolshevik revolution and its end in Stalinism, in which the Communists were depicted as pigs. He, Warburg, had faced all kinds of pressures against its publication, even from people in his own office and especially from his own very outspoken wife Pamela who evidently felt passionately that this was no time for ingratitude towards Stalin and the heroic Red Army who had played the main part in defeating Hitler.

I thereupon sat down in Warburg's office and read the typescript right through – with rising admiration.

This satirical, but more than that, this sad and haunting tale of how the domestic animals stage a successful revolution against Farmer Jones, only to fall under the much worse tyranny of the Communist pigs – this seemed to me a beautifully written allegory, with not a word too many or too few: at last Orwell had risen to his true stature as a writer.

I marvelled with what ease he seemed to have brought together the threads of his political thinking and of his literary imagination and in doing so had created a fable of such beautiful, inescapable simplicity. He had constructed his allegory in the manner of Swift. Employing the age-old folklore of talking animals, he had used his farming knowledge to create a whole world of recognizable animal characters. And withal, he had written a little fairy story in which children could weep over the end of the poor cart-horse Boxer, sent by the pigs to the knackers.

At the same time he had succeeded in ingeniously tracing the fate of the Bolshevik revolution. The pigs walking upright and the tyrannical boar Napoleon were the ruling Communists and Stalin. The expulsion of the pig Snowball, too clever by half, was that of Trotsky. The pains of Boxer in building the twice destroyed windmill were those of the Russian people under the Five Year Plans. The ending where the animals look from men to pigs and cannot tell one from the other referred to the wartime Teheran Conference of 1943, where Churchill, Roosevelt and Stalin had toasted each other as allies. The whole scene was lit up by phrases of genius such as the often-quoted 'All animals are equal but some are more equal than others', which precisely reflected the new class system in the Soviet Utopia.

Now, I don't know how far I saw all this at the first reading. As I realize now, I probably did not, but I certainly got the gist of Orwell's success. I felt that the special magic of *Animal Farm* lay in Orwell's loving and accurate description of the landscape and routine of work on the farm.

Returning to Fred Warburg, I recall that I made a pompous little speech. What was the matter with Victor Gollancz and other people who had sat out the war in London? I asked. Did they really think that Stalin, after victory in the bloodiest of all wars and already taking up a hostile stance against his wartime allies in a new global conflict, would let his policies towards Britain be affected by a little fable? I told Warburg how the Allied soldiers moving up from Italy had advanced eagerly to meet their Soviet comrades-in-arms only to be faced with extended bayonets. Warburg was indeed cynically amused by the whole row and had not the slightest intention of letting himself be deterred from publication in August.

I learned of the roundabout way the book had come to him. Orwell had written it in the winter of 1943–4. Gollancz, who had first claim, had of course turned it down flat. Orwell had had a fixed and false idea that Secker & Warburg had no paper ration to spare and so sent the manuscript to T.S. Eliot at Faber & Faber. Just as years ago Eliot had rejected *Down and Out in Paris and London*, so now he managed to turn down Orwell's work again, this time for the strange reason that *Animal Farm* was, as he thought, Trotskyist. Jonathan Cape, offered the book next, liked it himself but was unwise enough to show it for approval to a Foreign Office friend who was horrified at this slur upon our gallant Soviet allies and advised rejection. Depressed and thrown off his stride by these refusals, Orwell had wasted much time on notions of publishing the book himself as a pamphlet, before he turned up one day at

Warburg's office, looking particularly dishevelled as Warburg remembered, and had abruptly handed in the typescript and disappeared again. Warburg had accepted it on the spot (what a wise move for his firm this turned out to be!) and thought that it would do quite well, although one could never tell with so short a book. . . .

After a brief spell in the country with my family, I was back in London in July. Much had happened. Attlee's Labour Party had won the General Election; Churchill was out; Orwell's fellow-journalist Aneurin Bevan would now be able to realize his plans for public health and housing, and state ownership of the mines. As for Orwell, I thought that he might now see some of the democratic socialism enacted for which he had asked in *The Lion and the Unicorn.* Yet after the six long years of war which had seen so many setbacks, it had become harder to summon up political enthusiasm. Still, like most people around him, Orwell looked pleased at the Labour victory. But three weeks before *Animal Farm* was due out, the Americans dropped their atom bombs upon Japan. Like everyone else, Orwell was profoundly affected by this awesome, disastrous start to the nuclear age. Most people, like myself, managed to put it out of their minds, but one can see from his letters and writing that the thought of the nuclear devastation which he always saw ahead filled him with dark forebodings which never left him.

In view of the opposition *Animal Farm* had already aroused, I found him for the first time a little tense about publication. By now Stalin's Soviet armies stood in the very centre of Europe, with régimes based on secret police and censorship springing up behind them. Orwell knew that for all its fairy-tale guise, in *Animal Farm* he had put his views on the dark side of Communism squarely on the line at a time when most English people were still full of warm praise for the victories of the Red Army over those of Hitler.

He need not have worried. To be sure, the reception of *Animal Farm* was mixed, as one could have expected. A few Communists and sympathizers among critics (there were by now less of them) condemned it and even among friendly reviewers there were a few misgivings. For instance, in *Horizon*, Orwell's friend Cyril Connolly criticized the implication that like the boar

Napoleon on the farm, Stalin had basically ruled the Soviet Union by terror. Saying that every revolution was betrayed by the violence inherent in it, Connolly went on:

> 'The Soviet Union . . . is an immensely powerful managerial despotism where on the whole despite a police system which we should find intolerable, the masses are happy and where great strides in material progress have been made (i.e. the independence of women, equality of the sexes, autonomy of racial and cultural minorities, utilization of science to improve the standard of living, religious toleration, etc.). If Stalin and his régime were not loved as well as feared, the Animal Farm which comprises the greatest land-mass in the world would not have united to roll back the most efficient invading army the world has ever known – and if in truth Stalin is loved, then he and his régime cannot be quite what they appear to Mr Orwell (indeed Napoleon's final brutality to Boxer – if Boxer symbolizes the proletariat – is not paralleled by any incident in Stalin's career, unless the Scorched Earth policy is indicated).'[1]

One rubs one's eyes today: how had Connolly managed the disappearance of the millions of Russian peasants who starved during the collectivization exercise and the further millions of Soviet citizens sent at Stalin's orders to perish in the *Gulags*? In fact, in the heady days after Hitler's defeat, this rosy view of Stalin's realm was the one which prevailed among most non-political people in England.[2] However, as against such doubts, Orwell also had his full share of praise. *Animal Farm* received a perceptive appreciation from Graham Greene. It received unexpected praise in the *New Statesman* from its editor, Kingsley Martin. In a sense, the mixed reception by critics did not matter. From the day of publication, *Animal Farm* took off to become a steady international bestseller. There comes a moment in a writer's career when he finds himself treated suddenly with respect all round; and so it was with Orwell. There had been his journalism, his essays, and his earlier books. Now, with *Animal Farm*, he was suddenly established in the public eye as a major English writer.

I remember telling him so: he reacted to the comment

without any enthusiastic show of pleasure. By this time I had taken over from him as literary editor of *Tribune*, about which more in the next chapter, and we were talking over a drink in his first-floor flat in Canonbury Square in North London where he was then living alone. He told me that his adopted toddler Richard, staying with friends, would come to him when his new housekeeper arrived. He also said – it seemed to me rather sadly – that he had not yet been able to bring himself to dispose of Eileen's effects. I found myself almost looking round for Eileen – her bright presence seemed to brood over the dark, bare and uncomfortable-looking rooms.

On leaving I thought about Eileen and I have often thought about her over the years. I knew Orwell's second wife Sonia closely, but through the way the fortunes and separations of wartime went, I did not get to know Eileen nearly as well as I would have wished. And yet I have two basic thoughts about her. The first is that she had a very positive influence on Orwell's writings, especially on *Animal Farm*. The second is that Eileen's death was a blow to him from which in his personal life he never fully recovered.

These assertions, I know, are hard to substantiate. Indeed I find it difficult to get Eileen O'Shaughnessy who in 1936 became Eileen Blair into focus. In the recollections of her wartime colleague Lettice Cooper, and of her longstanding friend Lydia Jackson ('Elizaveta Fen'), who have written about her, her personality appears curiously elusive. Memories do of course become generalized. Stafford Cottman, Orwell's eighteen-year-old companion during his last days in Barcelona, told me that he remembered Eileen there quite clearly. She seemed to him a remarkably even-tempered young Englishwoman, 'like a pleasant young schoolmistress', as she efficiently handled the affairs and finances of half a dozen members of the ILP contingent. Michael Meyer, who as a young man saw a good deal of the Orwells at Canonbury Square during the latter part of the war, told me that he had a memory of her as an excellent cook, a bright, cheerful hostess, sitting quietly while Orwell talked ... in other words playing the suitable background role of a great writer's wife.

To go back to the beginning. When Eileen left her warm middle-class family background behind to marry Orwell and to cope with his principles about living in a spartan working-class manner in the isolation of Wallington, with his obsession (as it must sometimes have seemed to her) about writing something every single day, plus his many undoctored illnesses, did it always seem worth while to her? The evidence suggests that with the inevitable ups and downs she loyally supported her husband and his writings and received his reticent love in return; she identified herself with his views and causes; she followed him to the war in Spain. Even so, from all accounts the guiding force in her life was her love for her elder brother Lawrence. In her article 'George Orwell's First Wife' in the *Twentieth Century* magazine, her friend Lydia Jackson recollects Eileen as saying that her brother was the only person she could always count on. 'If we were at opposite ends of the world and I sent him a telegram saying "Come at once" he would have come. George would not do that. For him his work comes before anybody.'[3]

I talked about it with Margaret Branch, today a Jungian psychotherapist, who saw a good deal of Orwell and Eileen from the first year of the war onwards, when Eileen often stayed with her sister-in-law in Greenwich and was leading very much a life of her own.

Margaret Branch told me that her brother's death was such a shock to Eileen that for a time she became almost mute. 'One saw in her visible signs of depression. Her hair was unbrushed, her face and body thin. Reality was so awful for her that she withdrew – the effects lasted perhaps eighteen months. In her severe depression she was facing the dark night of the soul. Nobody could get through to her.'

These were the times in 1940 when Orwell, trying perhaps to help her, brought her a few times to Scarlett's Farm where she sat with us in silence.

Margaret Branch thought that her brother's death shattered Eileen's dream of life. 'Eileen was a dreamer. To marry Orwell and share his curious life-style at Wallington, she had to have a streak of mystical dream. She played at being a Wallington shopkeeper, at being a housewife, and at advertising the eating of carrots for the wartime Ministry of Food – she caught George's dreams from him like measles.'

From talking to people who knew Orwell and Eileen during the years of the war when I was abroad, from reading material in the Orwell Archives at University College and from some of the facts patiently unearthed by Bernard Crick in his biography, I think I see a shape of their wartime life and have come to some conclusions.

By the beginning of 1942, Eileen, however shaken by her brother's death, evidently had recovered her outward poise. For the next three years of the war, first in a remarkably dreary flat in Maida Vale and then, when bombed out of it by flying bombs, in a more presentable apartment in Canonbury Square, the Orwells enjoyed reasonable domesticity. They mixed well with the growing number of friends which Orwell's literary and journalistic work brought him as he worked first in the BBC and then on *Tribune*; Eileen resumed war work at the Ministry of Food, where her job was to help in the preparation of broadcasts which urged British listeners to make the best of war-rationed menus; say to consume a new kind of fish called snoek or to eat more carrots to see better at nights. . . .

I learned that Eileen herself and of course Orwell treated these official broadcasts with much irony. For Eileen, the care for Orwell's health and his writings remained the priority. Margaret Branch remembered her, during one of his periodic bronchial colds, rushing home from the Ministry each midday to prepare his lunch; she remembered Eileen later expressing her indignation against the successive publishers who in 1944 rejected *Animal Farm*. But, as a partisan of Eileen's she also noted, as did Lydia Jackson also, that while Eileen had her dream of somehow restoring Orwell's health through her love and care, her own health gave rise to growing anxiety: under the eroding stress of wartime life she appeared anaemic and undernourished; she neglected herself.

Still, at Canonbury Square there was now much more money coming in from Orwell's writings, as well as their combined salaries. Friends like Margaret Branch thought it was partly this which persuaded Eileen in spite of misgivings to agree to Orwell's urgings to adopt a child and it was then, in June 1944, that they adopted the newly born baby Richard Blair. Her misgivings stemmed from doubts about her own health and her strength in the years ahead. She had begun to suffer from bleedings; it must have been evident to her that there was something seriously wrong with her, although she also evidently tried to put the fact from her mind. How far Orwell was aware of her true condition is hard to know; he probably was not. The baby Richard soon became the great joy of his life; of Eileen's too, although she was not to nurse him for long.

In March 1945, which was when Orwell was away as a war correspondent for the *Observer* in France and Germany, Eileen went to stay with her sister-in-law Dr Gwen O'Shaughnessy in Newcastle. There at last she underwent a medical examination by a specialist, which was followed immediately by an operation by a leading local surgeon. From all the the evidence of her detailed letters included in Bernard Crick's biography[4] it is clear that Eileen had encouraged Orwell to go off, because she knew that her trouble was not, as she suggested to him, a minor one, but that she had growths in her womb. In a way which was all too human and understandable, particularly in wartime, she had postponed facing a serious medical examination. She had evidently worried about spoiling their chances of adoption if she were found to be ill and also, needlessly, about the financial cost to them of an operation – this was before the days of the National Health Service. In the event, the one possible mischance occurred; Eileen died under the anaesthetic in a perfectly proper operation. Orwell received the news of her death on 29 March 1945 in Cologne, where he himself lay ill.

I find Eileen's last letters to Orwell, written from Newcastle, which Bernard Crick quotes, most poignant and moving. They are everything that Orwell's own puritan letters are not; they are loving, intimate, personal, bright and informative in a chatty way, and they bring me to my other thought about Eileen. It has so often been remarked that unlike Orwell's other works, *Animal Farm* is a supremely well-written little satire. Its autumnal sadness is presented with the lightest touch, with not a word too many in a book not directly meant for children, but read by them avidly. *Animal Farm* has another distinction. Composed in the winter of 1943–4, it is the only work of

Orwell's which he is known to have discussed with his wife as he worked on it. Sequence by sequence, it is said, Eileen and he laughed about it in bed. Margaret Branch remembers hearing about its progress from Eileen, and she heard it said that Eileen's fellow-workers at the Ministry laughed about her reports of the story. And if *Animal Farm* is a tale so perfect in its light touch and restraint (almost 'unOrwellian'), I think some credit is due to the conversational influence of Eileen and the light touch of her bright, humorous intelligence.

All this is just my surmise. Though regrettably I knew Eileen only during the early part of the war when she was at her lowest ebb, I am sure that after her death Orwell's personal life was incomplete and in decline. This one did not notice at first, because for a year I met Orwell mainly at midday in Fleet Street at the offices of *Tribune*, which was the new focus of our acquaintance.

THIRTEEN

On and Off Tribune

WHEN ANEURIN BEVAN departed from *Tribune* into the initially enthusiastic *ambiance* of the post-war Labour Cabinet, his disciple Michael Foot took over the guidance of the paper, first from the editorial board and then as full editor. I thought Michael Foot a kind and gentle person, who was also a superb journalist, but I would not in 1945 have guessed at his future rise to political eminence. (In 1945 he was also still a true-blue democratic socialist, given to writing long articles about the sterility of the British Communists.)

My own news was that Orwell very badly wanted to end his literary editorship of *Tribune* and asked whether I would like to take it on. In the early summer of 1945 he wanted much more time to spend with Richard (now that he was a widower); with the war over, he naturally wanted to be free from office chores for his own writing; but, always dutiful, he did not want to let *Tribune* down: so what did I think? After my two years abroad during the war I liked the idea of what I thought would be a temporary part-time job while I looked around. With the aid of the deputy editor, Evelyn Anderson, with whom Orwell had become close friends, the matter was arranged.

When I went with Orwell to his little office at *Tribune* to take over, I found to my surprise that the drawers of his desk were stuffed with unpublished manuscripts of reviews, literary articles and poems.

'What on earth are all these?' I asked.

He sighed. 'Most of them are unspeakably bad,' he said, 'but I could not bring myself to send them back.'

I could see his dilemma, hovering between the high standards he set for his own writing and his desire not to hurt a struggling fellow-writer to whom a small *Tribune* fee might mean the difference between eating and not eating – or so he explained to me with what I thought considerable exaggeration. Torn between his high standards and generosity he let his famous honesty desert him. He had not answered some letters and in others had written that he had not yet got round to deciding about the particular piece but would do so presently.

Abroad during the war I had come across very occasional copies of *Tribune* which I read with interest. To my question about how Bevan and Orwell with their divergent temperaments had got on, Jon Kimche, who had left with Bevan at the end of the war, gave the reply that for all their mutual high respect for each other, they had never really communicated.

For instance, Kimche said, at one editorial meeting Bevan had made a pro-Zionist speech and Orwell countered by stating that the Zionists were only 'a bunch of Wardour Street Jews who have a controlling influence over the British press'.

Every one on the editorial board looked astonished at Orwell. 'Wardour Street' was a somewhat pejorative shorthand term for the ailing British film industry, some of whose leading entrepreneurs were Jewish. Kimche remembered that he afterwards tried to convince Orwell that the 'Wardour Street Jews' were mostly not Zionists, nor representative of Anglo-Jewry, nor controlled the British press, but as usual could not shake his opinion.

By and large, as Kimche reported, Bevan's and Orwell's minds ran on parallel lines without meeting. Thus at a typical editorial conference Bevan might deliver a rousing lecture on the nationalization of the coal industry when the war was over, *his* editorial for the week. After this Orwell would remark how depressing it was to be getting rid of Hitler, only to be left with a world dominated by Stalin, American millionaires and a tinpot dictator like de Gaulle: he might mention this in *his* column. Yet Kimche thought that this non-dialogue made for an exciting wartime weekly.

As I flipped through the back numbers of *Tribune* to look at Orwell's 'As I Please' columns (Bernard Crick has calculated that Orwell wrote 71 'As I Please' pieces touching on 231 topics), I was struck by the incisiveness of Orwell's opinions about everything. That inner voice of his which he could so

directly express in *Tribune* could sound like that of a latter-day
Dr Johnson, as he wrote about air raids or the price of tobacco
or popular English prejudice against American soldiers or the
lack of imagination of men who could fly through the clouds but
had not yet found how to eliminate the drudgery of washing
up crockery after meals.

All the same, among the dogmatic statements one could
trace a clear line: if Orwell did not much care for the defects of
British society, no, he did not like them at all, he knew that the
other side was worse. Thus when *The Times* upon the death of
James Joyce gave him what Orwell called 'a mean, cagey little
obituary' and refused to print T.S. Eliot's subsequent letter of
protest, Orwell had written scathingly:

> 'This was in accordance with the grand old English tradition
> that the dead must always be flattered unless they happened
> to be artists. Let a politician die and his worst enemies will
> stand up on the floor of the House and utter pious lies in his
> honour, but a writer or artist must be sniffed at . . .' [1]

However, if Joyce was an exile from Anglo-Irish philistinism,
Orwell had seen that this was as nothing compared with his
physical flight from the Nazis from France into Switzerland:

> 'One thing that Hitler and his friends have demonstrated is
> what a relatively good time the intellectual has had during
> the past hundred years. After all, how does the persecution of
> Joyce, Lawrence, Whitman, Baudelaire, even Oscar Wilde,
> compare with the kind of thing that has been happening to
> liberal intellectuals all over Europe since Hitler came to
> power? Joyce left Ireland in disgust: he did not have to run
> for his life, as he did when the panzers rode into Paris.' [2]

Well said, I thought.

Compared with his other writings, the literary reviews in the
back numbers of *Tribune* seemed to me mostly mediocre. With
all the obvious problems of wartime, he had not been a
particularly good literary editor. Kimche told me that he had
actually not often *sent* books out for review: news that he was a
soft touch had attracted a stream of callers to his Fleet Street
office to collect review copies or leave their articles and poems,

some of which he had then shoved forgotten into that drawer. Only contributions by personal friends like Julian Symons and Stevie Smith stood out. I was luckier: with the war over, I was given more pages and could draw on a whole string of talented young reviewers coming out of the forces.

As far as I could do so while slowly taking in the full details of Hitler's holocaust, I liked my first two years on *Tribune*. For a while my part-time job became full-time as I was inevitably drawn in on to the political side. While *Tribune* in the main busied itself with discussing Aneurin Bevan's interests in the National Health Service, public housing and nationalization, I contributed editorials and notes criticizing British policy in the Palestine conflict in which I felt deeply involved.

As Jewish survivors of Hitler's holocaust in Europe tried to dodge the British navy in making for the refuge of Palestine, opposition towards them among the Palestine Arabs erupted into violence. Guided by his pro-Arab Foreign Office advisors, the new British Foreign Secretary, that aging trade unionist Ernest Bevin, rather like a wooden man-of-war camouflaged as steel, became neurotically obsessed with trying against American opposition at all costs to prevent Jewish refugees from reaching Palestine, to prevent them indeed from leaving Europe. Ugly clashes and incidents took place. Within the Labour Party, the fight against Bevin was led by my wartime colleague, Richard Crossman. In the columns of *Tribune*, I wrote pieces highly critical of Bevin's policies. As I knew well, the Palestine Arabs had a case, but Bevin's policy was not that. It was an attempt made at the expense of the Palestine Jews to sustain British strategic military and political control over the Middle East, a policy which I thought had by this post-war era become a vain dream. I knew that Orwell completely disagreed with me: to him the Palestine Arabs were coloured Asians, the Palestine Jews the equivalent of the white rulers in India and Burma, an over-simplification from which he would not be budged, but then it did contain one sliver of truth.

This phase of the Palestine conflict came to an end with the emergence of the State of Israel after which I felt I could opt out, and did so. My main cooperation with Orwell was of course on the cultural and literary side of *Tribune*. That is, I tried to cooperate all round; as it was, I did not at first care too much for the post-war and post-holocaust world in which I found myself. I don't think that after Eileen's death, Orwell liked it that much, either, although outwardly he appeared at first unchanged in the absolute discipline of his busy life. After being turned down by a dozen American publishers because of its shortness, *Animal Farm* finally came out in New York with enormous literary and financial success. This success, plus the growing positive impact of his critical essays on the English language and kindred subjects, had at last brought him recognition as an international literary figure – I was amused to see how reluctantly he accepted this position. Again, while he had left his *Tribune* job and his 'As I Please' column was taken over by Bevan's wife, Jennie Lee, he maintained his regular literary link with the paper.

I have a distinct memory how, tall and looking thinner and still raggedly clad, he would during most weeks visit my little office at *Tribune*. Even as he entered, he would plunge into some major statement, usually political, often assertive, which was for him a way of making human contact. He would stay to talk on any subject from the new concept of the Soviet-built 'Iron Curtain' across Europe to the latest light novel which had arrived on my desk. He would sometimes discuss his contributions – in the first year after I took over from him he contributed some of the wittiest pieces he ever wrote for *Tribune*, dogmatically written but always with a light touch and that grain of inescapable truth.

In 'The Confessions of a Book Reviewer' he drew a most plausible portrait of a hack reviewer secretly hating the shiny new books which arrived for him in weekly parcels. In 'The Decline of English Murder' he noted an apparent change from the English Sunday newspaper tradition that murder was an emotionally-charged crime committed within a claustrophobic lower-middle-class family to a new pattern of purposeless gangster killings. In another essay he popularized the concept of 'Good Bad Books', those enduring popular bestsellers which for their sentimental sincerity he claimed to prefer (or really preferred) to creative literary works. And in 'A Good Word for the Vicar of Bray' he reflected – truthfully, I think – how much he would have preferred a leisurely, bookish, rural eighteenth-century life to his actual existence.

Sometimes I could push books or themes his way. Thus there landed on my desk a reprint of *Helen's Babies*, John Habberton's nineteenth-century fabulous American bestseller about the comic tribulations of a well-bred American bachelor left in charge of his sister's small boys. Orwell and I discovered that we had both as boys immensely enjoyed the harmless humour of this book, as indeed we had enjoyed many other American popular stories which, so Orwell claimed, had left some children of his generation with a detailed knowledge of the unfamiliar plants and animals of the American scene.

At any rate, he took *Helen's Babies* away with him to make it the starting point for one of his nicest, most penetrating light essays, 'Riding Down From Bangor'. In this he said that if the nineteenth-century characters in *Helen's Babies* were mildly ridiculous, they were yet enviable in their unthinking piety and striving for good morale. If popular American books of the period gave English children the picture of a world more colourful and with more freedom than their own, the cause lay in the buoyant American nineteenth-century belief in a better future:

> 'Nineteenth-century America was a rich, empty country which lay outside the mainstream of world events, and in which the twin nightmares that beset nearly every modern man, the nightmare of unemployment and the nightmare of State interference, had hardly come into being. There were social distinctions, more marked than those of today, and there was poverty ... but there was not, as there is today, an all-prevailing sense of helplessness. There was room for everybody, and if you worked hard you could be certain of a living – could even be certain of growing rich: this was generally believed, and for the greater part of the population it was even broadly true. In other words, the civilization of nineteenth-century America was capitalist civilization at its best.'[3]

A look back upon the golden past from the viewpoint of 1984? Or at least of 1946? Alas, so Orwell ended the essay, alas for the

American popular culture of the repellent horror comics of 1946!

After his visits to myself and others at *Tribune*, Orwell in 1945–7 often went on to a Fleet Street lunch with two outstanding writers and wits of his own generation, Anthony Powell and Malcolm Muggeridge, and Julian Symons, a younger writer who was both a friend and politically something of a disciple of Orwell's. Symons in a fond reminiscence has written that 'in a friendly and even affectionate way, Muggeridge and Powell would often lure Orwell away from sensible empiricism to wild flights of political fantasy'.[4] Malcolm Muggeridge in an amusing memoir has said that Orwell, an original in himself, could be extremely funny in the confidence with which he propounded his prejudices:

> 'Thus, he would come out with the proposition: "All tobacconists are Fascists!", as though this was something so obvious that no one could possibly question his statement. Momentarily, one was swept along. Yes, there was something in it; those little men in their kiosks handing out fags and tobacco all day long – wouldn't they have followed a Hitler or a Mussolini if one had come along? Then the sheer craziness of it took hold of one, and one began to laugh helplessly, until – such was his persuasiveness – one reflected inside one's laughter: after all, they are rather rum birds, those tobacconists.'[5]

Thinking back upon those years 1945–7, I feel, however, that in spite of gay lunches in Fleet Street, life for Orwell was far from lighthearted. Quite the contrary, I think that without Eileen he was solitary and at a loss. One could perhaps have noticed the signs of this more clearly.

Orwell together with Richard spent Christmas 1945 in north Wales with Arthur Koestler and his wife Mamaine and her twin sister Celia Kirwan, today Mrs Celia Goodman. Mrs Goodman has told me how she always remembered her astonished first glimpse of Orwell: a huge, gaunt figure standing waiting in the wintry December gloom of Euston Station, wrapped in an extra-long shabby military greatcoat, with Richard under one arm and a battered old suitcase in the other hand. Orwell's posture, she thought, conveyed both loneliness and his love for his adopted son which came shining through. She said that she felt immediately drawn to him.

Koestler has given a well-known account of that Christmas stay. Thus Orwell told him that when lying in his hot bath he often thought up excruciating punishments for his enemies. We agreed that this was fantasy: in real life Orwell was usually understanding and conciliatory when meeting personal opponents. As a critic in print he was of course very different. In *Tribune*, Orwell had just written a mercilessly scathing review of what Koestler in retrospect considered a lousy play of his. Ironically he asked Orwell: 'Why didn't you just say that this play was not worthy of a gifted writer, why did you just say it was muck, why did you write such a stinking review?' Orwell replied: 'Well, it was a stinking play.' No concessions for friends.

Koestler reported that he and Orwell went for a long country walk, with Orwell carrying Richard, Asian style, on his hip. They argued about the Palestine conflict; finding Orwell immovably opposed to Jewish immigration, Koestler says he thought it best to drop the subject. But then Orwell complained that the Labour Government had not yet unconditionally pulled out of India. Koestler said that on the day the British went, there would be 100,000 dead in Calcutta and a million elsewhere. To Orwell it made no difference. 'Let them kill if they want to,' he said. 'It's their business.' He added: 'At least there won't be a white man's burden any more.'

Koestler told me that something in the grimness of Orwell's tone made him look up sharply at him.

In May 1946, for nine months or so, Orwell resumed his weekly 'As I Please' column in *Tribune* and I remember an argument with him over the very first of these he proposed to write. In this piece, said Orwell, he wanted to attack the Labour Government, including his friend Aneurin Bevan. If they as socialists had really wanted to change British society, they should have done three things: abolish the public schools, abolish all titles and abolish the House of Lords. He wanted to say that instead Bevan had let himself be diverted into enlarging the National Health Service and the public housing sector and into measures of nationalization – all well and good but these were administrative reforms and so largely bureaucratic and not tackling the basic inequalities of British society.

I objected that Orwell could not signal his return to *Tribune* with a direct attack on Bevan who after all had been his own most generous editor on *Tribune* and who still had his informal link with the paper. In short, I laughed Orwell out of delivering his attack and this particular 'As I Please' was never written.

Looking back, I very much regret this. Orwell was of course right, as he so often was: the expensive, fee-paying public schools have remained the divisive factor in British society. But on second thoughts, should it not also have struck one's attention that in looking away from national health and public housing, Orwell seemed to have lost some confidence in the Labour Government's patient efforts to improve British social life – that his thoughts were elsewhere?

For it is now that one must ask what prompted him to take flight from his London life to settle in the isolated northern part of his remote Hebridean island of Jura? Work and lunchtime talk apart, how had he been living? Since he treated friends and acquaintances always alike, at the same time courteous and withdrawn, it was not easy to know. I have a memory of the first of a few visits my wife and I paid him in his Canonbury Square flat. This must have been early in 1946, on a cold winter's day. I know it was on a Tuesday, the free day of his young housekeeper, Susan Watson, whom we saw slipping away as we arrived. Since my wife worked with small children, Orwell wanted her advice about his handling of Richard.

The first thing that struck us was the utter cheerlessness of the awkwardly built flat. My wife said afterwards that it looked as if every door had a slice at the bottom sawn off so that cold draughts could whistle through the entire flat, and she advised Orwell to install draught excluders, which he promised to do. A coal fire burned in only one room, the sitting room – fuel rationing was then still in force. Orwell invited Mary to watch him bathe Richard. He did so in a steaming hot bath, but even here the window was open and a cold current of winter air was coming into the bathroom. When Mary remarked on this, he said: 'It's a good idea,' and quickly shut the window.

When he had finished bathing Richard, he picked him up, dripping wet and wrapped in an inadequate towel, and carried him through the icy corridor to the warm sitting room, where he sat down close to the fire with Richard on his lap and proceeded to dry him. When Mary told him that he must first quickly dry Richard in the bathroom and then wrap him in a proper large bath towel while carrying him through the cold corridor, he gratefully accepted the advice: again he said it was a good idea. But although Richard did not speak much, he looked a particularly healthy, bonny and laughing two-year-old; Orwell held him most lovingly on his lap; it was obvious that both father and child were thoroughly enjoying the whole experience. When Mary said that in her judgement he was handling Richard very well indeed, he gave one of his cryptic smiles. 'Yes,' he said. 'You see, I've always been good with animals.'

It was one of those typical Orwellian remarks that stuck in our minds, with its odd grain of truth: infants *were* in a way like animals in the way one had to handle them. Mary said after we left that it really seemed to her an excellent relationship. Orwell loved Richard and Richard adored his new father, and such genuine warmth on both sides was far more important than any little instances of Orwell's inexperience of details of babycare. She thought that after Eileen's death, it was wonderful for Orwell to have Richard to look after.

Yet from this and a subsequent visit, we also carried back an impression of Orwell showing his affection for his child amidst surroundings of strange, almost deliberate discomfort, almost background gloom. Looking back, I feel one should have sensed that, bereft of Eileen, he was no longer clear about his whole setting in his journalistic London life.

I received an impression of this setting when talking to Susan Watson, who at the time gave Orwell such excellent service. A polio victim as a child, separated from her husband, a Cambridge don, the young Susan Watson had come to keep house for Orwell at Canonbury Square for over a year in 1945–6, and so had a closer view of him than most people. She had arrived as Richard's 'minder' and housekeeper. Having herself had a cook-general in Cambridge, she could not cook;

but she quickly learned from recipes to provide Orwell with his Sunday roast beef and Yorkshire pudding, and the steamed puddings he loved. Susan said that Orwell paid her generously and treated her scrupulously, like a young sister looking after his infant.

On arrival, Susan found Richard a happy infant; Eileen had mothered him lovingly and well. So had Orwell; he told Susan that he himself had looked after Richard for three weeks and he had only missed his bottle once. As for the brooding sense of the absence of Eileen – when Susan asked what she should do with a wardrobe full of Eileen's clothes, it was as though he could not bear to think about this, and he said she could choose any she liked for herself, and when Susan demurred he insisted. Talking briefly about Eileen, he said that adopting Richard had been mainly his own idea: Eileen had been unwell and overworking to such an extent that he saw it as a way of keeping her at home. Not long after Susan's arrival, Christmas came and in return for a present from Orwell to her of a brooch, she shopped around laboriously to find him a pair of size twelve gloves.

For Susan it was a pleasant enough job, but from her memory Orwell emerged as a man very ill at ease with himself. Apart from a pretty scrap-screen with postcards of Gauguin and Cézanne and Victorian postcards, the flat, which consisted of a sitting room, Susan and Richard's small bedroom and Orwell's small study, was quite emphatically bleak, as my wife and I noticed on visits. Susan tried to improve the look by dyeing the sitting room curtains red, buying a cover of green hessian for the divan on which Orwell slept, and hanging a print of Douanier Rousseau above it, but the flat still looked bleak. Susan remembers Orwell's small study as crammed with a table and typewriter, a filing cabinet seemingly filled with Communist pamphlets and a much-used carpenter's workbench with a tool rack above it. As for my wife's suggestion to Orwell to install draught excluders on his doors, Susan said that he talked about it but never got round to it. Susan gathered from conversation – or was it a later conclusion? – that he thought people should live in some ways on a working-class level: but he gave the flat none of the loving care which she knew so many working men gave to their homes.

She noted that for all his work at his carpenter's bench, Orwell was not good at housework, but he loved making fires; he laid the wood most carefully. He also insisted on the precise preparation of very strong tea. He loved pretty flies and baits – he showed Susan a box of beautiful coloured flies for his fishing. He had another box filled with comic postcards, to be taken out and chuckled over with a visitor. He kept no wine or other drink in the house, but once quickly sent Susan out to buy a bottle of sherry: he was expecting Cyril Connolly and Sonia Brownell. On another occasion he was to lunch at the Ritz with 'the old Earl' – Bertrand Russell. For this he was to wear his best suit, a herringbone tweed which looked to Susan like a working man's best suit. He sent her out with precise instructions to buy him a pair of working men's braces; failing to do this, she went to Regent Street to buy him a pair of more ordinary braces, which he accepted without a word.

He was demanding to work for, simply because he was so demanding of himself. His habits – working or eating – were dominated by the clock. High tea with Richard was a high spot of the day. Tea was poured from so large and heavy an earthenware pot that Susan could only lift it with both hands. At first at teatime he would sit in silence. Then at a certain point he would turn his chair sideways and roll one of his interminable strong cigarettes: Susan knew this was a sign that he wanted to talk. He once or twice mentioned his early experience at St Cyprian's as something that Richard would be spared. Although she was sure that he was basically sad and lonely, he could also suddenly break into cheerful talk, imparting a sense of adventure and fun to the conversation. Later, when Susan read his essay on 'Boys' Weeklies' she thought that he had sometimes himself talked like a character from the *Gem* or *Magnet*. He was enthusiastically loving towards Richard. She thought a main pleasure of his week came each Tuesday, which was her day off, when he would himself bathe and feed Richard.

But of course the dominant fact in his life was his writing. He drove himself relentlessly, accepting almost every journalistic commission offered. He worked most mornings; then at night he would sit typing into the early morning hours, until 2 or 3 a.m. Susan, when waking at night, felt it was quite unusual if she could not hear the sound of the typewriter. He did not tell her of his tubercular condition so that she was terribly shocked when he had a haemorrhage, and she saw him walk down the passage with blood running from his lips. Should she call a doctor? No, no, no; doctors were no good; just bring him a jug of iced water from the ice chest; he had of course no such modern appliance as a refrigerator. Susan remembers keeping him in bed for a fortnight, and that he asked her to tell people who telephoned that he could see nobody and write no articles. But he soothed Susan after the haemorrhage, telling her that he would live until Richard was thirteen and that he would show her, Susan, where his files and papers were kept so that she could deal with them.

As I think back upon the story, I feel that Orwell fled away to Jura not only to gain peace to write his book but because by 1946–7 he found his London life apart from writing no longer tenable. He was of course busy enough, typing away nightly into the early morning hours, writing for *Tribune*, the *Observer*, *Horizon*, visiting and lunching in Fleet Street; by now there was also plenty of money coming in from the American sales of *Animal Farm*; but he must have found the solitariness of his widower's life deeply disturbing. This explains some of his odd actions at the time. I knew that after Eileen's death in 1945 he had had a brief (and unsatisfactory) affair with Sonia Brownell, the beautiful assistant editor of *Horizon*. I think I was also vaguely aware that he had proposed marriage to another beautiful woman, Koestler's sister-in-law Celia, who gently said no to him but remained his warm and supporting friend. But what I did not know is what has since come to light: that, as Bernard Crick describes in his biography, Orwell at the time proposed unsuccessfully to two and perhaps three more well-connected young women.[6]

His arguments in proposing were always the same: he was no great catch, his life expectancy was poor, but he was looking for a mother for Richard, and his wife could as his widow enjoy a fair income from royalties. These were hardly propositions to be put with any hope of success to self-reliant, post-war young women, but I think these proposals were not based on any real relationships; Susan Watson told me that he made one proposal on two days' acquaintance. There was an element of fantasy about these proposals (as there was, indeed, about his subsequent deathbed marriage to Sonia), a sign that his sense of personal identity in his life in London had become disturbed. Could his friends have done more for him in his loneliness? Given his complete reserve towards friends and acquaintances alike, I doubt it.

My last memory of Orwell during this period is associated with deep, deep fog. My wife and I and he had dined with Mrs Evelyn Anderson, his former *Tribune* colleague, who lived in Bayswater. That evening a pea-soup fog, still common in London at the time, had been descending so heavily that my wife had on the way abandoned our car. On emerging from the house we found the fog so thick that my wife said no, we would spend the night with Mrs Anderson. But not Orwell: one way or another he would return to Canonbury Square. My last glimpse of him was of his tall figure, looking grim and sad faced, as he strode off and disappeared into the fog.

Not long after, in May 1947, he wrote his last piece for *Tribune*, packed up and disappeared to his far-off Scottish island, there to write his new book. We were out of contact except by letter for over a year, and when my wife and I met him again in 1949, he was on his sickbed in a sanatorium and terminally ill.

FOURTEEN

Looking at the Future from Jura

W HEN ORWELL in the late spring of 1947 went to the island of Jura to settle down to write *Nineteen Eighty-Four*, he was no doubt putting his frail physical health at risk.

Some critics have seen his escape from London to the remoteness of Jura, together with the pessimism of *Nineteen Eight-Four*, as hinting at a certain death-wish in him. I think this much too crude a judgement, yet some questions remain.

One can easily understand Orwell's feeling that he absolutely had to get away from the journalistic pressures of his London life (he disliked London, anyway) in order to concentrate on his new book. He obviously found it hard to say no to journalistic commissions, yet with the money coming in from *Animal Farm*, he could now afford to limit himself to much less, and better paid, journalism – say, for America. So one can see why for the purpose of his new book he had to get away from callers and the telephone. But why as far as the isolation of northern Jura? In retrospect I tell myself that Orwell could have found a perfectly good refuge to write his book somewhere in the countryside of southern England, hidden away, but with the comforts and medical facilities he might need close by.

This safety was clearly never in his mind. The house he had found on Jura, Barnhill, was an isolated farm building in the primitive, empty northern part of the island. He had found Barnhill through the good offices of his friend David Astor, who as a boy had spent summer holidays on an estate the family owned in the populated south of the island. David Astor has said that when helping Orwell to make the arrangements for going to Barnhill, he believed that Orwell would use that

remote farmhouse only for summer holidays – he never thought
he would take up permanent residence there. To those who
considered it reckless for Orwell in his tubercular condition to
take himself to the north of Scotland, Bernard Crick has
answered that Jura, set right in the Gulf Stream, has in fact a very
mild if rainy climate. This may be correct, but is not the whole
point. David Astor, who was Orwell's loyal friend and supporter
to the end, has told me that it was the isolation of Barnhill in the
wild north of the island and the lack of civilized comforts
which troubled him when he thought of Orwell's stay there. The
nearest telephone to Barnhill was in a building five miles away
by road. Orwell on Jura did acquire a motor cycle and later a
large old car, but the road was so rough that in bad weather one
had to walk the last five miles. The complicated journey from
Barnhill to Glasgow for medical care could take up to twelve
hours by car, ferry and train. Barnhill was in no way a good place
for a man in Orwell's precarious state of health.

When I ask myself why he went there, I recall the reference I
found in his wartime diary of 1940 to 'my Hebridean island
which I shall now probably never see'. He obviously had
dreamed of living in the Hebrides for many years. He had
progressed through his life in sharply marked phases: Eton,
Burma, Paris, Wigan, Spain, Morocco, London, *Tribune* – now
perhaps the dream was of a Hebridean phase, mingled with the
ideas of *Nineteen Eighty-Four*. There may have been a subsidiary
reason. Writing to me from Jura, he advised me not to worry so
much about Palestine and Israel 'because we might all be blown
up in five or ten years'. I think he half-believed it and, looking at it
theoretically, he wanted to put the maximum distance between
himself and the atomic threat. It's a thought.

He had actually gone on a first reconnaissance of some weeks
to Barnhill in the summer of the previous year, 1946. Susan
Watson with Richard followed him a week or so later, but
finding Orwell's younger sister Avril in residence at Barnhill,
she knew that her own tenure would now be short lived and she
returned to London a week before Orwell did. From now on,
Avril was in charge of Orwell's household and of Richard.

So by the early autumn of 1946, Orwell was back as usual in
Canonbury Square. This was when he resumed his weekly 'As I

Please' column and his regular visits to *Tribune* for about another eight months. My wife and I visited him during that winter of 1946–7 on an occasion when Avril and Richard were out. The spartan life-style was still in force. I seem also to remember that he was quite seriously ill again with bronchitis during that winter, but in his ususal style he rose again from his bed to write and type as though nothing had happened.

Then, as the harsh winter of that year passed and spring arrived, he and Avril and Richard were off again to Jura and his intention was that this time it was to be for good.

The evidence is that he enjoyed the summer of 1947 at Barnhill, with its long northern daylight, as much as any period in his later years. He set himself up again as a semi-smallholder. He had tried to plant fruit trees and rose bushes and he planted vegetables. He kept chickens and a pig; there was much putting out of lobster pots and fishing. Susan Watson has related how already during the previous year's reconnaissance, Orwell enormously enjoyed taking her out fishing with well-baited lines.

Of the literary acquaintances Orwell invited, only his faithful long-standing friend Richard Rees came. Rees stayed for six weeks and arranged for a young Scotsman, Bill Dunn, to farm Barnhill for Orwell. Among other visitors were some of the odd characters Orwell always attracted, but his nephew and niece Henry and Jane Dakin and their younger sister, Lucy, also arrived (and probably contributed a touch of young normality). Henry Dakin has told the story of a famous expedition by boat, when, owing to Orwell's characteristic miscalculation about the tides and currents, he and Henry, with Lucy and Richard on board, were very nearly caught in the notorious Corryvreckan whirlpool. In the end the boat capsized; they were marooned for some hours on a tiny island, but all ended well although the ducking certainly did not do Orwell much good.

Sometime during that summer, Warburg's partner Roger Senhouse showed me the essay 'Such, Such Were the Joys' which they had received from Orwell but could not publish because of possible libel action. I was surprised by the vehemence of the boyhood memories in Orwell's mind. They seemed to explain a certain bitterness against his background.

From a letter in October 1947 I gathered that his new book was going well; the first draft was nearly completed. He also wrote that unfortunately his chest troubles were afflicting him again – and then came disaster. His feverish inflammation grew worse. A specialist in Glasgow diagnosed serious tuberculosis of the left lung and on 20 December 1947 he was admitted to Hairmyres Hospital at West Kilbride, near Glasgow. In a letter to me written from Ward 3 there on 31 December 1947 – what a conscientious correspondent he always was – he said that he had not been in good health on Jura for two or three months. I heard that an unfortunate accident had hastened his collapse. The story went that he had gone for a medical check-up to Glasgow while a large commercial convention was being held in that city and he had tramped from one full-up hotel to the next in heavy boots, carrying a suitcase weighted with purchases, finding a bed only when totally ill and exhausted. In his letter to me he wrote:

> 'I was very well last year, and I think this show really started in that beastly cold of last winter. I was conscious early this year of being seriously ill & I thought I'd probably got TB, but like a fool I decided not to go to a doctor as I knew I'd be stuck in bed and I wanted to get on with the book I was writing. All that happened is that I've half written the book, which in my case is much the same as not starting it. However they seem pretty confident they can patch me up, so I might be able to get back to some serious work some time in 1948.
>
> 'I am going shortly to start a little book reviewing for the *Observer*. I might as well earn a little money while I am on my back, & I've felt somewhat better the last week or so. The treatment is to put the affected lung out of action, which is supposed to give it a better chance to heal. It is a slow job, I suppose, but meanwhile it does me good to have proper nursing here. It is a nice hospital & every one is very kind to me. The next thing is to prevent Richard getting this disease, though I must say by his physique he doesn't look much like it at present.'[1]

My wife had begun to share with Orwell the contents of

parcels of delicacies such as crystallized fruit which an American friend worried by continued British rationing saw fit to send us and he always thanked us most punctiliously. Some weeks after admission to hospital, he did so in a letter to Mary (16.1.1948) in which he again wrote more optimistically about his health, his eventual return to Jura and of course about Richard:

> 'I think I am getting better. It's a slow process, but I feel somewhat better and they seem to think the X-rays show signs of improvement. I have air pumped into my diaphragm once a week, and later shall have it pumped between the ribs as well. Richard was blooming when I came away. He is now 3½ or a little over. He is still backward about talking, partly I think because he doesn't see enough of other children, but is bright and self-reliant in other ways. He is out helping with the farm work all day long, getting himself covered with mud from head to foot.'

Orwell remained for the whole first half of 1948 in Ward 3 at Hairmyres Hospital, where as usual he engaged in journalistic work and made notes for the impending second draft of his book. By a later inference I think he also liked listening to the soft Scottish working-class speech of his fellow-patients; his early prejudice against all things Scottish had long since disappeared and the patients were for him of the right class. But he did not return to Jura to resume intensive work on his book until well into July 1948.

I deeply regret now that I did not visit him in Glasgow. Looking back, I feel I did not fully realize the seriousness of his illness, nor how desperately he had tried to pour all his thoughts into the book he was writing on Jura. I twice half-made arrangements to visit him but was both times prevented – I had at this time my own problems in London. However, Fred Warburg did travel up to Glasgow and returned surprisingly optimistic. He thought that Orwell was recovering quite well and working again and might soon be out of hospital – he was unfortunately quite wrong there. Through the friendly services of David Astor, a supply of the still rare drug oreomycin had been flown to Orwell from America and he was busily noting the side-effects of the treatment in his diary. I was encouraged by reading (though I think this was very much later in 1948) a longer essay he wrote called 'Writers and Leviathan'.[2] In this he advised writers to take part in the sordid business of party politics as citizens, as human beings, but not as *writers*, for there they had to remain free – he did not see how this split in a writer's active life could in practice be avoided. It struck me that these might be second thoughts about the writing of *The Lion and the Unicorn*.

We corresponded intermittently (I later found I had kept only two of his handwritten letters of the time) mostly about the affairs of *Tribune*. In his letters he expressed the strongest disapproval of *Tribune*'s current stand against American foreign policies, such as the rearmament of West Germany. Even so, I was surprised when many years later I discovered that in a letter to Julian Symons on 2 January 1948 he wrote about *Tribune* that 'the evil genius of the paper has, I think, been Crossman, who influences it through Foot & Fyvel. Crossman & the rest of the gang thought they saw an opening for themselves in squealing about foreign policy, etc.'[3] Flattered though I should have been to be coupled with the future leader of the Labour Party, this was fantasy. True, I had been in touch with Richard Crossman about Palestine/Israel, but this had been earlier on; by 1948, I had opted out of the political side of *Tribune* and in any case, ever since my Anglo-American war service, I had been as strongly pro-American and opposed to Left-wing anti-Americanism as Orwell was.

Nor was the apparent change in *Tribune*'s political stand which so irritated him due in any way to Richard Crossman. The real point was that Aneurin Bevan had been growing restive within the Labour Cabinet about what he regarded as the lukewarmness of his colleagues already well before he was to leave the Cabinet – which he did the following year – to found the Left-wing secession called 'Bevanism'. I think that *Tribune*'s criticisms of US policies reflected Bevan's restiveness. I merely replied to Orwell that I was glad he still kept so regular an eye on *Tribune*.

The winter of 1947–8 was exceptionally cold and severe, rationing actually being tightened, but it passed; the tardy spring passed; I heard from Fred Warburg that in July Orwell was back on Jura working on his book. The only visitor this time was Richard Rees. In retrospect I think that Orwell must have worked desperately hard and long hours, often sitting up in bed, in correcting and rewriting the first typed draft of *Nineteen Eighty-Four*, because by November he had already finished the job – and then had a brief mini-collapse.

Now we come to what seems in retrospect a minor setback which yet had tragic consequences for Orwell. Faced with his much-corrected and criss-crossed typescript, he had asked Warburg to send a typist up to him in Jura. Warburg and his partner, Roger Senhouse, tried to find a girl willing to leave for Jura both in London and in Edinburgh, but without success. I can remember the time quite well: London was wintry and rationed, people were weary, there was still an acute shortage of trained secretaries, let alone one to brave the Scottish wilderness. However, while waiting for someone to be found by Warburg, Orwell told his agent Leonard Moore not to bother with similar efforts, and in the end no secretary from any source appeared. Recalling the incident, Warburg has written: 'I had to cable my failure to Orwell, who finished the revision early in November and typed the MS himself. This failure on my part still haunts me. It was perhaps the last straw.'[4]

Warburg should have felt like that, for it *was* the last straw. Surely there is always a price at which such matters could be arranged, and no financial price should have been too high to get a typist to Orwell in his state of health. However, who knew how desperate his state of health was? This is just being wise in hindsight. The point was that, aching to be finally rid of the book which he had worked on for two years and thought about for many more, Orwell sat down impatiently to type out the long second draft of *Nineteen Eighty-Four* by himself. Susan Watson has told me how already eighteen months earlier on Jura she had watched Orwell, while unwell, work himself into a state of exhaustion. She said that he always felt the cold badly and sat up in bed working in an old, seedy dressing-gown with a frayed belt. His bedroom was uncomfortable. He had an iron bedstead; the room had a smoky grate – Orwell sometimes smoked kippers there – and it had a Valor paraffin stove, also smoky, which made moving patterns on the ceiling.

It was underneath these patterns that Orwell in November 1948 sat feverishly – he really had fever – clean-typing *Nineteen Eighty-Four*, including the Appendix on Newspeak. If he really did it in less than a month, he must have typed 5,000 words a day, a considerable effort even for a perfectly fit man. For Orwell with his fever and his fast-deteriorating left lung, it was heroic but disastrous. Not surprisingly, after finishing the typescript and sending it off to Warburg in early December, he had another horrible collapse and this time, as I think he half guessed, it was critical. He was not to rise from his bed again.

Of all this at the time I had only an inkling through Fred Warburg who himself only recognized the full extent of Orwell's deteriorating health when it was too late. Years later, when I more or less knew the facts, I remember asking Orwell's second wife, Sonia, why he had so desperately boxed himself in on Jura over *Nineteen Eighty-Four*. I said that he must have realized that typing was becoming an exhausting labour for him; he must have seen that his publishers and friends had failed to conjure up a typist for him in the wintry isolation of Jura. Why then did he not think of simply coming south with his typescript to avail himself of professional help? Sonia said: 'Oh, George was perfectly aware that he could come to London and engage an efficient secretary, but as he saw things, leaving Jura was just not on. It would have meant an upheaval in his whole consciousness of himself which he did not want to face. Besides, all his life he had ignored his illnesses up to the point where they got too bad, when he went to bed and waited to recover as he always did. Perhaps he thought that this time, too, he would recover; or he just refused to think.'

In the end, in Orwell's journey to Jura and his stay there to write *Nineteen Eighty-Four*, there remain some questions to which we do not know the answers.

FIFTEEN

Terminal

THE LAST PHASE of my contact with Orwell is so
melancholy that as I think back I prefer to do so in
literary terms – Orwell's literary terms.

When Fred Warburg received the typescript of *Nineteen Eighty-Four* in December 1948, it excited him immensely. He felt that the novel was devastating in its picture of future totalitarian doom, so much so that he immediately dictated a five-page appreciation of it for his office colleagues. He proudly showed me this document in which he incidentally described Orwell's strange Utopia as a savage attack on socialism, quite wrongly I think.

He also let me see the typescript, which I had to read very quickly; and I remember how at the first hasty glance I was taken aback: the book was not what I had expected. I felt that the love story between Winston and Julia was not convincing; the scenes of Winston's final torture seemed a little crude; the scenery of the novel seemed to me to be taken too directly from the shabby, bombed wartime London which after all was in the past. True, such touches as the picture of Big Brother who might or might not exist and the daily two minutes' hate before the telescreen were most ingenious; the description of 'Ingsoc' as a totalitarian society that could never be overthrown had its pages of strange power and the final exit line where Winston Smith weeps as he loves Big Brother was, as usual, brilliant. However, if I ask myself honestly whether I realized at this first hasty reading that here was a book against which, in a sense, all subsequent history was to be measured, the answer is that I did not. It was only at a second reading of the book in print in the summer that I quite changed my mind and felt that with all its defects the book had a unique power of stirring the imagination – it was a work of some genius.

Orwell himself meanwhile was, as I heard, bedbound in a sanatorium at Cranham, high up in the Cotswolds, and in the spring my wife and I visited him there.

On a wintry day the sanatorium looked a bleak place and the visit was a major shock to us: Orwell was so much worse, so much thinner and frailer in his critical illness than we had expected. True, mentally he seemed in perfect control, but in body, there he lay flat on his back in bed, looking terribly emaciated, his face drawn and waxen pale – without doubt he was dangerously ill. Constrained by the shock, I tried to tell him how much I had liked his book. He commented a little sadly that because of his illness, the book might have turned out duller and more pessimistic than intended.

We were accompanied on our visit by Olga Miller who wrote her entertaining satirical political verses unfailingly each week in the *New Statesman* under the pen-name 'Sagittarius'. Orwell had known her at *Tribune*. Olga determinedly cheered us with her witticisms as we talked about London life. She told how in 1945 she had written a poem about the Allied crossing of the Rhine into Germany over the bridge left mysteriously intact at Remagen. As a result she was asked to appear for interrogation by security officers of US military intelligence, no less, but Richard Crossman had managed to talk them out of it. Orwell shook his head over the boneheadedness of military intelligence. I watched him fall into the teasing style of conversation he liked to adopt with my wife. I recall Mary saying: 'George, do you remember how at Scarlett's Farm you showed me your unopened Income Tax demands and said they couldn't get blood from a stone? Well, George, no more worrying about the Inland Revenue with all that lovely money coming in from *Animal Farm*.' He answered with a sigh: 'It may look like it, Mary, but it's all fairy gold, fairy gold ...' This was in fact a reference to the dreaded Inland Revenue again, to whom he had apparently paid away more than half the previous year's income because he was only now making proper arrangements through an accountant to spread his earnings.

As we drove back to London I remember how Olga Miller said that even in bed, Orwell seemed in his person and interests characteristically unchanged. However, that was in spirit. As for his physical state, we felt dismayed by the severe advance of his illness. He still engaged in very occasional journalism and a few weeks later I was surprised to receive a long and firmly handwritten letter from him. In this he discussed the political placing of Graham Greene – both a Catholic and almost a fellow-traveller, he thought. In the letter he also reproved me for repeatedly criticizing contemporary novelists in *Tribune* because they would not write realistically about the English post-war scene. This could not be done, he went on; any novel written purely about the contemporary scene would be mere *reportage* and so outdated almost before it appeared. A true novel had to be lived with in the mind for years before being written down (I knew that this was certainly so in his own case). He also reminded me that nearly all the worthwhile books about the 1914–18 war only appeared up to ten years after the event. I took his point and told him so, adding that I had evidently not made myself quite clear. What I objected to was that many English novelists were still writing in a class-bound pre-war manner about a post-war England whose class structure and whole mood were so very different. (I must have been waiting for the new school of English post-war novelists.)

In a letter on 15 April I got bad news from Cranham. He wrote:

'I have been horribly ill the last few weeks. I had a bit of a relapse, then they had another go with the streptomycin, which previously did me a lot of good, at least temporarily. This time only one dose of it had ghastly results, as I had built up an allergy or something. I'm a bit better now, but I can't work and don't know when I shall be able to.'

Fred Warburg, who with his wife Pamela had visited Orwell again, reported that he had given his new number one author a lecture about preserving his health at all costs, even if it meant that for a longer period he would be able to do only very partial work. Pamela in particular felt that the Cotswolds sanatorium was inadequate. She was convinced that Orwell should now be seen by their friend Dr Andrew Morland, a Harley Street chest specialist who in earlier years had attended D.H. Lawrence.

Warburg also thought that Orwell should be brought to London for the best possible care. I later heard from Pamela that Dr Morland had seen Orwell and, according to her, thought he had just a chance of partial remission, but that there was equally a danger of further relapse. For the moment Orwell could not even think about systematic work, as on a book – Pamela was emphatic about this.

On 15 June 1949, *Nineteen Eighty-Four* was published in a first printing of 25,000 copies. Warburg, whom experience had rendered cautious since we first met, thought that in spite of his own enthusiasm for the book there was a risk in such a large printing. He was of course quite wrong, because from the day of publication, Orwell's pessimistic Utopia has never ceased to sell steadily in a score of countries. Success was immediate. Apart from a few carping Communists, reviewers were enthusiastic. V.S. Pritchett in the *New Statesman* compared Orwell to Swift. A most perceptive critical appreciation appeared in the *Times Literary Supplement*, written, I learned, by Julian Symons. The novel was published on the same day in New York, where it was given understanding praise by that sensitive critic, Lionel Trilling. Here, alas, was an uneasy paradox: Orwell, who in life might have little future as an active writer, had on the strength of a book about the future become a leading writer of the time.

As for myself, on the BBC's Third Programme I took part in a radio conversation about *Nineteen Eighty-Four* with Orwell's friend Malcolm Muggeridge. Because we knew that Orwell would be listening from his bed, Muggeridge suggested that after paying due tribute to his grim vision of the future (predictions were always wrong, Muggeridge suggested, but the worst were probably the best), we should make our conversation as lighthearted as possible. For instance, when talking about the famous torture scene where Winston Smith, tied to a couch, has a cage with rats placed over his face and so surrenders totally, Muggeridge and I concurred in observing that the scene reminded us of small boys in a boarding-school dormitory talking boastfully about various forms of torture. In the end one boy says: 'I'll tell you what's the worst thing. You're all tied up and a cage full of stinking rats is put over your face. First one rat bites your eye. Then another bites your lips. Then another starts eating your nose.' At this point the dormitory prefect calls out, 'Silence, all of you! Lights out!' End of the torture conversation.

We heard from Orwell that, listening in bed, he had laughed out loud. A crumb of solace, anyway.

Not long after, Fred Warburg told me that he was again visiting Cranham as Orwell was very worried because in America *Nineteen Eighty-Four* was being billed in Right-wing circles as an all-out attack on socialism, which had never been his intention. As I remember it, my comment was more or less that one could easily see how such a misunderstanding could arise – I also had pondered about the name 'Ingsoc' Orwell gave to his future society. But of course *Nineteen Eighty-Four* was *not* a savage attack on socialism; it was a warning about a possible type of state tyranny which called itself socialist. In 'Writers and Leviathan', Orwell had written that it was a weakness of the Left to suppose that with the overthrow of capitalism, something like democratic socialism would inevitably take its place. There was no such inevitability: with the abolition of capitalism, who knew what régime might follow? *Nineteen Eighty-Four* was an allegorical warning against the worst possible consequence. Taking political questions calmly as was my wont (except about the European Jews) I said that Orwell need not worry; his novel was far too good to be made merely an object of extreme Right-wing propaganda; such publicity would soon die down and the book would find its place in modern thought on its merits.

It occurred to me afterwards that Orwell might not have time to wait for this. On his return from the Cotswolds, Warburg did indeed issue a press statement protesting against the depiction of *Nineteen Eighty-Four* not as a warning but as an attack on socialism. He said that he had put out the statement at Orwell's special request, but I think he was quite pleased to take charge of the matter. He was always a publisher who relished intellectual battles.

He also said that arrangements had now been made for Orwell to place himself in Dr Morland's charge. It seemed to me high time. In August we had at the last moment to cancel

another trip to Cranham to see him. He wrote to me
(11.8.1949) rather ominously:

> 'I was very sorry indeed to put you all off last Sat., and I hope
> I did not throw your arrangements out too much by doing so.
> I had what they call a "flare-up", meaning a sudden burst of
> high temperature, etc. It doesn't usually last very long but it
> is very unpleasant and of course I am barely human while it
> is happening.'

At the end of September 1949 Orwell was brought to the
private wing at University College Hospital in London, under
Dr Morland. In the first days of October I received my last
letter from him. He asked me to thank my wife for her gift of tea
and some crystallized fruit; little enough! A few days later I saw
him at UCH and noted that his illness had made frightening
progress. He was not only thinner but more motionless as he lay
stretched out in bed. For the first time I really took it in that he
might die soon. The knowledge hovered like a dark shadow in
my mind as I now visited him fairly regularly during the next
three months until the end.

At the same time, as one does on such occasions, I tried to
keep the thought from the front of my mind and to converse
normally; one always hoped that he might as on previous
occasions recover, have some period of active remission. In
this spirit his friends registered acceptance of his strange
marriage to the beautiful Sonia Brownell who was such a vital
figure in the London literary élite. The marriage ceremony in
late October took place in his hospital room, as arranged by
David Astor. Orwell's motives were perhaps obvious: he was in
love with Sonia and had the dream, as he told friends, that
marriage could prolong his life by giving him something more
to live for. My wife and I were fond of Sonia, we liked her
intellectual wit and infectious laughter; she had become quite a
close family friend; but we did not question her about the
marriage – we felt we could not.

At any rate, to the general satisfaction Sonia now took over
Orwell's affairs. With death presumably imminent in his mind,
he made a new will and a literary testament. Sonia told me that
in the latter he wanted nearly all his early work suppressed or at

least never reprinted. She had argued with him against this. He was not the only famous author to want to expunge his literary life and I told her to go on arguing. She said that Warburg and other friends had given the same advice.

Concerning his desire to have his early creation expunged, I feel that two points must be made plain. Contrary to what has sometimes been implied, there was in the end no self-pity in his make-up. Apart from a brief word to my wife that after a slight haemorrhage the previous night he had thought he was 'a goner' (a word he liked), I heard him make no references to death. To the end he kept his discipline; he kept up his lively interest in current politics, newspapers, literature, life in general. He was stoical. Visits to his hospital bed might be melancholy; they were never depressing.

Secondly, although it turned out that way, *Nineteen Eighty-Four* was not meant by him to be his own personal literary farewell. On the contrary, his mind remained stocked with projects on which he had wanted to work up to the moment his strength gave out. As he said to someone: 'Can one die if one has an unwritten book in one's mind?'

The most ambitious unwritten project was one he had carried in his mind for years of a three-volume novel, unpolitical and dealing with personal relationships. (I later learned from his notes that a possible title for it had been 'The Lion and the Unicorn'.) In his hospital room at UCH he also talked of his longstanding interest in that isolated band of rebels, the nineteenth-century anarchists. He wanted to read Alexander Herzen again. He had also long intended to write an essay on Joseph Conrad, whom he admired for having brought a European dimension into the provincialism of English literature. Also, Conrad had shown that men were always solitary and that political life offered no moral guidance. He thought him *en rapport* with his age in posing the choice for society of autocracy or anarchy.

But I think that most of all he regretted not writing a long essay on Evelyn Waugh for which he had been making notes before he had to abandon his work. I recall him as saying something like: 'The point about Evelyn Waugh is that he disproves the Marxist theory that a worthwhile writer has to be

in tune with the basic political and economic trends of his age.'
Waugh wrote about an imagined English landed aristocracy
which in the real world had long abdicated from true social
leadership. Even so, said Orwell, for all that they held opposed
political viewpoints, Waugh was the best English writer of his
generation.

Of course, Orwell went on, Waugh had moved step by step
from satirizing his landed aristocracy towards identifying
himself with them, as he finally did with such fatal results in
Brideshead Revisited: here he had truly exposed his soft centre.
The thought brought Orwell to a favourite comment I had
heard him make before, that the turmoil of modern life gave a
writer only fifteen years of true creativity: after this he could
only repeat himself less well. He thought Evelyn Waugh had
reached this stage (there he was wrong – the war trilogy was
still to come) and he himself, quite apart from his illness, had
probably done so.

I think it a great pity that this essay on Evelyn Waugh was
never written. Since they were contemporaries and from much
the same social class, it might have been as interesting a social
and philosophical comment on English life and class structure
as the essays on Dickens and Kipling. Waugh had actually
visited Orwell at the Cranham sanatorium where they talked
and apparently liked each other. Malcolm Muggeridge,
another exact contemporary, has written with telling irony that
he would have loved to see the two of them together:
'Complementary figures ... [Waugh's] country gentleman's
outfit and Orwell's proletarian one and both straight out of the
pages of *Punch*.'[2] A nice picture, and one gets the point; yet the
two eccentric dressed-up exteriors also covered the solitude and
displacement of two true writers.

Among other plans for the future Orwell talked about was
the education of his boy Richard. Reminiscing, he told me
(what he had told me before) how he had met his schoolfellow
John Strachey who had once been as near as dammit a
Communist and was now a pretty moderate Labour Cabinet
Minister under Attlee; Strachey had said he was sending his
son to Eton because after all it offered the best education.
Orwell remarked that he disagreed and was totally against

boarding schools. There were state schools, of course, but as a compromise he had put down Richard as a day-boy at Westminster. But that was still eight years away and he hoped that by that time public schools might be abolished – plans for a non-existent future. (In fact, Richard, in Avril's charge, went to a local school in Scotland.)

The New Year came and the half-century, while Orwell lay helpless in his hospital bed and his tuberculosis weighed him down without respite. In early January 1950 he startled me with the news that plans had been made for him and Sonia to go by air to a sanatorium high up in the Swiss Alps. A spell of thin mountain air, putting less pressure on the lungs, was then still thought a suitable treatment for TB sufferers. After giving me the surprising news, he went on to wonder (I later learned that he did so with several visitors) whether the Swiss sanatorium would be able to provide him with the strong, dark brew of Indian tea he liked. He thought that the clear Alpine water might be unsuitable.

Shades of the Magic Mountain! I remember how at some point in this conversation I experienced that clarified feeling of cold reality breaking in upon deliberate illusion as, with oneself in health, one talks to a friend who may be near death. Knowing Switzerland well, I suddenly felt certain that Orwell could not make it; he was no longer in any physical state to endure the journey by air and then by car along the winding snow-covered roads high into the Alps. With his emaciated face he seemed as one looked at him a Ghandi-like figure. His body was by now so skeletal that it was hard to find any flesh on his thigh for his regular injections. The idea that he could undertake such a complicated Swiss journey with Sonia suddenly seemed a fantasy.

Still, perhaps I was wrong, I thought, perhaps there was some hope. Dr Morland had suggested that, considering how acutely Orwell had abused his TB-racked body on Jura, he had since then shown a modicum of resistance. I tried to tell myself that perhaps he could still enjoy some remission. And so I came to my final visit, in which chance made me the last of his friends to talk to him. I can just remember that it was a nice and easy conversation in which we recalled our early schooldays and I said, yes, I might visit him in his Alpine sanatorium. The next morning, on 22 January 1950, I heard that during the night after a final haemorrhage he had died quickly.

Being both a complete agnostic and deeply attached to English tradition, Orwell had in his will asked for a Church of England funeral service and burial. As he was a member of no church this posed some difficulties. The funeral service was arranged by Malcolm Muggeridge and took place at Christ Church halfway up Albany Street, London NW1. In a cold church on a wintry London morning, in a somewhat sparse gathering, I found myself looking at some familiar faces and a few unfamiliar ones. The interment, which was arranged by David Astor, was to be in the rural churchyard of All Saints Church in Sutton Courtenay in Berkshire. The headstone was to bear the simple legend Eric Arthur Blair, 1904–1950.

After the funeral service, my wife and I went to lunch with Malcolm and Kitty Muggeridge, whose Regent's Park apartment we were to take over. Muggeridge, as his published diary has recorded, mused on the strange fact that the majority of participants in Orwell's Church of England funeral service had been Jews and unbelievers.

Afterwards, Sonia came to stay with us for a week in the country and for another week with Arthur and Mamaine Koestler in north Wales, and then went on to pursue her wayward further life. My wife and I always remained fond of her and in 1980 I visited her during her last months in hospital as I had visited Orwell thirty years earlier.

As for myself, with Orwell's death in January 1950 a decade of my life came to an end which had been very different from anything that came before – or anything that came after.

PART THREE

Appreciation

SIXTEEN

Orwell in his Century

I REMEMBER not long ago exchanging memories of Orwell with Julian Symons and my saying that one could watch a picture being built up of Orwell as a completely eccentric, slightly saintly and slightly absurd, major prophet; and that in this portrait it was hard to recognize the very different and much more ordinary figure of the Orwell we had known. Eccentric? That he certainly was, as in his ragged way of dressing, but in knowing him over the years one could simply take such eccentricities for granted: he was just a friend who was also a particularly good writer. As a – then – young woman of his acquaintance recalled, even if he only rarely talked intimately, he was always easy to talk to, he listened, he was interested in you, he never tried to overawe you, he was always courteous.

As for his being a prophet, to be sure as a conversationalist he could be opinionated. Julian Symons has written that he was unperceptive in not trimming his views to his audience: 'He might identify nationalism with Fascism in the presence of an Irish nationalist, or talk about the corrupting nature of Jewish violence in front of an enthusiastic Zionist.'[1] But as a prophet he could also be wrong, not only in assertions such as that which stuck in Muggeridge's mind that all tobacconists were Fascists, but wrong in some of his major statements.

He predicted, for instance, that the ever-growing power of the state would make any action against it by the individual impossible. Well, we have on the contrary witnessed the striking vulnerability of some modern states to action by determined small groups of urban guerrillas. Even in Moscow small groups of dissidents have achieved surprising publicity, for a time at least. Orwell also said that the novel as an individual art form could not survive under Communism. The notion has been disproved by the impressive 'dissident' novels of Pasternak, Solzhenitsyn and Sinyavsky. Orwell would also have been surprised by the powerful expression of individual feelings in Soviet autobiographies like those of Nadezhda Mandelstam and Eugenia Ginzburg, which make their Western counterparts look pallid. Had he lived on, he would no doubt have revised his ideas about writers under the Soviet régime – as a critic he could be flexible as well as inflexible.

And yet, he *was* a prophet whose work posthumously became part of the literary folklore of the late twentieth century and in this process his position became transformed. In the essays he wrote during his lifetime, he addressed the small groups of intellectual readers of small-scale magazines like *Horizon* and *Polemic*. Since his death, he has become a writer with an impact upon the imagination of the mass reader and there has been no halting this transformation. *Animal Farm* and *Nineteen Eighty-Four* have sold internationally in millions of copies. Their slogans, continually quoted, have become a regular part of the modern political idiom. In the quick way the young catch on today, the two satires have become required reading in schools. Bright fourteen-year-olds avidly read *Nineteen Eighty-Four* as a set book for their examinations; younger children read *Animal Farm*.

The impact of Orwell's thought has also transcended frontiers. One notes how some situations under Communism have been variously described as 'Orwellian' by Soviet writers like Solzhenitsyn. East European intellectuals, indeed, have often expressed surprise that Orwell, who had never visited a Communist country, should so faithfully have understood the essence of life under Communism. As for the US, as just one among countless examples, an American professor told me that at the start of her course in political science, she regularly asked her students as their first task to read, and to comment on, Orwell's essay, 'Politics and the English Language'. I have recently been told how in many West German schools, Orwell's essays feature prominently in studies of modern English writers.

And so on. A point to note is that Orwell's impact has seemed to grow regardless of criticisms levelled against his work, and this goes for some leading Marxist critics. For instance, in the essay he called '*Nineteen Eighty-Four*: The Mysticism of Cruelty',[2] Isaac Deutscher, that eminent biographer of Trotsky and one-time guide of the New Left, tried in 1954 to put Orwell in his place as a talented but politically naive outsider. It was unfortunate, he wrote, that poor Orwell encountered Communism at such a bad moment in 1937, the time of Stalin's Moscow treason trials and of the Communist propaganda lies about the POUM in Spain. Not being a systematic political thinker, Orwell let the picture of Communism in his mind become stuck in this particular moment. He did not realize, as he, Deutscher, as a trained Marxist historian did, that beyond Stalin's dictatorship, the Soviet system was bound to develop either towards Bonapartist adventurism, or more likely towards great liberalization.

Neither of these developments has of course taken place within the rigid Soviet Union. Looked at today, Deutscher's essay reads already like the tired and dated political journalism of the fifties. By contrast, Orwell's reflection of that ominous moment of world history in 1937, which he caught in *Homage to Catalonia* and *Nineteen Eighty-Four*, remains as grave a warning as ever. Somehow, the impetus of Orwell's writing has effortlessly survived this and similar Marxist critiques.

Attempts to explain this impetus and pin Orwell down in a phrase have proved tempting. He has been described by one notable critic as a writer who went native in his own country. This is only partly true. He did seek to fashion some sort of native English proletarian life-style for himself and he did rough it with English tramps. But he roughed it only for a brief while and then largely in search of material. If with Eileen he tried to run the Wallington village shop, this was only a sort of game; and, as for roughing it on his trip to Wigan Pier, as John Beavan has pointed out,[3] Orwell did not during his journey ever try to penetrate into the warm and close family lives of the true English natives – the average employed, respectable, comfortable English working-class majority. Nor did Orwell ever 'go native' in the sense of settling to live with, say, Welsh hill farmers or Nottinghamshire miners or with a working-class woman. On the contrary, more than half the later acquaintances with whom he rubbed along were fellow-Etonians or Jewish intellectuals, while the women he liked were pretty classy: not much going native there.

He has been described as 'the wintry conscience of his generation'. Again, yes and no. His exact contemporaries – Greene, Powell, Muggeridge, Waugh, Koestler – were fully able to make up their own consciences, as were 'Auden & Co.', who followed three or four years later. Orwell's major appeal has on the contrary been to the conscience of the generation that has grown up since his death and quite remarkably so on all sides of the political spectrum. Neil Kinnock, an outstanding younger leading figure in the British Labour Party, has told me that during his youth in Wales, his literary and political heroes were Aneurin Bevan and George Orwell. He told me: 'For some reason I read *Nineteen Eighty-Four* first and couldn't get it out of my mind. Then I read *Homage to Catalonia* and was enthralled. But when I read the last chapter of *The Road to Wigan Pier* in (I think) the summer of 1956 when I was fourteen, my instincts at last had words and I knew not only that I was a socialist but why I was a socialist.'

Were I personally to venture a one-sentence judgement, I would say that more than any writer I can think of, Orwell by sheer concentration and drive transcended the limitations which he partly inherited but also partly created. I remember him as determinedly leading his would-be proletarian existence, keeping a blinkered gaze firmly fixed on popular mass culture and on major contemporary issues of political morality – and on little else. It seems to me that in this way he excluded large areas of the artistic and aesthetic imagination from his life. True, as he had shown in *Inside the Whale*, he had as a younger man keenly followed the twists and experiments in the course of the modern movement in literature; to the end he read and wrote about Joyce, Eliot and Pound. Yet, looking back, I feel that he was not interested in being part of the aesthetic avant-garde of his time. More than that, he could appear – I say 'appear' – uninterested in the arts. There is in his collected letters and diaries no mention of going to a picture gallery or to a concert. From his two years in Paris, if he did appreciate the visual achievements of the *Ecole de Paris*, he brought back no testimony. He spent months in Catalonia, but makes no mention of Picasso; he was concerned with Mussolini's Italy but not that of the Renaissance. In part, his turning away from what would today be called the élitist arts was by inclination, in part a deliberate act. When he stated[4] that he would far rather have written music-hall ditties like 'Come Where the Booze is Cheapest' or 'Two Lovely Black Eyes' than 'The Blessed Damozel' or 'Love in a Valley', there is no reason to doubt his earnestness (although I do think he would have liked to have written 'Prufrock'). All in all, the way he excluded such a large slice of the aesthetic imagination from his critical outlook made for a narrowness which as a writer he had to struggle hard to overcome.

While as a journalist and novelist he had considerable gifts of description, he was also handicapped by gaps in his imaginative powers. Apart from satire, he found it hard as a novelist to draw rounded characters (unless, of course, they were those of animals). He found it particularly hard to draw the characters of women and to see his heroines as independent human beings, not just social influences impinging on an Orwellian anti-hero. Since he liked to write love scenes, this was a major shortcoming which he also had to fight against.

There was another limitation he had to transcend. As I saw him, Orwell set himself to write of the limitless immorality of totalitarianism without having any close knowledge of, or even as it could seem a special interest in, Hitler and Hitlerism and Nazi Germany – the supreme revolutionary force for evil active in his lifetime.

This is a fairly large statement to make, but I think it is borne out by the facts. The one journalistic piece Orwell wrote about Hitler, comparing his face to that of a tortured Christ, is pretty silly. His one serious reference to Nazism, which he there overrated, was in his essay on H.G. Wells. There is almost no mention in his writings of Goebbels, Goering and the other larger-than-life Nazi leaders. I think he knew little of Sauckel's empire of millions of expendable slave labourers, at least in precise detail. There is no mention in the index of Orwell's collected writings of Auschwitz, that hell on earth; indeed, very few references at all to the Nazi concentration camps. As I have mentioned earlier, Orwell even seemed reluctant to use the word 'Nazi' as opposed to the neutral term of 'Fascist' Germany.

Now, one can argue that since all the wartime propagandists around him, some of whom had earlier been benign towards Hitler, were prattling about the wickedness of Nazism, he may have felt that he could leave the topic to them. This was probably the case, but I think there was more to his avoidance of writing about the Nazi atrocities than that. I had felt that I broadly agreed with him about the atrocities committed in Stalin's Soviet Union, even if he was more closely involved with them than I was. But preoccupied as I had been before, during and after the war with the career of Hitler and the Jewish tragedy of the holocaust, I was aware that the world I looked upon was not precisely that which Orwell saw.

Which brings me with my background inevitably to the Jewish question. Here I knew that Orwell and I differed diametrically in our respective attitudes towards the Palestine Jews and their violent opposition towards that unfortunate British Foreign Secretary, Ernest Bevin. As a convinced anti-Zionist, Orwell was disturbed by my unequivocal support at the time for the creation of the State of Israel. Looking back, I would readily concede that in regarding the Palestine conflict as one between right and right, as my friend Richard Crossman described it, I disregarded the susceptibilities of the Palestine Arabs. On the other hand, I considered Orwell's assumption that the shattered Jewish survivors of the holocaust should simply resume their lives in Central Europe as pretty fair insensitivity.

But our differences over Jewish issues went beyond Palestine and Israel. In a letter Orwell wrote to Julian Symons from Jura[5] he said: 'I have no doubt that Fyvel thinks that *I* am antisemitic.' Well no, I never would have said that. Orwell's friend Malcolm Muggeridge, however, did. In his reflections on Orwell's funeral service, he wrote: 'Interesting, I thought, that George should so have attracted Jews because he was at heart strongly anti-Semitic.'[6]

Put baldly like that, I would not agree with such a statement. Orwell's attitudes towards 'the Jewish issue' were much more ambivalent. Not of course his attitudes towards individual Jews. In becoming the writer he did, he was inevitably drawn into Jewish contacts. Many of his later acquaintances were at least ethnically Jewish, like Arthur Koestler, Fred Warburg, Jon Kimche, Evelyn Anderson on *Tribune*, myself (even Julian Symons was half-Jewish). The majority of Orwell's early American supporters were also Jewish. It was unthinkable that he should ever have been openly anti-Semitic. But his ideological views concerning the assimilation into British culture of a strong Jewish ethnic minority were a different matter.

He tried his hand at some personal study of war and post-war anti-Semitism in Britain, about which he wrote a few short articles. His conclusions were, first, an admission of surprise at the vehemence of some of the anti-Jewish sentiments he encountered. Secondly, he decided that whatever arguments the anti-Semites tried to marshal to justify their opposition towards Jews, their feelings were basically irrational. Thirdly, however, he concluded that such widespread dislike of Jews had to have a cause; all such popular feelings had causes. He came to this conclusion uneasily, since he rather liked to identify himself with popular feeling and here he could not do so. He did not really get far with his researches into anti-Semitism. Since he knew little of Jewish history (but who except Jews does?) and had no feel for it, European anti-Semitism was much too large, too old, too historic, too complex a problem for his type of amateur social research. But just occasionally, the ideas of his early upbringing, in which he said that Jews featured only as objects of scorn, did come out.

The only time I can remember having a real argument with him was over an article entitled 'Revenge is Sour' which he published in *Tribune* of 9 November 1945. In this he described how shortly after fighting ended, he was shown round a prisoner-of-war camp in south Germany by a young Viennese Jewish officer in a US captain's uniform whom he tried hard to like but clearly could not. He related how he watched this Jewish officer shout at, and kick, a captured ss-officer who, one-time torturer though he probably had been, now looked to Orwell only a pitiful being in need of psychological treatment.

Orwell observed quite shrewdly how he thought that the
Jewish officer was exerting his new power over his personal
enemy not because he enjoyed it, but because he *felt* he ought to
enjoy it; and he then went on in a brief aside:

> 'It is absurd to blame any German or Austrian Jew for
> getting his own back on the Nazis. Heaven knows what
> scores this particular man may have had to wipe out; very
> likely his whole family had been murdered; and after all,
> even a wanton kick to a prisoner is a very tiny thing
> compared to the outrages of the Hitler régime.[7]

That was all he wrote of the background, which I thought
quite out of proportion. I said to Orwell that here in Hitler's
so-called 'Final Solution of the Jewish Question' one had the
greatest deliberate crime committed in man's history, yet all
Orwell did was to mention it in one brief and dismissive
sentence in a lengthy article telling how one Jewish officer
kicked one ss-man, an action Orwell referred to as 'getting his
own back'. This was surely standing history on its head. How
conceivably could the relatives of the six million murdered Jews
'get their own back' on the Nazis? Moreover, what was
Orwell's point in referring to this particular man throughout
the article simply as 'the Jew' – 'the Jew' did this, 'the Jew' did
that, or worse, 'the little Jew' did the other? Did this naming not
imply that the man was not a Viennese, as he had been born,
nor the American officer he had now become, but simply 'the
Jew' and so an alien.[2]

My outburst ran something on these lines and I can
remember that Orwell's reaction was one of sheer astonish-
ment: he obviously thought that I was hypersensitive and
overreacting. I don't believe that I had any effect on his views
on the responsibilities for the Nazi crimes – in the same article
he wanted Britain to protest against the Soviet expulsion of
Germans from East Prussia as a crime – but I think he took my
point about language. He never again referred to anyone
simply as 'the Jew'.

The argument after which Orwell wrote that I thought him
anti-Semitic, which I did not, was a different one. It concerned
what I considered the pretty hostile anti-Jewish references in

T.S. Eliot's early verse of the twenties. Orwell maintained that Eliot's observations were not directly anti-Semitic, and legitimate barbs for their time. He was of course not the only one to hold this view. At any rate, what he said was that yes, Eliot's verses could be regarded as a cultural attack on certain Jews, but one had to distinguish between what was said before Hitler came to power and what was said after, that is, before or after 1934 (he got the date a bit wrong). In the twenties, anti-Jewish references were not out of order. They were only on a par with the automatic sneers people cast at Anglo-Indian colonels in boarding houses.

My answer was that the cases were not at all on a par and that to draw an arbitrary dividing line between anti-Semitism permitted and not permitted in the year 1934 was to take a very parochial English view of the matter. I described how already in the Russian civil war, the 'Whites' had engaged in wholesale massacres of Jews as responsible for the downfall of Russia; and how in the German Weimar Republic of the twenties, the enemies of that Republic were manically proclaiming that the Jews were to blame for Germany's defeat in 1918, for the inflation, for everything, and so leading European history into its disastrous phase of war and slaughter. I said that in singling out Jews as enemies of his imagined European culture, Eliot, great poet though he might be, had been politically naive and placed himself in the wrong camp.

I said also that as for Eliot's famous ironical definition of the cultural enemy as 'Chicago Semite Viennese', if he thought that Viennese Jews had emigrated in numbers to Chicago, he was off the mark; but that in pre-1914 Vienna there *had* been a genuine problem of Jewish identity. Sigmund Freud as psychologist, or Gustav Mahler as musician, Artur Schnitzler as dramatist, Theodor Herzl as a Zionist journalist – they and other Jews, collectively creators of culture on a considerable scale, all faced the same problem of having to do so within a Viennese society where anti-Semitic pressure against them was overt and popularly sanctioned.

I went on that it could be said on Eliot's behalf that he clearly had little knowledge of these problems of identity for Jewish writers and artists in the Vienna of the *belle époque*. Even as I said this, however, I remember noticing from Orwell's reaction that he himself also had no idea whatever of the intellectual Jewish problems in pre-1914 Vienna. By 1946, it was for me still the world of my father's youth, but for him an unreal world with which he had no concern.

I discovered later that some time after our argument, both in a letter and in an article, he repeated his view that after 1934, literary anti-Semitism would have been wrong, but before that date it was no more than the sneers cast at Anglo-Indian colonels. He always liked retaining his thoughts in the identical words.

So we each stuck to our view. A few years later, when I remarked to Arthur Koestler that I could always agree with Orwell about the injustice of British rule in India and the injustices under Stalin's Communism, but that when I talked about the Jewish fate in Europe I found him curiously distant, Koestler made what I thought was an apt remark. 'Probably Orwell's imagination was limited,' he said, 'as the imagination of each of us is limited. We can all produce only a limited amount of calories of indignation.'

That was really the point. As a friend, one took Orwell as he was; and, as if to show that he knew more about such things than one might think, he did call his last rebel in *Nineteen Eighty-Four* Emmanuel Goldstein and modelled him on Trotsky. As a friend, too, one knew that he had more than sufficient calories of indignation to make him the great writer he was.

SEVENTEEN

Impressions on Re-reading Orwell (1)

YEARS AGO, I think, I had read everything that Orwell had written – he is eminently the sort of writer with whose work one can do that. On re-reading this work recently, the novels, journalism, letters and all, I had a striking sense of familiarity: I realized that not only the gist of what he wrote but some of the very words and phrases had remained in my memory. Both subject matter and style were Orwell himself; any page of his was instantly recognizable; he wrote like nobody else. Some critics have defined this distinctive manner of writing as a chain of firmly laid down propositions, as a pared-down, puritan style, but I think that his individualism goes even further.

Ever since I read 'Such, Such Were the Joys', in reading Orwell I have had in my mind the image of Orwell as a small boy at St Cyprian's, rejecting Mrs Vaughan Wilkes's orthodoxies and advances and instead setting down his experience and opinions in his own inner voice. That inner voice was a very special one, resolutely defining his status and position in life, and so was already the voice of the adult writer into which it was to develop.

Reading Orwell, I often seemed to hear him speaking in his rather high-pitched voice. For instance, I remembered how on visits to *Tribune*, he would, on entering, at once break into some major topic of conversation, political or stylistic. Similarly with the openings of his novels and reminiscent essays. In his constant task of self-definition, he had at once to fix the place, the time, the condition and state of mind of his Orwellian hero before plunging into the work.

Perhaps almost obsessionally, he had to fix the time; I had to smile a little as I looked upon this trait. His first novel, *A Clergyman's Daughter*, begins: 'As the alarm bell on the chest of drawers exploded like a horrid little bomb of bell metal, Dorothy, wrenched from the depths of some complex, troubling dream . . .' In the novel, *Burmese Days*, we start with the magistrate, U Po Kyin, sitting on his verandah: 'It was only half past eight, but the month was April and there was a closeness in the air.' Then there is the start of *Keep the Aspidistra Flying*: 'The clock struck half past two. In the little office at the back of Mr McKechnie's bookshop, Gordon – Gordon Comstock, last member of the Comstock family' and, as we know, twenty-nine and rather moth-eaten already, 'lounged across the table'. In *Coming Up For Air*, the time fixed in the opening sentence concerns only the day – 'The idea really came to me the day I got my new false teeth' – but all readers of *Nineteen Eighty-Four* know how at the opening the clocks are striking thirteen as Winston Smith enters Victory Mansions. Always clocks and the time!

As with the openings of the books, so with their endings. They are each so definite that one feels the whole book was written to lead up to them. In *Burmese Days*, we learn that Elizabeth, the very ordinary English middle-class girl who has jilted poor solitary Flory and so caused his death, marries and becomes 'what nature has designed her from the first, a burra memsahib'. In *Keep the Aspidistra Flying* we end with Gordon Comstock, reformed, employed and married, about to become a father: 'Once again things were happening in the Comstock family.' From the start Orwell must have determined to reprieve him. But in *Nineteen Eighty-Four*, at the end poor Winston Smith, defeated and doomed, can only weep as he loves Big Brother. One feels that the novel led inexorably to this climax from the start.

I believe that one reason why Orwell's early novels, with all their flaws, appear still so readable to the young, lies in the determination with which, from start to finish, he portrays the defiant Orwellian hero – Orwell, lonely against the world! His early patroness, Mrs Mabel Fierz, told me that while she regarded the early novels at the time as the immature works of a young writer, she also felt the novels had a savage intensity

about them, which may be why they have endured. Another
reason may be the vivid descriptive passages which here and
there each novel includes. A few critics have tried to dismiss his
style as that of a journalist (say, as compared to that of his
friend and fellow-Etonian, Anthony Powell), but this is quite
wrong. Orwell's style is only *deceptively* simple; avoiding all
clichés, he weighed every word. If the result could sometimes
seem logical and bare, he did occasionally let himself go in
gentle descriptive passages, as for instance when he tried to link
his love for nature with his feelings for women. There are such
passages in *Burmese Days*, describing how the hero, Flory, has
taken his beloved and conventional Elizabeth out shooting in
the jungle and has shot and killed a leopard. The beaters
squatting round the dead leopard stroke his beautiful, soft
white belly. Orwell writes:

> 'Presently two of the beaters cut down a tall bamboo and
> slung the leopard upon it by his paws, with his long tail
> trailing down, and they marched back to the village in
> triumph.
>
> Flory and Elizabeth walked side by side across the stubble
> field . . . The sun was going down beyond the Irrawaddi. The
> light shone level across the field, gilding the stubble stalks
> and striking into their faces with a yellow, gentle beam.
> Elizabeth's shoulder was almost touching Flory's as they
> walked. The sweat that had drenched their shirts had dried
> again. They did not talk much. They were happy with that
> inordinate happiness that comes of exhaustion and achieve-
> ment, and with which nothing else in life – no joy of either the
> body or the mind – is even able to be compared.[1]

The evening sunshine, the beloved girl at his side – this
young man' vision of happiness was followed in his next novel,
Keep the Aspidistra Flying, by another such expedition in which
Orwell lets his anti-hero, Gordon Comstock, wander with his
girl Rosemary through the empty Thames Valley countryside,
where the leaves are turning to 'fairy gold'. It is Gordon's intent
to make love to Rosemary in the open, but he finally fails to do
so, feeling inhibited by having only sixpence in his pocket.
(Orwell told me that after publication he had several letters

from young men reporting a similar predicament.) But later, in *Nineteen Eighty-Four*, he made the experience positive again. He has Winston Smith make love for the first time to his girl Julia in a rural setting outside the detested London of 1984, under the dappled light and shade of trees, with bluebells thick on the ground and ring doves droning overhead ... That Orwell on Jura, now in his forties and writing his nightmare novel, should have clung to his youthful vision of combined love for nature and for women is, I think, rather touching. It shows what a fuller writer he might in slightly different circumstances have become.

Re-reading Orwell, I found other instances suggesting this same point. Trying to elucidate why *The Road to Wigan Pier*, Orwell's study of industrial blight in 1936, should still be so moving and readable today, some critics have delved into the contacts and background of his journey across the industrial north of England. They have found that his experiences, conversation and even his diary notes were in reality sometimes not quite the same as represented in the book. However, to stress this is surely to discover the obvious. To explain the difference between background and book one need cite only the following passage, where Orwell, travelling by train from Wigan through a 'monstrous landscape' of slag-heaps and grey slum houses, saw a young woman kneeling behind a house, poking a stick up a blocked waste pipe. He wrote in a celebrated passage:

'I had time to see everything about her – her sacking apron, her clumsy clogs, her arms reddened by the cold. She looked up as the train passed and I was almost near enough to catch her eyes. She had a round, pale face, the usual exhausted face of the slum girl who is twenty-five and looks forty, thanks to miscarriages and drudgery; and it wore, for the second in which I saw it, the most desolate, hopeless expression I have ever seen.

'It struck me then that we are mistaken when we say that "It isn't the same for them as it would be for us", and that people bred in the slums can imagine nothing but the slums. For what I saw in her face was not the ignorant suffering of the animal. She knew well enough what was happening to her – understood as well as I did how dreadful a destiny it was to be kneeling there in the bitter cold, on the slimy stones of a slum backyard, poking a stick up a foul drainpipe.'[2]

Orwell's diary notes show that he in fact saw the young woman in a back alley, not from the train; but whatever the circumstances, this is of course pure novelist's technique: from one glimpse of a young woman, Orwell builds up an entire character, an entire life. I think the reason why *The Road to Wigan Pier* has remained read from the depression of the thirties to that of the eighties is that to his factual accounts of unemployment and slum life, Orwell has added pages which are those of a powerful novelist writing in his best descriptive form.

A powerful novelist. Reading through Orwell's earlier works, I felt ever conscious of the narrowness, the social and emotional limitations he had to struggle to transcend and did transcend: if he had not had to start life with such deep-rooted guilt feelings, if he had not at St Cyprian's come to regard himself as a relentless outsider, if only his health had been more robust, if Eileen had not died untimely and if he had not lived in an era of wars, dictatorship and atom bombs which he felt he had to reflect in his writing, I think he might well have excelled as a very different kind of writer, certainly as a humorous writer or a descriptive writer. The three-volume 'unpolitical' novel he still had in his mind at the time of his death might well have become his own *Buddenbrooks*.

I was reinforced in this view of him in looking at his journalism, in which he at the end became so very assured and fluent. I found myself particularly impressed by the special, slightly longer pieces he wrote for me on *Tribune* in 1945–6.[3] This was after Eileen's death, when he was emotionally at a very low ebb, but this fact did not show itself in the light touch of these delightful articles – how well I remembered them! There was 'Some Thoughts on the Common Toad', which in his awakening in the spring, Orwell said, had 'about the most beautiful eyes of any living creature'. There was 'The Sporting Spirit', where he pointed to the absurdity of believing, as was increasingly the case, that 'running, jumping and kicking a ball are tests of national virtue'. Then finally there was 'Riding Down From Bangor', in which, as I said earlier, he nostalgically tried to define the reasons why mid-nineteenth-century American capitalist civilization, as reflected in its popular literature, seemed so spacious, optimistic and buoyant. Since most journalism dates almost overnight, I thought it remarkable that these little articles still read so well, but then they were not *ordinary* journalism.

More important in Orwell's work, of course, were the longer essays. Reading them, I noted again how little they seemed to have dated, even an essay like 'Politics and the English Language' where Orwell took his examples of appalling political language from the journalism of the forties. He had an anticipatory ear for jargon; his irony is as telling as ever and one can see why the essay has remained a school and university set-piece. Most of the important essays seem to have withstood the erosion of time; partly, I think, because they are all written in that pared-down style without nuances in which the full meaning appears immediately. Arthur Koestler had a good comment about them. The essays, he said, 'were like beacons, throwing a steady light on their time'. Reading them, I sometimes seemed to hear Orwell's actual dry voice and chuckle, since he regularly tried out the same themes in conversation as in his writings.

In his views he was also remarkably retentive. Experience seemed seared into his memory, reduced to essentials. For instance, his essay 'How the Poor Die', describing his stay while very ill in the Hôpital Cochin in Paris in 1929, was not written until seventeen years later, in 1946; but he remembered in detail not only the gruesome deaths of wretched patients in his ward, but also his own conclusion: 'It's better to die violently and not too old. People talk about the horrors of war, but what weapon has man invented that even approaches in cruelty some of the common diseases?'[4]

One cannot help but notice how much the essays are exercises in self-definition. Particularly when he wrote about well-known literary personages, about Swift, Dickens, Kipling or Koestler, one can see Orwell seeking to define their standpoints in order to outline his own. In the case of Swift, *Gulliver's Travels* had of course been his favourite reading as a small boy, and as the author of *Animal Farm* he must have been aware of some parallels. Thus it was not surprising that in his Swiftian essay, 'Politics *vs* Literature',[5] written in 1946, he found Swift a political rebel who was driven towards a Tory anarchism by the follies of the progressive party of his day – not unlike himself? He also thought Swift to be far-sighted. In Book III of *Gulliver's Travels*, about the mad scientists, he saw Swift as exposing 'what would now be called totalitarianism in his portrait of a spy-haunted police state with endless heresy hunts and treason trials'. As for the society of the Houyhnhnms, the horses Swift thought so laudable, Orwell saw this society as built on a basis of 'we know everything already, so why should dissident opinions be tolerated?' It followed that this equine society, where there could be no freedom and no development, was in essence totalitarian. In his conclusion, he saw Swift as possessing 'a terrible intensity of vision, capable of picking out a single hidden truth and then magnifying it and distorting it'. Again, there is an element of self-definition here.

One of Orwell's earliest essays was his long, enjoyable study, 'Charles Dickens'.[6] As Mabel Fierz confirmed to me, already as her young literary protégé Orwell had revealed himself as an enthusiastic Dickensian, knowing the books, the characters, the dialogue almost by heart. He need therefore not be taken too seriously as he first built up the case against Dickens: that as an artistic stylist set beside Tolstoy and Flaubert he was a giant dwarf, that he had his bourgeois snobberies – how dare Uriah Heep aspire to Agnes? – and that he could not draw true working-class characters, and so forth. Orwell, indeed, soon turned to Dickens's positive aspect. If Dickens stood for bourgeois morality, he said, who after all was more bourgeois in moral outlook than the British working classes of Dickens's day and after? Dickens remained so popular, said Orwell, precisely 'because he was able to express in comic, simplified and therefore memorable form the native decency of the common man'. It was this same common decency, Orwell concluded, in bringing the essay inevitably back to his own situation when writing in 1939, which made Dickens stand out so admirably as 'a nineteenth-century liberal, a free intelligence, a type hated with equal hatred by all the smelly little orthodoxies which are now competing for our souls'. One can feel that the whole essay was written to lead up to this well-known, ringing conclusion.

In 'Rudyard Kipling',[7] Orwell characteristically began his essay with the remark that Kipling had been despised by five literary generations of enlightened persons, but at the end of the day they were forgotten and he was still there – why? Orwell clearly wrote his essay, if no longer as an obedient son of the *Raj*, as a son nevertheless. To be sure, Kipling could be a jingo imperialist; his mysticism had suspect Fascist elements; he could at times write in the worst of taste, as in his patronizing poems about British soldiers, falsely reproducing their lower-class slang. Even so, said Orwell, apart from his gift for vivid words, Kipling had one great asset his critics lacked – his sense of responsibility: 'Kipling sold out to the British ruling class . . . . This warped his political judgement, for the British ruling class were not what he imagined, and it led him into abysses of snobbery and folly, but he gained a corresponding advantage in having at least tried to imagine what action and responsibility are like.' Responsibility was the one thing Kipling's Left-wing detractors had never tried to imagine, Orwell said.

In his search for parallels, he also emphasized another of Kipling's assets. He was the only modern writer to have added commonly used phrases to the English language, such as 'East is East and West is West', 'the white man's burden', 'What do they know of England who only England know?' or the famous 'Paying the Danegeld'. When Orwell said that this last phrase was often used without knowledge of its origin 'by people of Left-wing persuasion', he had not yet written his main satires and added his own phrases to the English language. But I wonder – did he already have the feeling (did he always have the feeling?) that it was within him to do so?

Reading his wartime essay, 'Arthur Koestler',[8] in which he endeavoured to define Koestler's political ideas and thereby to clarify his own, I thought the essay stood out for the number of striking statements it contained within its small format. Twentieth-century English literature, so Orwell began, had been dominated by foreigners, like Henry James, Conrad,

Shaw, Joyce, Yeats, Pound and Eliot. (Foreigners? Fellow-foreigners?) No Englishmen could write about their disillusion with despotic Communism with the same sense of first-hand experience as Continentals had done – true enough. And then, in an often-quoted sentence: 'The sin of nearly all Left-wingers from 1933 onwards is that they wanted to be anti-Fascist without being anti-totalitarian.'

Considering Koestler's novel *The Gladiators*, which described how revolutionary Roman slaves under their leader Spartacus in 73 BC tried – and failed – to set up their idealized communal 'City of the Sun', Orwell contrasted it with Flaubert's *Salammbô*. Flaubert in his slower-moving time, he said, could still think himself into the stony cruelty of antiquity. Koestler, writing in the troubled atmosphere of 1938, had to make his Spartacus a modern proletarian dictator in disguise. (When I asked Koestler about this comment, he agreed with it.) But as for Orwell, was he already thinking about the problem of making Winston Smith a real man of the future, not the present?

From *The Gladiators*, Orwell went on to consider *Darkness at Noon* and then Koestler's subsequent statement in which he described himself as a complete short-term pessimist who could only keep out of all politics, but at the same time as a long-term optimist about man's ultimate ability to attain a much better life. Orwell objected explicitly to this notion. He said that Koestler's long-term optimism revealed that he still thought of an earthly paradise, of his own 'City of the Sun', as something desirable. Orwell regarded this as hedonism and as Koestler's weak point. Koestler told me that he had tried to argue repeatedly with Orwell that what Orwell called his hedonism was only his own presumably greater love of life, but to no avail: for Orwell he was docketed as a hedonist. Orwell gave his reasons in the conclusion to the essay. Perhaps the earthly paradise was just impossible, he wrote, perhaps suffering was ineradicable from human life, perhaps 'even the aim of socialism is not to make the world perfect but to make it better'.

When Orwell wrote this in 1944, he was still working on *Tribune* alongside Aneurin Bevan and looking forward to the advent of a post-war British Labour Government. Unlike

Koestler, who had opted out of all party politics, he was still ready to confirm his hopes that such a Labour Government would make the world a little better. But the essay also shows that more deeply he was pondering on the unattainability of that ambivalent earthly paradise, which was the subject of his two great satires.

EIGHTEEN

Impressions on Re-reading Orwell (2)

HOWEVER INTERESTING the essays, Orwell's prestige rests in the end on *Animal Farm* and *Nineteen Eighty-Four*, and as I read the two books again I was struck by their contrast. *Animal Farm*, which he wrote in 1943–4, when reasonably happily married and with Eileen an appreciative listener as he worked on it, seems a sunny tale of the countryside. By contrast, *Nineteen Eighty-Four*, which he wrote four years later when struggling against illness on Jura, is all inferno, a story of permanent metropolitan darkness.

To be sure, *Animal Farm* is also a story of frustration and cruelty. From the first page onwards, the revolt of the domestic animals of which it tells is predestined to fail. The final scene when the bewildered animals look from their ruling pigs to the neighbouring men and cannot tell which is which, is already inherent in the opening where the old boar Major talks of a glorious revolutionary animal Utopia to come. But the events in between, as they gently unroll on Animal Farm, seem bathed in a permanent, benign sunshine. I remember how when I remarked on it, Orwell half admitted that he loved his farm whose workings and seasons he painted in such precise detail.

This loving detail was one reason for the astonishing success of the little allegory. There are others.

One can see that for adult readers there was the relentless fairy-tale logic of his satire on the course of the Soviet revolution. Orwell had turned over *Animal Farm* in his mind for a long time, but I recall his saying that what triggered him was the wartime Teheran Conference of 1943, where before the photographers, Churchill and Roosevelt smiled upon their monstrous tyrannical ally Stalin, who fought at their side against their monstrous enemy, Hitler. He also thought that the time when Western readers looked upon Stalin's tyranny through rose-coloured spectacles was most suitable for his attack upon it. He was not the first to suggest that in revolutions, the talk of democracy, liberty and the classless society was as a rule a cover for the ambitions of a new class elbowing its way to power, but the simplified fairy-tale form in which he presented this thesis was a touch of genius – it made the conclusion seem inevitable.

Even as read today, all the elements of the political satire fit perfectly. The animals, who after the overthrow of Farmer Jones sing revolutionary hymns as they parade on Sundays, still represent the first, brief libertarian enthusiasm of the Soviet revolutionaries, even if this far-off phase, so soon doomed, is today hardly remembered. The inscrutable boar Napoleon with his fierce dogs is still Stalin to the life. The boar Snowball, too clever by half, is still like the expelled Trotsky, whose political testament still has its followers. The building of the windmill, twice destroyed by human invaders, still resembles the once so hopefully publicized fulfilment of the Soviet Five Year Plans, as the animals toil for their new masters, the pigs.

But if on today's reading, *Animal Farm* is still a most convincing political satire, one can also see why it survives even more as the supreme modern intellectual fairy tale for children. Oddly, it was not Orwell's intention to provide children's reading. Remembering the incident from her housekeeper days in 1945, Susan Watson told me that after the successful publication, Orwell spent a full day rushing from bookshop to bookshop, asking for *Animal Farm* to be moved from the shelves of children's books where he often found it automatically placed.

Ultimately of course in vain. So successfully had he thought himself into the age-old European folk tradition of talking animals, that for children who read him he turned the domestic animals on the farm into immediately recognizable and memorable and sometimes lovable characters. Lovable above all was Boxer, the great cart-horse, poor in intellect but large in muscle, who could only say 'Comrade Napoleon is always right' and 'I must work harder.' With Boxer, as a child's favourite there is Clover, the gentle, maternal mare; there is the cynical old donkey Benjamin who observes everything with detachment (Koestler told me that during Orwell's Christmas visit to them in 1945, he and his wife called him 'Benjamin'). There are the savage dogs, the recognizably silly sheep – it is the believability of these characters which has turned *Animal Farm*, like *Gulliver's Travels*, into favoured children's reading: perhaps this is the fate of all the best satires.

On re-reading the little book, I found that two passages above all had remained in my memory. The first concerned the political satire. A leading character in the story is the porker Squealer, Napoleon's spokesman who alternately cajoles and threatens. After the first revolutionary burst of equality among animals, Orwell has the pigs (like the Soviet bureaucrats) come immediately into their own. The crucial change occurs on Animal Farm when he lets the other animals discover where all the milk now goes: it goes with the windfall apples from the orchard into the pigs' private mash, and Squealer, the propagandist pig justifies this to the animals in what I remember Orwell considered the key speech in the story. The pigs were not eating this mash out of selfishness, Squealer said, reproving the protesters, but out of duty. Science had proved that apples-and-milk mash was absolutely necessary to the well-being of a pig:

> ' "We pigs are brain-workers. The whole management and organization of this farm depend on us. Day and night we are watching over your welfare. It is for *your* sake that we drink that milk and eat those apples. Do you know what would happen if we pigs failed in our duty? Jones would come back! Yes, Jones would come back! Surely, comrades," cried Squealer almost pleadingly, skipping from side to side and whisking his tail, "surely there is no one among you who wants to see Jones come back?" ' [1]

The second passage concerned Orwell's loving picture of his farm. Turning the pages, I found myself remembering Orwell, with Eileen, in his happier days during the war thinking about the farm he would have liked to run, for that is what *Animal Farm* also is. Hence the convincing picture of the farm, as he carefully describes its changing seasons of sowing, reaping and storing for the winter, its arduous toil in the fields, the orchard, the cowshed, the chicken run. Animal Farm is seen as a real farm, set in a timeless English Edwardian landscape in the pre-motor-car age. In describing its workings, Orwell throughout plays fair. To run the farm, Napoleon needs to buy oil, nails, string, iron for the horses' shoes. Even though it had originally been decreed that the hens could keep their eggs, Orwell shows why on the contrary Napoleon has to sell the eggs outside. But while acknowledging necessities, he always returns to the enticing beauties of the farm. There is a scene near the end of the book where the years have sped by, most of the animals can no longer remember the revolution, but the mare Clover, gentle, worrying Clover, is still around. From the knoll of the windmill, with other animals huddling round her, she can see most of Animal Farm:

> 'The long pasture stretching down to the main road, the hay field, the spinney, the drinking pool, the ploughed fields where the young wheat was thick and green, and the red roofs of the farm buildings with the smoke curling from the chimneys. . . . The grass and the bursting hedges were gilded by the level rays of the sun. Never had the farm appeared so desirable a place.'[2]

No wonder that even the tyrant Napoleon seems at the end only a drunken old utter scoundrel of a boar (as Stalin might have seemed to his Western allies at Teheran). Perhaps the only repellent character remains Squealer whom Orwell uses to demonstrate that a despotism requires constant deceit to keep the masses in order. As Squealer expounds the laws of Animalism and explains why the pigs must always reinterpret them, ending with the immortal 'All animals are equal but some are more equal than others', Orwell has him progressing from *doubletalk* to *doublethink*, and so preparing the way for *Nineteen Eighty-Four*.

The world has lived very nicely with *Animal Farm* but uneasily with *Nineteen Eighty-Four*. It is fair to say that Orwell's last work has, more than any book published since 1945, subtly affected the popular impression of the way history has been proceeding. The book contains obvious elements of his private nightmare – the hero's loneliness and guilt, memories of London's wartime squalor, his phobia about rats, images of a boot on a face . . . And yet, out of his *private* nightmare Orwell by his supreme effort produced a book profoundly and prophetically related to the *public* problems of the time, an allegory that after his death has become like a measuring rod of history.

This impact is all the more remarkable because at first sight, as one reads it today, *Nineteen Eighty-Four* has a few very evident faults. True, the imaginary future Orwell wrote about back in 1948 still has a very ingenious look – he had good insight into the shape of history to come. The world of 1984 which Orwell drew was dominated by three totalitarian superstates – Eurasia (Soviet Union), Eastasia (communist China) and Oceania (the US) and for a writer looking ahead in 1948 this was not a bad guess. He saw Britain as Oceania's Airstrip One – again not a bad guess, but then the American connection simply drops out of his story, leaving Britain alone as a totalitarian Oceania. As such, in Orwell's picture, it is ruled to the last detail by the all-powerful Party, which is headed by Orwell's nice invention of a mythical protector, Big Brother, the fount of all wisdom and virtue – and of absolutely total ruthlessness. (Well, we have since Orwell's death seen the temporary rise of some similar figures.) The Party is divided into the mysterious privileged minority of the Inner Party and Orwell's chosen victims (his own social class), the harassed Outer Party members who are constantly watched over by the Thought Police for deviation,. dissenters being tortured within the Ministry of Love and vaporized.

In this coherent inferno, the watching is done through ubiquitous telescreens – Orwell's single mechanical invention for the future – through which the Party simultaneously broadcasts lying propaganda and has everybody watched all the time for possible heresy. (Again, this is not a bad broad forecast of today's mounting Government supervision of citizens by computer storage of information.)

But now we come to the Proles, the vast working-class majority of the population who do not count in Orwell's Britain of 1984; and here he seemed to stumble. His picture is of a completely demoralized British working class:

> 'The Proles were born, they grew up in the gutters, they went to work at twelve, they passed through a brief blossoming period of beauty and sexual desire, they married at twenty, they were middle-aged at thirty, they died, for the most part, at sixty. Heavy physical work, the care of home and children, petty quarrels with neighbours, films, football, beer, and above all, gambling filled up the horizon of their minds.'[3]

This picture has not only little connection with the real organized and motorized British workers of the eighties, taking their holidays in Florida; it was an old-fashioned view even at the time when Orwell wrote in 1948. Since he severely censured Kipling for writing patronizing poems about soldiers who dropped their aitches, his own laboured attempts to reproduce Prole cockney speech are curious. Altogether, it is odd that Orwell, when writing on Jura in 1948, should in his Proles produce a picture of the British workers that looks like one taken from his childhood. Other faults in the book strike the reader. Orwell presents his totalitarian Party as deliberately unideological, neither nationalist nor Communist, which seems unlikely. His dirty, run-down London of 1984 with its bomb gaps is no city of the future but the bombed wartime London he remembered. The sinister canteen in the Ministry of Truth where the hero Winston eats is obviously based on the innocent wartime canteen of the BBC, which he also remembered.

And so on. Yet these faults hardly matter. The point is that the reader is soon caught by the sheer power and cohesion of Orwell's nightmare vision of a savage, totalitarian society – above all, one in which nothing can change. Orwell's Party rules Oceania by a system of *doublethink* under which two opposed opinions can be held simultaneously. Thus, while it derides every principle of English socialism, Orwell has the Party call its philosophy 'Ingsoc'. In the name of Ingsoc, under the Party's *doublethink*, London is forever dominated by the skyscrapers of the Ministry of Truth, where lies are fabricated, the Ministry of Love, where prisoners are tortured by the Party, and the Ministry of Plenty, which arranges strict food ration-ing. Within the nightmare, life is forever unchanged. The clocks of London strike thirteen. Big Brother glares from giant posters and his eyes watch the citizens through the telescreens. In his cubicle in the Ministry of Truth, the hero Winston Smith sits forever changing and falsifying past copies of *The Times* in keeping with current Party edicts, because the Party maintains that whoever controls the past controls the future. Every day, there takes place the two minutes' hate, during which the always defeated, yet equally undying traitor Goldstein appears hatefully on the telescreen, until pushed away by Big Brother. In the canteen Winston's colleague Simes is too knowing and so is vaporized by the Thought Police – it is inevitable. Life is shabby, the streets of London are shabby but Party parades are held in their full glory – Winston's girl Julia marches regularly in the ranks of the Anti-Sex League.

Into this nightmarish vision of the future, in which all details dovetail, Orwell has as it were projected himself into the story in the shape of his wretched hero Winston Smith. Whereas in Orwell's other novels the ending is implicit in the telling, Winston's doom is conveyed *explicitly* from the start. He is described as knowing himself doomed when he defies Party rules to keep an individual diary. Doom comes nearer to him and his girl Julia when they start to have an affair. It becomes inevitable when they visit Inner Party member O'Brien and offer to join the traitor Goldstein's army. When arrested, Winston is tortured and brainwashed by O'Brien within the Ministry of Love. His final and ultimate doom arrives when he is taken to room 101 'where the worst thing in the world happens', the worst thing in Winston's case being that a cage of rats is placed over his face, whereat he collapses, totally recants and becomes an automaton, loving Big Brother.

Since I first read *Nineteen Eighty-Four*, a neat *ad hominem* critique of it has been put forward by Anthony West,[4] who noted the similarity between Winston Smith's fate in 1984 and Orwell's memories of St Cyprian's as told in 'Such, Such Were the Joys'. As Mr West saw it, the mounting pattern of fear in which Orwell envelops Winston paralleled the fears which he himself recalled feeling at St Cyprian's, leading to the climax of the dread summons to the headmaster's study for the inevitable beating. Mr West goes on: 'Whether Orwell knew it or not, what he did in *Nineteen Eighty-Four* was to send everyone to an enormous Crossgates (St Cyprian's) to be as miserable as he had been.'

The critique is neat, but, firstly, Mr West was in part discovering the known. I recall how Orwell himself told me (although I don't think he wrote this anywhere) that the sufferings of a misfit boy in a boarding school were probably the only English parallel to the isolation felt by an outsider in a totalitarian society. Secondly, and more important, since Orwell always wrote autobiographically, touches of his private nightmare do recur in his writings. As I have myself suggested, one can if one likes find memories of his own loneliness as a boy woven into the sense of isolation felt by Winston Smith. Perhaps without the neuroses of Eric Blair the works of George Orwell might never have been written, but to reduce Orwell's achievement to these neuroses is naive.

After all, when composing *Nineteen Eighty-Four*, he was touching on the problems of very real dictatorship while writing in the horrendous dictatorial age of Hitler, Stalin and others. With a tremendous, exhausting psychological effort, adding no doubt elements of his private nightmare, he tried through the experiences with which he endowed the hapless Winston Smith to look deeply into the collectivist future he saw ahead. As I have said, his immediate model for his totalitarian Oceania was Stalin's Soviet Union, but I think his vision was much wider. As he wrote in the book, by the fourth decade of the twentieth century, all the main currents of political thought were authoritarian. The earthly paradise had been discredited at exactly the moment when it had seemed, through technology, to become realizable. These words in *Nineteen Eighty-Four* are put into the mouth of the rebel Goldstein, but there is no reason to think they are not Orwell's own. In previous writings he had stressed that bourgeois individuality was going, the bonds of family, locality, religion, craft and profession were going. In their place a new collectivism was spreading in society, whether in work or life or leisure. But it also appeared to Orwell in 1948 that the new collective did not bring the earthly paradise any nearer. Not only that, it appeared to him that under the threat of violence and the nuclear terror, the new collective could become grotesquely dehumanized. It is as a permanent warning against the danger of the dehumanized collective in our society that *Nineteen Eighty-Four* has survived and should be seen to have survived.

Two concluding points. When Orwell told me that because he thought ill health had affected it, he was dissatisfied with *Nineteen Eighty-Four* (he wrote to Julian Symons that he had 'ballsed it up') I think that his dissatisfaction was mainly directed at the third part of the book, where Winston is interrogated and tortured by O'Brien. From my first reading, one passage had particularly remained in my mind, that in which O'Brien explains that to Big Brother and the Party, power and the infliction of torture on victims are not only justified for their own sake. They are also justified for ever.

> '"If you want a picture of the future, imagine a boot stamping on a human face – forever . . .
>
> "And remember that it is forever. The face will always be there to be stamped upon. The heretic, the enemy of society, will always be there, so that he can be defeated and humiliated over again . . . The espionage, the betrayals, the arrests, the tortures, the executions, the disappearances will never cease."' [5]

I remember how at my first reading I had thought that here Orwell was really piling on his private nightmare a bit, yet the words must have made an impact on readers and been specially remembered. I found the passage used as comment in articles on the tenth anniversary of the Soviet crushing of Dubcek's liberal Communist Czech régime and on the twenty-fifth anniversary of the Soviet crushing of the Hungarian revolution; and on the occasion of the crushing of Solidarity in Poland in 1981–2, I found it said in the press that to Comrade Brezhnev, the Soviet boot must be on the face of the satellite countries forever. Like other Orwellian sayings, it has proved to be prophetic.

My last point concerns the Appendix on 'Newspeak'. The American Book of the Month Club at first wanted him to omit it. Fortunately he resisted, for his account of how his Party rulers in Oceania were busy eliminating large numbers of common English words from existence and substituting newly knocked-up words for others in order to make heretical thought impossible – this is almost the best touch of satire in the whole book. It is hard to resist the temptation to quote Orwell's own eloquent example of the substitution by the Party of new words for old to stop heretical thought:

> 'Consider, for example, such a typical sentence from a *Times* leading article as *Oldthinkers unbellyfeel Ingsoc*. The shortest rendering that one could make of this in Oldspeak would be: "Those whose ideas were formed before the Revolution cannot have a full emotional understanding of the principles of English Socialism." But this not an adequate translation. To begin with, in order to grasp the full meaning of the *Newspeak* sentence quoted above, one would have to have a clear idea of what is meant by *Ingsoc*. And, in addition, only a person thoroughly grounded in Ingsoc could appreciate the full force of the word *bellyfeel* which implies a blind, enthusiastic acceptance difficult to imagine today; or of the word *oldthink*, which was inextricably mixed up with the idea of wickedness and decadence.'[6]

I noticed how in her splendid autobiographical account of her political imprisonment under Stalin, the Soviet author Eugenia Ginzburg referred to Orwell's comments on totalitarian society with an apparent certainty that her references would be understood. When I mentioned this to a Russian friend – well, she was lucky enough to have come out of the Soviet Union five years ago – she said: 'What do you mean? With his *Newspeak* and *Doublethink*, Orwell wrote for us! No Westerner could understand him as intimately as we in the Soviet Union felt he understood our lives.'

NINETEEN

The Orwell Legend

URING HIS LAST YEARS Orwell had clearly made many good friends. I recall how when he died, the tributes from his friends all seemed to express what I myself felt, a sense of sudden deep loss. A unique personality was gone from us.

David Astor told me that he felt he had lost an invaluable mentor in his efforts to maintain the *Observer* as a liberal, humanist, tolerant Sunday newspaper. V.S. Pritchett, Anthony Powell and Arthur Koestler wrote their appreciative recollections. Koestler said that it was inadvisable to meet one's literary heroes in the flesh but Orwell had been the exception. Julian Symons wrote warmly about the kindness Orwell had shown to him as a young writer. Richard Rees, who had first helped him on the *Adelphi*, projected some of his mild saintliness on to his dead friend. Orwell's lunchtime companion, Malcolm Muggeridge, was more detached when he wrote in his diary on 26 January 1950: 'Read through the various obituary articles on George by Koestler, Pritchett, Julian Symons, etc., and saw in them how the legend of a human being is created.'[1]

Not a bad forecast, but I don't think that Muggeridge, or indeed anyone at that early date, knew how large the legend of the creator of Animal Farm and Big Brother was to loom.

The reason was that both as a writer and a man, Orwell fitted so remarkably – if alas posthumously – into the way in which life and politics have developed in the second half of our century. For example, he knew that the great march of the moderns in literature, the arts and music had by this time very much run its course. In the age of Hitler, Stalin, appeasement and war, a different era had arrived, in which the key question for intellectuals was no longer one of literary or artistic experiment carried to its limits, but the simpler humdrum question of defending freedom of speech and the legal rights of the citizen, as well as truth in the language of politics.

I come back to the way he seemed to have prepared himself all his life for this new era. As a boy at prep school, at St Cyprian's, he had built up a firm position for himself as a social outsider, as an observer sceptically commenting on what he saw, at first in an inner voice and then in print. This position he retained for life. When as writer and journalist he became too popular, too central a literary figure in London, he fled to the remoteness of his Scottish isle, to be an outsider again.

In his years of latency at Eton he all the same took a close look at the British governing class. As a policeman in colonial Burma he recognized the use of force by the white Sahibs to support their rule, and well before the time he saw its coming end. In Paris and London he acquainted himself with society's down-and-outs. In Wigan he saw the impact of the great economic depression. In the Spanish war, he met the phenomenon of Communist misrule head-on. At the wartime BBC and on *Tribune*, he learned about propaganda and socialist polemics respectively. It was all training, all a search for material, for the shaping of his views about his time.

In shaping these views, he might often be wrong in detail, and sometimes on major issues, as in his ideas about 'Fascist Germany'. But one reason for his posthumous impact, particularly on young readers, was his special talent for recognizing the underlying trends of his age. He had a sharp nose (he often used the simile of smells) for the direction in which the political and cultural events of the twentieth century were tending. (I concede, for instance, that in 1946 he foresaw more clearly than I how Zionism would lead to Israeli militarism.) Many of his contemporaries found in Marxism a new religion with which to tidy up the loose ends of modern history. A smaller minority, like Evelyn Waugh, found a similar explanatory faith in Catholicism. As opposed to these, Orwell remained the supreme agnostic. By this I don't just mean that he rejected 'the smelly little orthodoxies' which he described in his essay on Dickens. His agnosticism went much further. He accepted few received opinions without independently, sometimes obstinately, examining them, judging everything on its merits. When he spoke of the declining ability of the English ruling class, the endurance of the British workers during the Great Depression, British behaviour in Burma, Communist behaviour in Spain, Allied behaviour in bombing civilians during the war – all such attitudes he had personally observed, reflected upon and then judged.

His judgements might not be precisely correct every time, but I think it is his sceptical agnosticism which in particular appeals to readers who grew up after Hitler and Stalin had drawn their line across history, in that second half of the twentieth century he never saw. They were readers who had lost their own illusions, about the United Nations or the promises of the Soviet paradise, about unreal expectations of freedom in the Third World and even the hope that social democracy at home in the West could do more, as Orwell said, than improve society by a small measure.

As an agnostic – and here again lies his appeal – he was a great anticipator of the shape of things to come. *Nineteen Eighty-Four* showed that he was fascinated not only by the future but by the question of the past. Today we seem afloat amid a facile nostalgia for the fashions and artifacts of the past, but this is a relatively new attitude. When Orwell was writing, in the sombre forties, the past seemed to lie behind one like a heap of dull wreckage. Orwell was among the first to try to resurrect the legitimate values of the past, even to indulge himself with a certain nostalgia. If he had long left his upper-middle-class background behind, he never thought that its ideals of public service and patriotism were simply to be mocked and rejected. He endowed all the heroes of his novels, even Winston Smith wandering amid fantasies in the year 1984, with that nostalgic memory of a 'golden country' of rabbit-cropped pastures, an overgrown copse and a still pool with fish, a memory which he had himself treasured since childhood.

Looking back, he saw Kipling as a gross imperialist, but as a writer with a sense of responsibility. Looking back further, he saw Dickens as a nineteenth-century liberal lacking the coarseness to think, as Orwell's contemporaries did, that all social ills could be cured merely by altering the *shape* of society.

In 1946, a time when pro-capitalist views were not fashionable˙ among intellectuals, in 'Riding Down From Bangor' he described mid-nineteenth-century America as capitalist civilization at its best. In *Nineteen Eighty-Four* he tried to show how the future needed the past with Winston's concern over half-forgotten nursery rhymes and his purchases of a ledger of beautiful old white paper and a watery-coloured Victorian paperweight.

More anticipation. As mentioned before, Orwell in *Keep the Aspidistra Flying*, in 1936, let his young middle-class hero, Gordon Comstock, try desperately to 'drop out' of respectable society and do without money. In the rigid, hierarchical English class society of 1935, Gordon had no such option: but how closely his rages against the 'Money-God' correspond to the motivation of those many middle-class young men and women of our own time who (buttressed of course by social security) have 'dropped out' into their alternative life-styles in precisely Gordon's manner. Orwell was an anticipator, too, in his preoccupation with language, meaning and thought. In his insistence upon concrete precision instead of abstract fudging in political writing, in his ingenious invention of the *Newspeak* of 1984, and in his enduring concern with the possibility of controlling thought through control of language, he seemed to anticipate the flowering of the – for a time – famous Oxford school of linguistic philosophy, and of the science of linguistics in general.

One of his crucial anticipations was, of course, of the way in which totalitarian Communist societies would develop. Admittedly the Soviet society of today is no longer monolithically totalitarian as it was at the peak of Stalin's great terror. Still, in its rigid insistence on the central bureaucratic control of everybody and everything, in its enduring restriction on individual expression and in the use of KGB police force against dissidents, it can still be reasonably described by the adjective 'totalitarian', and Orwell's forecast of the world dangers inherent in such Communist totalitarianism was a major piece of political thinking. After all, he had sketched out the take-over of power by the pigs in *Animal Farm* long before Tito's former Yugoslav colleague, Milovan Djilas, in his *The New Class* drew his well-known profile of the new self-perpetuating Soviet ruling class. He wrote his *Nineteen Eighty-Four* long before Czeslaw Milosz in his Nobel Prize-winning *The Captive Mind* described the enforced Soviet imposition of a distorted political mass fantasy upon a captive population.

He not only knew Communist life in his own time; he had an image of its future. In O'Brien's interrogation of Winston by shock treatment in the Ministry of Love, there is a point where he shifts dramatically from merely accusing Winston of political *thoughtcrime* in daring to oppose the Party. He says that in his puny individual opposition, Winston has simply shown himself as *insane* – and the purpose of his torture was to cure him of his insanity. It is as though Orwell had anticipated the switch of the KGB from Stalin's former mass purges to the present method of singling out Soviet political dissidents and incarcerating them in psychiatric hospitals like the Serbsky, where they are treated by drugs against exaggerated belief in their individuality and against paranoid delusions of reforming the Soviet system.

Not long after re-reading *Nineteen Eighty-Four*, I was glancing at Christopher Booker's witty report on the Olympic Games of 1980 in Moscow, *The Games War*.[2] Reading Booker's impression of his first visit to Moscow, with its solemn centre overshadowed by four towering skyscrapers, I had an odd sense of familiarity and next learned how Booker himself was reminded by Brezhnev's Moscow of Orwell's imaginary London of 1984 dominated by its huge skyscraper. As Booker related how he and other foreign journalists had to walk the last stretch to the Olympic Lenin Stadium between two unbroken, solemnly staring ranks of Soviet soldiers, conveying an awesome show of Soviet armed strength, while behind them on giant posters the face of Brezhnev proclaimed 'Peace!', one might really have been among the *doublethink* of *Nineteen Eighty-Four*. It was as if Orwell, when writing in 1948, had been able to anticipate the Moscow of the Olympic Games of 1980.

But to return to the central theme of Orwell's thought, to his main message as expressed in his essays and *Nineteen Eighty-Four*. It was a simple, straightforward message. In spite of his nostalgia for his childhood pleasures and his appreciation of the virtues of his early background, he had travelled far from the whole culture and way of life of his conservative, very English, one-time imperial, native upper-middle class. As he liked to say, it was all up with this class. (Towards the very end of his life, as he lay in the Cotswolds sanatorium, on Sundays when crowds of upper-middle-class visitors arrived, he noted down his dislike of the 'fatuous self-confidence ... the fundamental ill-will' he felt was expressed in their voices.)

Instead, he became and remained a socialist. He regarded himself as belonging to the radical wing of the British Labour Party and continued to believe that its measures could make the life of the British working classes somewhat more humane and better.

And yet, he was profoundly afraid of what he saw as a larger, inevitable social change which was simultaneously in progress: the growth of a dehumanized, technological collective life lying ahead, particularly within the Big Soviet State in the East, but for that matter also within the State of depersonalized Big Business in the West. (The machines mechanically turning out 'prolefeed' novels for the masses in *Nineteen Eighty-Four* are a satire directed against American-style pulp fiction.) He was afraid of the loss of personal freedom as the collective society took over. He was afraid of violence as the moral checks of the old bourgeois order crumbled – see the essay 'Raffles and Miss Blandish'.[3] And he was of course afraid of the implications of nuclear terror.

And so we come to the crux of what he strove for in life. Both in his own life and his writings, he expressed the basic dilemma of his time, and also of our time which has followed after his death. The dilemma was that with Hitlerism and Stalinism, with two world wars and the nuclear arms race, an end had unmistakably come to that optimistic belief in man's inevitable progress, about which he had still read and been taught in early youth. The outlook of his English imperial upper-middle class, the glaring inequalities of Western capitalism – from these he turned with a weary shrug: he was formally a socialist. Yet at the same time he knew that the Marxist Utopia was hollow. He felt deeply pessimistic about the new collectivist manipulation of men and women which technical progress made possible in the society taking shape.

And so, in this dilemma, he called for the practice of the only possible virtues which he thought were possible in our time. He called for the reassertion of belief in personal freedom of speech; for the use of precise, truthful language in politics; for the equality of all citizens before the law; above all, for common decency and compassion in the conduct of political affairs. Simple virtues perhaps; his genius lay in his knowledge that in the dilemma of our time, these simple virtues might well be all we had to cope with the problems of our time crowding in upon us. It is as the great anticipator of our modern dilemma and the advocate of the only virtues at our disposal that I like to remember Orwell.

And, of course, as a lovable person. He was naturally contradictory in character, like everyone else. He was an anti-imperialist, yet quite strikingly in looks, and somewhat in manner, he remained a Sahib. In his writings he was a fierce critic, yet in person a gentle and considerate friend and acquaintance. He wrongly thought himself physically un-attractive, yet was strongly attracted towards beautiful women: well, he was not the only man in this predicament. He was happily married, yet not altogether a perceptive husband. He abhorred violence, yet served as a soldier. He was not good with his hands, yet tried hard to be a householder, a smallholder, a fisherman, a carpenter. He genuinely wanted often to be anything but a writer, yet insisted on the discipline of a spell of writing every single day.

With these contradictions, and in spite of his withdrawn personality, he was with his gentle manner a most attractive man, an intellectual critic with an endearing streak of some-times childlike simplicity. As I like to remember him, it is in an admittedly uncharacteristic moment of general optimism, in the magic year of 1940, when he wrote *The Lion and the Unicorn* which he ended with the following peroration:

'It is good-bye to the *Tatler* and the *Bystander*, and farewell to the lady in the Rolls-Royce car. The heirs of Nelson and of Cromwell are not in the House of Lords. They are in the fields and the streets, in the factories and the armed forces, in the four-ale bar and the suburban back garden; and at present they are still kept under by a generation of ghosts. Compared with the task of bringing the real England to the surface, even the winning of the war, necessary though it is, is secondary. By revolution we become more ourselves, not less. There is no question of stopping short, striking a compromise, salvaging 'democracy', standing still. Nothing ever stands still. We must add to our heritage or lose it, we must grow greater or grow less, we must go forward or go backward. I believe in England, and I believe that we shall go forward.'[4]

It has not turned out quite like that; the generation of ghosts is still around; but farewell, George.

Notes

CE: *The Collected Essays, Journalism and Letters of George Orwell*, edited by Sonia Orwell and Ian Angus, four volumes (Secker & Warburg, 1968)

Prologue

1 T.R. Fyvel, 'A Writer's Life', *World Review*, , 16 June 1950
2 T.R. Fyvel, 'George Orwell and Eric Blair', *Encounter*, 70, July 1959
3 Peter Stansky and William Abrahams, *The Unknown Orwell* (Constable, 1972), and *Orwell: The Transformation* (Constable, 1979)
4 Bernard Crick, *George Orwell: A Life* (Secker & Warburg, 1980)

Chapter 1 **Orwell's Background**

1 *Nineteen Eighty-Four* (Secker & Warburg, 1949), Penguin, 1954, p.1
2 'Such, Such Were the Joys', *Partisan Review*, New York, Sept. 1952; *CE IV*, p. 330
3 'Shooting an Elephant', *New Writing*, Autumn 1936; *CE I*, p. 235
4 *The Road to Wigan Pier* (Gollancz, 1937), p. 155

Chapter 2 **Education of a Genius**

1 'Why I Write', *Gangrel*, Summer 1946; *CE I*, p. 4
2 'Such, Such Were the Joys', op. cit.
3 Stansky and Abrahams, *The Unknown Orwell*, op. cit.
4 Cyril Connolly, *Enemies of Promise* (Routledge, 1938)
5 'Such, Such Were the Joys', op. cit.
6 Ibid.
7 'Why I Write', op. cit.

Chapter 3 **Eton – and then Burma**

1 *The Road to Wigan Pier*, op. cit., p. 175
2 Christopher Hollis, *A Study of George Orwell* (Hollis & Carter, 1956)
3 Stansky and Abrahams, *Orwell: The Transformation*, op. cit.

4 'A Hanging', *Adelphi*, Aug. 1931; *CE I*, p. 44
5 *The Road to Wigan Pier*, op. cit., p. 178
6 'Shooting an Elephant', op. cit.

Chapter 4 **Down and Out?**

1 Stansky and Abrahams, *The Unknown Orwell*, op. cit.
2 *Down and Out in Paris and London* (Secker & Warburg, 1949), p. 5
3 Ibid., p. 6
4 Richard Mayne, 'A Note on Orwell's Paris', in *The World of George. Orwell*, ed. Miriam Gross (Weidenfeld & Nicolson, 1971)
5 Humphry Dakin in conversation with the author, 1958
6 *Down and Out in Paris and London*, op. cit., p. 139

Chapter 5 **Orwell as a Young Novelist**

1 *A Clergyman's Daughter*(Gollancz, 1935), Penguin, 1964, p. 258
2 *Keep the Aspidistra Flying* (Gollancz, 1936), Penguin, 1962, p. 21

Chapter 6 **Becoming a Socialist**

1 *The Road to Wigan Pier*, op. cit., p. 198

Chapter 7 **The Spanish War and Truth**

1 *New English Weekly*, 23.7.1936; *CE I*, p. 225
2 *Homage to Catalonia* (Secker & Warburg, 1938), p. 4
3 Ibid., p. 314

Chapter 8 **The Detour**

1 *New Statesman*, 28.8.1937; *CE I*, p. 283
2 Letter to Stephen Spender, 15.4.1938; *CE I*, p. 313
3 'Not Counting Niggers', *Adelphi*, July 1939; *CE I*, p. 394
4 *Folios of New Writing*, Autumn 1940; *CE I*, p. 535

Chapter 9 **Meeting Orwell**

1 *Time & Tide*, 5.2.1938; *CE I*, p. 295

Chapter 10 **Searchlights**

1 Fredric Warburg, *An Occupation for Gentlemen* (Hutchinson, 1959)

2 *The Lion and the Unicorn* (Secker & Warburg, 1941), p. 38
3 Ibid., p. 99

Chapter 11 **Anticlimax**

1 *Observer*, 22.2.1942

Chapter 12 **On to *Animal Farm***

1 *Horizon*, Sept. 1945
2 I see that in my own review in *Tribune* I dealt inadequately with the
   political satire involved
3 Elizaveta Fen, 'George Orwell's First Wife', *Twentieth Century*,
   August 1960
4 Crick, op. cit., pp. 326–30

Chapter 13 **On and Off *Tribune***

1 'As I Please', *Tribune*, 10.3.1944; *CE III*, p. 106
2 Ibid.
3 'Riding Down From Bangor', *Tribune*, 22.11.1946; *CE III*, p. 242
4 Julian Symons, 'Orwell, a Reminiscence', *London Magazine*, Sept.
   1963
5 Malcolm Muggeridge, 'A Knight of the Woeful Countenance', in
   The World of George Orwell, op. cit.
6 Crick, op. cit., pp. 334–6

Chapter 14 **Looking at the Future from Jura**

1 Letter to the author, 31.12.47; *CE IV*, p. 386
2 'Writers and Leviathan', *Politics and Letters*, Summer 1948; *CE IV*,
   p. 407
3 Letter to Julian Symons, 2.1.48; *CE IV*, p. 393
4 Warburg, *All Authors are Equal* (Hutchinson, 1973)

Chapter 15 **Terminal**

1 Letter to the author, 15.4.1949; *CE IV*, p. 497
2 Muggeridge, op. cit.

Chapter 16 **Orwell in his Century**

1 Symons, op. cit.
2 Isaac Deutscher, *Heretics and Renegades* (Hamish Hamilton, 1955)

3 John Beavan, 'The Road to Wigan Pier', *World Review,* June 1950
4 'Good Bad Books', *Tribune,* 2.11.1945; *CE IV,* p. 19
5 Letter to Julian Symons, 29.10.1948; *CE IV,* p. 449
6 Muggeridge, *Like It Was* (Collins, 1981)
7 'Revenge is Sour', *Tribune,* 9.11.1945; *CE IV,* p. 3

Chapter 17 **Impressions on Re-reading Orwell (1)**

1 *Burmese Days* (Gollancz, 1935), Penguin, 1967, p. 164
2 *The Road to Wigan Pier,* op. cit., p. 18
3 *CE IV,* pp. 40 ff.
4 'How the Poor Die', *Now,* 6, Nov. 1946; *CE IV,* p. 223
5 'Politics *vs* Literature', *Polemic,* 5, Sept. 1946; *CE IV,* p. 205
6 'Charles Dickens', in *Inside the Whale* (Gollancz, 1940); *CE I,* p. 413
7 'Rudyard Kipling', *Horizon,* Feb. 1942; *CE II,* p. 187
8 'Arthur Koestler', *Focus,* 2, 1944; *CE IV,* p. 234

Chapter 18 **Impressions on Re-reading Orwell (2)**

1 *Animal Farm,* op. cit., p. 29
2 Ibid., p. 59
3 *Nineteen Eighty-Four,* op. cit., pp. 60–1
4 Anthony West, *Principles & Persuasions* (Eyre & Spottiswoode, 1958)
5 *Nineteen Eighty-Four,* op. cit., p. 245
6 Ibid.

Chapter 19 **The Orwell Legend**

1 Muggeridge, *Like It Was,* op. cit.
2 Christopher Booker, *The Games War* (Faber, 1980)
3 'Raffles and Miss Blandish', *Horizon,* Oct. 1944; *CE III,* p. 212
4 *The Lion and the Unicorn,* op. cit., p. 126

Index